PINK
SUNGLASSES
AND
YOGA PANTS

PINK SUNGLASSES AND YOGA PANTS

31 REFLECTIONS ON BIBLICAL FEMINISM

TARA J. HANNAH

ISBN: 978-0-578-48704-5

Typeset in Morandi Light by Raphaël Freeman, Renana Typesetting.

Printed in the United States of America

22 21 20 19 19 – 5 4 3 2 1

To all the women and girls
who have ever felt powerless
because of a religious teaching.
Here are your Pink Sunglasses.
+
Yoga Pants fit every body.

CONTENTS

ACKNOWLEDGMENTS

Eva, you told me I could write, so I believed you!

Maleah, thank you for polishing me up and being a safety net in sharing my faith.

The members of Christian Feminism Today, I'm indebted to you for sharing your faith with me. You are my friends forever.

The members of Christian Biblical Equality, your persistence is changing the world. This book could not have happened without your many resources.

Joel and the women at Oakbrook Church, thanks for listening to me.

The women and men who support me in YOGATHEA®, you are my tribe. Breathe the Peace!

Mom, your life has taught me I can be my own woman. Thank you for keeping faith (and asking me if I'm bringing the kids to church). My kids are lucky to have you as Grandma, and my husband really *does* enjoy arguing politics with you.

My husband and children, thanks for keeping our home clean while I ignored you to write this book. And thanks for checking on me while I was holed up at my desk to give me a hug or tell me you can't wait until this is finished…to read it of course! I love you!

INTRODUCTION

*What matters is precisely this; the
unspoken at the edge of the spoken.*

– Virginia Woolf[1] (1882–1941),
English writer

When my daughter was becoming a toddler, she walked into walls. The blunt impacts with the wall became a daily occurrence with her newfound bipedal skills. Initially she bounced off the wall and onto her bum with an "uh-oh," but as her stride quickened she would crash abruptly and then scream. Navigating her environment required most of her concentration, so she didn't talk or interact much. Eventually she withdrew from trying to make it past the wall. It's hard to negotiate with a wall.

Things changed when my little Sunshine was thirteen months old. She could *see* the wall through little coke-bottle-bottom lenses that had been carved perfectly into the most adorable reddish-pink plastic frames. The pediatric ophthalmologist told me she was legally blind, but her vision was treatable with bifocals, eye patches, and, perhaps, surgery. Her new, thick polycarbonate

---

1. Believed to be from a diary entry dated June 21, 1912.

PINK SUNGLASSES AND YOGA PANTS

bifocal lenses ended her war with the walls. Greater vision opened up her world, and she moved past the wall. Empowering my daughter with vision was like plugging her into a wall. As she found her power to move, be curious, and interact, it transformed her into a force.

In the way my daughter walked into walls, unable to see them, I have walked, slammed, and crashed into hard, invisible religious walls – walls built and preserved by an ideology that denies women the right to be the owners of their own power. Each time I hit a wall I knew something was missing, something I couldn't see. I searched Scripture and couldn't see past the walls of unnamed women – women owned as wives, used as concubines, thrown away as prostitutes, stolen as booty, raped and raped some more, sacrificed, demonized sexually, or instructed to submit to men. Meditating on Scripture, I couldn't figure out if God created woman *for* man or *despite* man. These walls, and more, almost knocked the faith out of me.

Looking back, I can see how asking questions about God's value of women only pushed me deeper into an abyss of more questions. I questioned God and was accused of being unfaithful, when in fact my questions stemmed from faith. My questions cost me relationships. It's painful for me to discuss the censoring, demeaning, diminishing, and the direct and indirect rebukes that I would have never experienced in my Christian faith if I had been born male. There are many unspoken words at the edge of Scripture, leaving uncertainty at best when focusing on women, if women are even mentioned in Scripture at all. I've searched and researched, meditated, asked, and spent a small fortune on books, seeking to formulate these unspoken words about women. I haven't articulated them all, but these thirty-one reflections are a decent start!

Perhaps I'm naïve in saying this, but I believe the Bible is for all of us, even a woman who asserts feminism. As I mentioned this writing project to women, I received a variety of responses. Secular women confessed faith, sharing they were lost to find a place to be both Christian and feminist. Christian women gave me a trifecta of responses. Many were ready to prepurchase the book before it was even written, as they are thirsty to understand how Scripture supports them. A pastor's wife and an elder's wife – the establishment – handed me a silencing tactic, telling me they already felt empowered as women of faith. These women obviously felt secure inside the religious walls they helped to build, and they did not want me to rock the boat in their peaceful waters of church. And, finally, there were women hunkered inside the thick citadels of religion, reflexively defining feminism as a heretical f-word. These woman-fortified religious walls have stood as a protection for war (perhaps against the illuminati?) and the women are completely blind to how their theological walls imprison them.

Women can be the fiercest defenders of a Christian theology that teaches the power of women is complementary, not equal, to men. I know many women who find security in submitting their power to men as a decree of faith, because the idea of receiving "divine protection" through man comforts them. It also permissibly allows them to shirk responsibility in the "final" say of spiritual matters. Feminism is an ideology, not a gender, so not all women are feminists. This also means that men are not the enemy. As the mother of three sons, and wife to a husband, I understand boys and men face their own sexism and can feel limited in some ways to live as a man. While many of these reflections are topics pertinent to men, I discuss sexism solely through a feminine lens, advocating for women to own their power. With that said, I hope men will read along to encourage the girls and women in their lives to own their power. Dads, buy a copy of the book for your daughters!

The journey into the valley of questioning God about the

power of women has been thorny and painful for me. I have cried many tears, been accused of sinful intentions, called derogatory names (by Christians), instructed to be silent, told to go home and ask my husband, and have been denied the opportunity to discuss this with church authority (possibly because I am a woman or because they didn't have the answers – I am not sure. Maybe I was just supposed to be silent?). Pastors who were supposed to guard my faith have wrongly questioned it because I questioned them! I'm not a theologian, historian, or a scholar. I work in healthcare, teach yoga, and try to get enough sleep so I'm not a big crank. I'm simply a woman who had some questions and didn't let God off the hook until I found my answers or, at least, some of them anyway. I'm delighted to share with you what I wrestled out of God!

My life has had many callings: the call to graduate school; to be baptized; to marry my husband and have children; the call to apologize; the call to produce a Christian yoga video; the call to pull over and check my oil, which happened to save me from being involved in a car accident. The list goes on and on. Writing this book has been more than a calling to me; it has felt like a moral obligation. As I scaled the religious walls, I saw the danger and found myself accountable to give the warning to Christian women and men in the way the lookout was accountable to warn Israel:

> You, human one, I've made you a lookout for the house of Israel. Whenever you hear me speaking, you must give them warning from me. If I pronounce a death sentence on wicked people, and you don't warn them to turn from their way, they will die in their guilt, but I will hold you responsible for their blood. (Ezekiel 33:7–8)

My burden and privilege is to sit on those religious walls and blow the horn on the traditionally accepted theology that conceals the power of women. I won't lie; I've enjoyed tearing a few of the walls down as well. Though I do not hold back on my criticism of the church and its pervasive and systematic oppression of women, I understand the church is a large soup of opposing flavors that has been aging for more than two thousand years. Much of what church serves warms and nourishes the soul. But churches also can serve a cold faith. And when the messages of Scripture are not properly preserved, people are served up a downright rotten mystery stew. Ultimately, though, the ubiquity of the church is the people – you and me. I'm not looking to make church the enemy but to call churches to repentance through each individual reader. It's the small everyday ways by which we support women in using their power that add up to big changes. Sexism affects our everyday lives and has a profound impact on the faith of women. We owe it to the girls and women we love, and those who we have not met, to defend their right to be both Christian and feminist in the church.

The thirty-one reflections in *Pink Sunglasses + Yoga Pants* are written as devotionals that pull a feminist concept from Scripture. They uphold the Bible as an authority but recognize that the Bible is a collection of poetry, letters, history, traditions, and legend. These reflections are for anyone who finds it even the slightest bit unbelievable that Christian women are supposed to submit their power. I hope they will inspire action in your everyday life and change how you see faith. Telling the truth about sexism is not easy, especially when it's entangled with religion. So use this book as a reference. Show the skeptics how sexism is alive and well in church, and offer them a different lens through which to see Scripture. And be warned: religious sexists can be the most toxic kind of sexists. If you decide to go into battle with them, don't let them poison you; and this goes for family, husbands, and pastors.

I come from privilege, and I'm sure that will be evident through my stories. While I see how the walls in Christianity create a hierarchy of flesh, I recognize that I, too, have blind spots and may be contributing to walls that do not restrain me but restrain others. There are many kinds of women, and I cannot possibly understand all of them. I have not yet reached the age of a "mature" woman, and I do not understand what it's like to be a teen growing up with the Internet. I understand that black and brown women face issues I may never understand, and gay women sometimes must fight to be classified as women. Please know it is my heart to unite us and empower each woman through what I have learned. I hope my writing will serve as a bridge for all women (and yes, men) to walk over the thorny valley of questioning, and past the invisible religious walls of sexism, to find a place to join power as equals in doing the important work of the church. I hope my writing will give each of you the spiritual lens to see God's brilliant light beyond the walls that have concealed God's power in women. May these reflections deconstruct the sexism in your faith and pull the scales from your eyes as you claim God's power that is inherent in you!

> Before I created you in the womb I knew you;
> before you were born I set you apart;
> I made you a prophet to the nations.
>
> (Jeremiah 1:5)

PART 1

POWER TO HER

I can still make her my slave, for she does not know how to use her power.

– The Wicked Witch of the West
in *The Wonderful Wizard of Oz*

I
___

UNLIKE A NATURAL WOMAN

*Authenticity is the daily practice of letting
go of who we think we're supposed to
be and embracing who we are.*

– **Brené Brown (1965–)**,
American professor and author

L ike many preschool girls, my daughter had a dollhouse with the obligatory miniature furniture and family. It was basically a cubic, wooden frame, which stood twenty-three inches tall so all the rooms could be accessed by the open sides and roof. The dolls had wooden spheres for heads, with no faces, and wiry bodies, so they could sit in chairs or stand holding the baby with their stiff arms and tiny, spherical hands. We would sit on her bedroom floor and play dollhouse, as she placed her brother's *tyrannosaurus rex* on top of the dollhouse frame and roared, "I'm going to eat you!"

My daughter's *T. rex* roared like King Kong as he (or she) invaded the dollhouse and ate the family. I made the young brother escape and had him crying because he was an orphan now. My daughter wasn't too concerned about that. The *T. rex* rounded up the gang of dinosaurs, and they had a jumping off the roof of the house contest, clawing their plastic feet into my carpet with more "roars" and "arghs." My daughter had a few dolls and stuffed animals but didn't pretend with them much. When she outgrew the dollhouse, she inherited my old Barbies and liked those a bit more than the traditional dolls she ignored; maybe because Barbie was an independent woman who could be whomever she wanted to be? Rather than the traditional Barbie play – shopping, getting married, or having lunch – my daughter's Barbies conquered the world with their superpowers! Malibu Barbie and the Brooke Shields Barbie-like doll went on missions. They were unstoppable with their master plans and abilities to fly, shoot, crush, freeze, electrocute or more – clothes were optional for all missions.

I remember playing with those very same dolls, which back then usually had a fashion show, went swimming, or took trips. I yearned for the Barbie Dream Pool, so my dolls could hang out in luxury, but I had to use the bathtub instead. Sometimes, if I could sneak them out of the house, I took my Barbies to explore in the woods. Once, my Malibu Barbie battled with my brother's Darth Vader in the backyard. I buried him for his funeral after their battle; Darth Vader has been missing ever since, and my younger brother still holds this over me. I can't help it if Barbie beat Darth Vader!

"Sugar and spice and everything nice, that's what little girls are made of" and how we groom them to be. This sugar and spice candy-coating starts with the onesies baby girls are dressed in that say "Princess" in glitter letters across their chest. Guilty. I love glitter – and pink – so there was no shame for me in dressing my big-cheeked baby-girl in glittery pink; girly-girl bling wasn't a prescription, however. We feed girls a steady diet of fairy-tale princesses, sparkles, beauty shop, and dolls to care for (and not conquer the world with); narrowing their vision to explore anything outside the boundaries of sweet femininity. Even if our daughters are dinosaur-loving, dirt-bike-riding, fort-building girls who use their Barbies to kill off Darth Vader, when it comes time to face God on Sunday morning, moms usually get a bow in their daughter's hair and doll them up to be more like a sugar-plum fairy than an adventure seeking prodigy. The good Christians at church add some sugar with "Cutie-pie," "Pumpkin," "Baby-Doll," "Sweetie," or "Princess"; that list can go on and on. By the time my daughter was ten she responded to "Honey" or "Sweetie-*anything*," with "You're not my mom (or dad)." She felt their comment was too personal, and she did not want to be seen as sweet; she wanted to be smart! Yet she was stilled judged on how sweet (or unsweet) she gave her reaction.

The sugar, spice, and nice recipe for how girls, and even women, are to be is not necessarily how we really are. This is especially true in many Christian environments, where there's an unspoken rule stating women in a bad mood are not welcome. These churches teach a fairy tale of how God created women sweet, soft, and nurturing, or "naturally feminine." The "naturally feminine" teachings are inconsistent with any creation narrative but are used to hold girls and women in a space that is anything but sweet. The "naturally feminine" police in my own life said girls don't naturally grow up making their Barbies kill off Darth Vader; they must have learned it from somewhere – from my older brother who was the preacher? – yet when girls play house, that's presumably how God created them – "naturally feminine."

As I tried to figure out where "naturally feminine" was located in the Bible, I learned it is not a biblical idea but a product of natural law, a Greek moral code that influenced the New Testament writers. The Greeks described the nature of their customs as "natural law" and believed them to be divine will from God or "God's law." "Natural law" and "God's law" were assumed to be synonymous so people with alternative practices, beliefs, ethnic backgrounds, or customs were considered to be "unnatural" barbarians or heathens and in need of being cleansed. Women were "naturally" gentle and subordinate to men because that was the societal expectation.[1] The symbiosis of natural law and God's law largely dissolved in the Renaissance, but not without the execution of Joan of Arc "for wearing men's clothing" and innumerable supposed witches.[2] Our postmillennial Christian society recognizes the diversity of cultures and people, yet is less willing to sanction women who don't sweeten up with the "naturally feminine" frosting.[3]

"Natural feminism" is not supported biblically as a characteristic created inherent to women, but many Christian circles teach it that way. They turn the nursery rhyme of sugar and spice into a theological behavior code. During my fundamentalist years I tried so hard to please God by fulfilling the "naturally feminine" expectation. As a girl who was unashamed to kill off Darth Vader at the hands of my Malibu Barbie, the "naturally feminine" expectation allowed me to be vulnerable and express my emotions. The church, however, made my vulnerability a permanent state of virtue, which didn't give me the space or encouragement to move beyond my vulnerability and develop my power. Basically, I handed over my lethal Barbie attitude and wasn't allowed to have it back to fight more battles. I was compelled to believe that I was created incorrectly, flawed, or in sin for feeling more spicy than sweet, so I became a harsh judge of myself and other women. At church, ideals of femininity and righteousness were baked together like hard candy because they were unable to see

1. Aristotle, *Politics*, trans. Benjamin Jowett (Kitchener, ON: Batoche Books, 1999), 4–7. Aristotle is considered the "father" of natural law. His writings greatly influenced New Testament thought. Much of his philosophy on natural law can be found in this work.
2. Rosalind Miles, *Who Cooked the Last Supper: The Women's History of the World* (New York: Three Rivers Press, 2001), loc. 112, 2097, Kindle.
3. Cristina L.H. Traina, *Feminist Ethics and Natural Law: The End of the Anathemas* (Washington, DC: Georgetown University Press, 1999), 1–11, 80–87.

the influence of natural law in Scripture. It's a painful testimony because my fellowship was unwilling to authenticate my power beneath the "natural" candy coating they used to cover me.

Christians become limited to see valuable lessons from Jesus when our doctrines are "all Greek" to the power of women. For example, Jesus told a parable about not losing heart in persistency in prayer.[4] The story was about a remorseless judge and a persistent widow.

> **Jesus:** There was a judge living in a certain city. He showed no respect for God or humanity. In that same city there was a widow. Again and again she kept coming to him seeking justice: "Clear my name from my adversary's false accusations!" He paid no attention to her request for a while, but then he said to himself, "I don't care about what God thinks of me, much less what any mere human thinks. But this widow is driving me crazy. She's never going to quit coming to see me unless I hear her case and provide her legal protection."
>
> (Luke 18:2–5, The Voice)

The only decent character in the story is the woman; however the unwillingness to see women with power has blinded many preachers, and even scholars, from seeing that we treat God in the same way the judge treated the widow. The candy-coating of women not only covers our eyes but covers our ears to hear God's subtle and persistent voice that whispers to us to care, be just, and not lose heart. We can step into the role of judge. We can decide whether we will care about God and justice for those without rights. It's within our power to care and influence just

---

4. Scholars cite translation difficulty about verse 18:1, which, more accurately, is translated "not to lose heart" instead of "not to give up." See Arland J. Hultgren, *The Parables of Jesus: A Commentary.* (Grand Rapids, MI/Cambridge, UK: Eerdmans, 2000), 252.

causes. Our internal prejudices of women have rewired us as unable to see God outside the boundaries of what we believe to be natural. Using the picture of God as a widow may "embarrass" us. The widow is without legal standing, poor, and unable to testify in court. Even so, she used her power. The question begs to be answered, "Will [Jesus] find anyone who still has faith," when the persistent whisper of God is ever ignored?[5] Our Bibles define true religion as caring for the "widows who suffer needlessly and resisting the evil influence of the world" (James 1:27, The Voice).

Can a weak old lady be powerful? We tend to underestimate the widows in the Bible. We overlook their cleverness and power as they shatter the helpless stereotypes to get the job done.[6] In Bible times a widow was considered to be a drain on society because she was often too old to bear children and unable to produce income. "Old" *should* be an honorable distinguisher

---

5. Shannon J. Kirshner, "A Standing Applause Sermon," Views from the Edge, October 18, 2016, https://gordoncstewart.com/2016/10/18/a-standing-applause -sermon/.

6. In Genesis 38 we find the story of Tamar, who made sure she had a place in society and a family by dressing up as a prostitute and sleeping with her father-in-law in order to become pregnant within the family line. Her son, Perez, would be listed later in Matthew 1 as being in Jesus' direct family line. The widow of Zarephath receives an honorable mention in Luke 4:26 for sheltering Elijah in 1 Kings 17:9–24. Ruth and Naomi were widows who changed the story of the Jews and made up their own rules for marriage. Amy-Jill Levine. *Short Stories by Jesus: The Enigmatic Parables of a Controversial Rabbi*. (HarperCollins, 2014), 239, 242. The law did give some protection to widows because they were to marry the next closest male relative. This is why Tamar was righteous to pretend to be a prostitute and conceive a child with Judah, because according to the law she was owed a husband to provide her a child from that family, and Judah the patriarch didn't provide it to her. See also Tan Ching Sueng Belinda, "Tamar is Righteous, but Judah Is Not: A Narrative Analysis of Genesis 38" (master's thesis, Singapore Bible College, May 2017).

(Leviticus 19:32; Proverbs 16:31), yet is typically protested by women because it implies the opposite of "sweet". Old is swallowed as "sour," "bitter," "harsh," and "stale" – something to be set aside or discarded. When we lose the power of the widow – a seemingly worthless and powerless woman – we lose the challenge of the Bible in our own lives. If we want to be on the side of truth and justice, as the widow, we must relish the power of each girl and woman. When we judge, they'll never be sweet, attractive, fresh, young, established, affluent, smooth, tight, keen, pure, respectful, gentle, soft, likable, kind, intelligent, assertive, persistent, vigorous, competent, natural, feminine, spiritual, or godly enough.

So let's own up to being like the unremorseful judge; every day we make decisions to say yes or no to God. Despite my being the woman who was pressed to submit "gracefully" to a "natural feminine" role – to keep my "right" relationship with God – I was still a judge. We are all judges in our lives; and God is constantly whispering into our tightly wrapped lives, so that we may find life, despite a dead or unhealthy situation.

In my case, saying yes to God meant moving beyond spiritual ideas that felt natural to me. Leaving my fundamentalist church after nineteen years was counterintuitive and took vast amounts of space and contemplation. God became more than a Father but a depth without boundaries or handles that I needed to brave. I felt as if I was falling (even after I had landed), but that was the consequence of my sitting so high in a seat of judgment, deciding how God, women, and all other people should and shouldn't be. Letting loose of my old anchor, I said yes to a bigger God and took a leap of faith outside the safe boundaries of a church with people I had grown to love. They said I was "falling away" from God, so I prepared to crash, but instead I was carried up high and taught to soar!

Just as an eagle stirs up its nest, *encouraging its young to*
    fly,
    and then hovers over them *in case they need help,*
And spreads its wings and catches them *if they fall,*
    and carries them *up high* on its wings.

                (Deuteronomy 32:11, The Voice)

2

MIRROR, MIRROR, OFF THE WALL

*Sometimes the very thing you're looking
for / Is the one thing you can't see.*

– From the song "Save the Best for Last"
performed by Vanessa Williams (1963–),
American entertainer and Miss America 1984[1]

walked down the runway of my first beauty pageant at age eight. It was at the Village Mall on a Saturday afternoon, and I clearly remember my private lament that I could be outside playing instead of dressing up and doing this. When I look back at the pictures, my soft smile showed absolutely no teeth, and I can tell I was burdened. But, even at such a young age, I was proficient at hiding my irritation, so if I was angry about not being able to ride my bike or read my books in my secret clubhouse in the woods, I didn't show it. As a good contestant, I obediently acted the way I was expected to act. I complied with dressing up, standing up straight on stage, and following the trail of masking tape Xs. I even smiled at the judges while my feet were squeezed into the

---

1. "Save the Best for Last," Written by: Phil Galdston, Jon Lind, Wendy Waldman-Parker, Lyrics © Sony/ATV Music Publishing LLC, Universal Music Publishing Group, Kobalt Music Publishing Ltd., Round Hill Music Big Loud Songs.

black patent leather Mary Jane one-inch heels I had worn the previous Christmas. There's a lot to think about when competing in pageants. The carrot Mom dangled in front of me (as if I had a choice whether or not to participate) was that I would become confident in presenting myself in public. She probably took me out for ice cream, too, but I don't remember.

I won the pageant.

The interview must have been the part that got me the points because my dresses were from Kmart; and as I said, I didn't use a toothy smile. As we girls were lined up on stage, my presentation was vastly different from the frilly dresses, polished smiles, and hairspray-caked 80s hair of the girls who stood next to me. My shoes were black; the other girls wore white. My naturally curly hair was on the verge of frizz, in a side ponytail of banana curls that Mom had sculpted around her index finger with a wet brush. We didn't use curling irons, and I wore very little makeup. Mom entered me into another pageant a couple of months later; I won that one, too, with a little (very little) fancier dress and hair. I was never great at team sports, but somehow I came to dominate the pageant world. Evidently I was princess material!

By the time I was twelve I had enough rhinestone tiaras for every girl in my class. I could flash my "natural" pageant smile like nobody's business and give my elevator speech about who I was and how I wanted to change the world (which wasn't *that* dear to my heart, because I don't remember what it was!). I was the picture of an all-American, privileged, young beauty princess, standing up straight and wearing a crown on my head.

My price in the social contract was to maintain my "natural" pageant smile and hide any discomfort. Showing my pain – outside of shedding an honest tear for a social cause, or because my parents were fighting, or I was being judged in tighter dresses and higher heels would break the magic aura I was supposed to deliver and could destroy the unlikely possibility of my creating world peace!

In spite of all the grief beauty pageants get from feminists, I do believe they were instrumental in my development of self-presentation. Mom was right, again. After becoming "the fairest of them all" with my olive skin, dark eyes and hair, I learned to use my personal presentation to manage the world around me. I'm still confident (enough) going into interviews or being looked at. I know how to speak to a crowd and, of course, smile and wave!

Pageant feminism empowers girls to speak publicly, attend college, and become community leaders. The pageant world has a darker side, however, because participating in a pageant requires submitting to male gazing, which results in the sexual objectification and malaise of the woman. So let's be real; I would be a liar if I said I have never used male attention to gain access to power. Flashing my "natural" pageant smile and buttering a man up with beauty-queen charm has opened doors for me; but that isn't a power that will move the world, unless you're Queen Esther.

Queen Esther of the Bible is sometimes described as a beauty queen who fought for social justice with her good looks. I once heard a narrow-minded Bible-talk (small group) leader elevate Queen Esther's morality for being "the fairest of them all"; that is, the most righteous of them all. His message taught that submission to male sway is what makes a woman moral and beautiful and, therefore, diminished Queen Esther's courage and character in saving the Jewish people. This "princess" theology upholds Queen Esther for her submission and amiable femininity, veiling her rebellious actions, which caused her to risk execution.

A closer (and more accurate) unpacking of the book of Esther reveals Queen Esther's suitor, King Ahasuerus (Xerxes I), was basically a sex trafficker and likely serial rapist. This king forcibly gathered many of his kingdom's virgins into slavery, setting the most beautiful of them aside for his sex pageant as he searched for a replacement for his former queen. These young women were given beauty treatments for an entire year presumably to prepare them for competition in how well they could impress the king in bed. As the winner of this sexual beauty pageant, Esther won the prize of queen...Miss (sexually violated) Persia? Queen Esther survived in this sexual hierarchy to confront her "master," even though as queen there were no laws to protect her. She risked her life to become an informant, and rightfully so, I might add. Esther wasn't a docile woman; rather, she used her charm to tap into the power she needed for bringing "world peace" to her people. She understood God's truth as a greater moral authority than any man-made law; and she was right to bravely manipulate the system with her pageant charm. She hid all her pain and discomfort, and smiled and waved when she was supposed to, while being brave enough to stick her nose into the king's political business though her predecessor, Queen Vashti, was deposed for doing much less.

Evidently it takes more than seven eunuchs to fetch a sitting queen (Esther 1:10–12).[2] My sexist Bible-talk leader villainized Queen Vashti, portraying her as a disobedient pagan who deserved exile because she didn't submit to her drunken husband's demand that parade herself as his beauty queen in front of a gathering of drunken men. I can't say I blame her. Queen Vashti is to be admired for refusing to be eye candy for inebriated men. Both this king and my Bible-talk leader clearly believed it is okay for a beautiful woman to be an ornament of male power without regard to her other virtues.

The Bible doesn't define what "wearing her royal crown...to display her beauty" means (verse 11, NIV). Was she to strip down

---

2. Eunichs were sexually castrated male servants of the king.

to her crown? Was she supposed to smile and wave like a pageant queen? Verse 10 describes the king as being "in high spirits" from the wine, after seven days of his no limits drinking bash (which sounds as though it could rival any spring break beach party), so it's probably reasonable to assume he was plastered. With how the Bible describes the drinking during this seven days, I, personally, visualize the palace as being the site of a multikegger frat party, littered with men who were passed out, had urinated on themselves, vomited, and had lost their shirts somewhere.[3] If these men are anything like the guys I saw in college, the longer the party, the higher the spirits, the crazier the dares, the wilder the stunts, and the more unrestrained sexual aggression towards women. All-you-can-drink private parties are dangerous places for females, even in the ancient days before the rape pill.[4] Queen Vashti was right to "disobey" her husband's call.

To my bewilderment I know Christian men and women – such my former Bible-talk leader – who have expected their adolescent daughters to avoid drunken parties; yet, out of the other side of

---

3. You may read the entire interaction in Esther 1. The Bible describes this event in detail with bling furniture and mosaic flooring of crystal, marble, and mother of pearl. Unlimited **royal** wine was served in individually crafted golden goblets. The rule about the drinks was "No limits!" The king had ordered everyone serving wine in the palace to offer as much as each guest wanted (Esther 1:8). Being nobody was required to drink, there may have been, just maybe, one half-sober person there.

4. I personally never attended a frat party and avoided most house parties because I believed them to be dangerous. I did see the passed-out guys in the yards the next morning. In college I watched women whose lives were forever changed because of something that happened at a party. I would like to think I would be like Queen Vashti and not attend her husband's party, but I don't know if I'm as strong as she was. A great resource to delve into the issues and dangers of sexual violence on college campuses is Vanessa Grigoriadis. *Blurred Lines: Rethinking Sex, Power, and Consent on Campus* (New York: Houghton Mifflin Harcourt, 2017).

their mouths, they condemn Queen Vashti. They hold an exegetical beauty pageant, judging Queen Esther as righteous for showing her beauty and bravery, and Queen Vashti as immoral for bravely avoiding a brothel (to ironically celebrate her beauty). These Christians uphold Xerxes and his drunken "inner circle" verdict as God's law. They regard Vashti's power to say no as a threat to their "right" to gawk at and control women.

My former Bible-talk leader argued this was God's lesson to make sure all the women would remain "in their proper place." The "proper place" of *what*? To be lusted over whether she liked it or not? I seriously disagreed with the morality of his teaching that it is okay to parade a woman's beauty in front of boozy men, without her consent, just because her husband told her to. I knew this man on a personal basis and was certain he would be furious if his daughter's husband ordered her to perform in front of other men in some home video or at a party. When Bible teachers debase Vashti, they are aligning their value of women with the pagan drunkards of Xerxes and his council, who saw women as sexual ornaments of their power. Vashti made the respectable decision and avoided dehumanization. She wielded her power of no, even at the cost of losing her crown.

Despite both queens' radical nature, princess theology softens Queen Esther's image to fit a narrative that hides her real power and demonizes Queen Vashti for wielding hers rightfully. It is unfair to compare these two uniquely righteous queens in a perverted moral beauty pageant. Queen Vashti and Queen Esther both endured harsh treatment in risking their lives for what they believed to be right, they used their power in very different ways to serve and survive. It's notable how Esther risked her life and saved an entire nation of people, people who were ancestors to Jesus, not with waging a war but strategically flashing a pageant smile. Like both women, we each have different virtues and powers and should focus on honoring the strengths of each woman instead of competing with them to be "the fairest of them all."

Princess theology teaches women's righteousness as a pageant competition where women compete to be the most compliant to man-made standards of "spiritual" beauty and charm. Man-made Christian rules present "contests" in a superficial pageant judged by both men and women. I've seen and even competed in these "fairest of them all" moral competitions. Replace "fairest" with "modest," "best mother," "most hospitable," "most influential," or "purest." Some churches are full of Christian women who are competing to be the most compliant to church standards of moral beauty and pleasantries, as if the worst thing they could do is disappoint someone. These women keep a warm smile on the outside, while they hide their discomfort and pain. They live by a complex moral code created to judge women, assigning standards of beauty – inner and outer – as indicators of virtue. Losers are shamed as not good enough or even labeled as sinners. At times I've been threatened with the label of "disrespectful" or "bitter." Even though I no longer attend a church with this subculture, I still hear a voice inside me warning that I am not supposed to oppose a man directly. I'm still realizing I can't fight every battle with a smile and dress, using my pleasant pageant "world peace" voice.

We live in a world that honors "the fairest of them all" and abhors female power. It's no secret that a woman who submits to male attention has access to power, however gaining power in this way is essentially borrowing someone else's strength and not necessarily tapping into her own "inner character." If a woman is promoted to a leadership position in church she should be able to keep her authentic voice. It's important for each woman to find her power from within and not just be a puppet of another's power.

Standards of beauty have always been deeply ingrained in me, even to the point of my smiling to earn love and care as a child.

After all, I had a pageant mom and later attended a church that taught princess theology. As I grow older, I try to not be like the older villain queen in Snow White, unable to see my own beauty in the mirror when a younger more beautiful woman passes by. As Queen Vashti was cast aside for a younger queen, older women, too, are cast aside and disqualified to access the stage. These mature women have a character and strength from within, and they are some of my favorite people to be with and learn from. Mature women are the most powerful women I know because they have found God's power from within them and no longer rely solely on "outward beauty."

A mature Christian woman has learned that life is not a contest to be "the fairest of them all." A woman's appraisal does not require submission to male gaze or male power; that's princess theology. Instead, each woman reflects a unique power beyond being poised with a flashy pageant smile. It can take a bit of reflection to see this "inner beauty" of ours, and it may require taking down the mirror to understand what's beneath the veil. Christian women become veiled to their power when conditioned to self-value by the "outward beauty" of princess theology. But our lives are not called to be a commendable performance. We are called to use our power to reflect God's glory. We are called to "act with great confidence" in understanding this hope (2 Corinthians 3:12) and be transformed by seeing God's glorious Spirit in the mirror instead.

> All of us are looking with unveiled faces at the glory of the Lord as if we were looking in a mirror. We are being transformed into that same image from one degree of glory to the next degree of glory. This comes from the Lord, who is the Spirit.
> (2 Corinthians 3:18)

3

NO SUCH THINK

Sexy doesn't have to come with the
price tag of being dumb.

– Alecia Beth Moore (aka, PINK, 1979–),
American singer and songwriter

f you ever want to be treated as a "dumb blonde," become an aerobics instructor. As a brunette – and one who could never, ever pull off being a blonde – I typically don't advocate for blondes, but I'm going to stand arm in arm with my blonde sisters for a moment. Let's do this, ladies! If any group of women get the candy coat, it's blondes. Blondes, especially slender blondes, are held to an impossible image that requires a perma-smile and childlike demeanor. It's as if they must put an "ies" or exclamation mark at the end of their words: "ouchies," "oopsies," "besties," and so forth. If blondes are mad, people treat their anger with "kid gloves," as if their vexation is a cute pout or they are incapable of emotionally processing a real problem and shouldn't be taken seriously. Blonde jokes are still socially acceptable; and it has occurred to me that dumb blonde jokes don't apply to blonde men, which reveals dumb blonde jokes' true identity: dumb women jokes, at the expense of blondes. These "jokes" reduce women's intelligence to hair color and undermine women's credibility.

I was once told I was blonde and had dyed my hair brown. This person was trying to insult me and insinuate that I lacked intelligence. A guy with whom I competed for top grades in school publicly, and regularly, called me an "airhead"; he, too, suggested I was dumb. I've never been told a dumb aerobics instructor joke; however, there is a stereotype in that role and some sort of invisible sign on your head that says, "Don't take me seriously" because of my spandex.

Some of my most significant ministry work has been done in yoga pants. No joke. In my almost three decades as a yoga and fitness instructor I have listened to hundreds and hundreds of women share their intimate stories with me in the sweaty, casual space after class. It's sort of like being a bartender or hairdresser where the ladies tell all, but at a gym. I have listened to stories of women who were surviving abuse, adultery, family dysfunction, and illness; helping their kids in school, going back to school, and raising toddlers, teenagers, and grandchildren; dealing with marriage dysfunction, taking care of parents, living with a husband's illness, explaining their divorces to their church friends, paying bills, giving their daughter a cell phone, and the list goes on and on. I know they tell me more than their pastor or counselor because I'm not an official. I'm the non-threatening, don't-have-to-take-serious yoga and fitness instructor. I also know I give great advice, because so many women come back to my class and tell me so. I love to hear and see how their stories are progressing as they become stronger, more fit women; and it's one of my greatest privileges to be on the journey with them as they transform their lives and health. Watching women morph from their first day, tiptoeing to the back corner of class and wearing an oversized tee shirt, into strutting confidently into the front row with matching tank top and yoga pants is an enduring pleasure of my life. Helping women transform doesn't just happen by jumping around and smiling a lot with an excited voice in class each week. It comes by understanding the science of diet and exercise. And, more importantly, it comes by helping motivate women to overcome their emotional barriers. You see, sometimes okay, more than sometimes – women dumb themselves down, but not in the way you might think.

Before I start this conversation, I'm want to be very clear: being *fit* and being *sexy* are two separate things. I know many fit women who do not feel sexy, and I know many sexy women who are not fit. Sexy is a comfortability and confident expression within the body. The world has a plethora of female, sexy expressions; and being fit doesn't necessarily make you comfortable or confident in your own skin. That said, the perceived stereotype is that *fit* is synonymous with *sexy*. So, for sake of this conversation, to understand how women dumb themselves down and don't reach their fitness goals, I must make fit synonymous with sexy, so we'll call it *fit-sexy*.

One of the greatest barriers I see standing in the way of women achieving their fitness goals is their prejudices towards fit-sexy women. For example, women will come to class with the belief that their marriage will get better if they get in better shape. However, as they start getting into shape, they find the opposite to be true. Each time I've helped a wife change her figure, the dynamic in her marriage changes, often because the husband now must deal with his wife receiving attention from other men. Husband aside (that's *his* problem, not hers), the wife must decide if she can be both a good wife and fit-sexy. I've seen many, many women give up on their goal of health because they cannot accept that fit-sexy and "good wife" can be portrayed in the same image of a woman. Other women start having difficulty in their sex lives because they now look more like the women in porn videos (the ones some of their husbands watch).

Yes, that's what you get when you discuss marriage or sex with me after class; I'll challenge you about your stereotypes towards fit-sexy women and why you don't want to become "sexy." I've also met victims of sexual assault who fear the new attention they are getting, to the point of major anxiety. I always validate these women and encourage them to not give up their health for a rapist. I also ask them to make an appointment with their therapist promptly and tell them I will be follow up with them because I care.

The strict, religious women who come to my class, despite my spandex, have voiced to me their fear of becoming sinful because they are getting fit; in their eyes, sexy is bad. In these examples, each woman boils down the credibility of a wife or woman to an image or appearance. She struggles to accept she can be both fit-sexy and credible, because she internally dumbs down *sexy* (at least the stereotypical fit-sexy). It's the same prejudice as people who shell out mean-spirited blonde jokes or dumb woman jokes to put women back into their place of being an image. We've all heard a woman dish out a dumb blonde joke. Guilty. But here's the thing: in our society, being a sexy and credible woman is like being queen; the power is there, but sexism wants to preserve women as an image and is not interested in the intelligence behind the good looks. A woman can be sexy *or* credible, but she pays a price to be both.

Despite the empowered lives and strong bodies I've helped to shape, some people still see me as a superficial, self-absorbed, and, perhaps, even materialistic chick in spandex. An aerobics instructor. They clearly don't understand how wisdom can be delivered from a woman in yoga pants. I started teaching fitness in college. It was a natural fit with my dance background and collection of VHS step aerobics tapes. Back in those days of side ponytails and sweatbands, the dumbing down of us skinny chicks in unitards was worse than it is today, or maybe I was just younger and more susceptible. I was called "baby" and "girl"; and if I eye-rolled the person or bawled them out about the sexism, they moved to "kid" instead. The problem with these names is that they, too, dumbed down my talents. They caused me to question my maturity, adulthood, validity, and power. As I'm aging and not so easily dumbed down, the comments are migrating to accusations of "rude," as if my seemingly discourteous behavior caused me to lose my head. It has occurred to me that black women are dumbed down with accusations of "angry" and "rude," and mature women with "nag," as if they, too, lost their minds. The dumb downs undermine women's credibility so they don't have to be taken seriously. It's arduous treatment based on an image. If you haven't been the topic of a blonde joke, or lost credibility because of a "sexy" appearance, age, or skin color (that somehow makes you volatile), you've certainly experienced the dumb down if you are female and drive a vehicle. Don't get me started on that one.

Throughout my life I have found it difficult to manage the dumb downs. In my teenage years I learned to exhibit a much different demeanor when I talked with guys. I smiled more and said less. In fact, the less I said the more they liked me, which begged the question of whether they really liked me at all. I dumbed myself down. Eye contact and a variety of smiles can say a lot; perhaps that's why selfie photos are so popular these days with teen girls and young women. There is no shame in a great selfie, but put some smart words as a caption and allow yourself to be seen as both (appropriately) sexy *and* credible.

Contrary to all the dumb downs to women, the book of Proverbs portrays Wisdom as a feminine being who has understanding and strength. Her name is Lady Wisdom, and her voice is heard by all humanity. She is not immature, childlike, or temperamental. Women – especially blondes in spandex or black women in a weave – are rarely recognized for their inherent Lady Wisdom. In fact, Lady Wisdom has been largely lost in translation. She was with God before the very first events of creation and offers a powerful promise of hope for one who is willing to listen to her.

PINK SUNGLASSES AND YOGA PANTS

So now listen to me, my children:
    those who live by my ways will find *true* happiness.
Pay attention to my guidance, *dare to* be wise,
    and don't disregard my teachings.
The one who listens to me,
    who carefully seeks me in everyday things
    and delays action until my way is apparent, that one will
        find *true* happiness.
For when he recognizes *and follows* me, he finds *a peaceful*
    and satisfying life
    and receives favor from the Eternal.

                            (Proverbs 8:32–35 The Voice)

Lady Wisdom is a powerful reminder of God's intricate instructions beyond the face of a single "Father." *Sophia*, the feminine noun used in the New Testament for wisdom and is linked with Christ as an ingredient for salvation.[1] "He became wisdom [*sophia*] from God for us. This means that he made us righteous and holy, and he delivered us" (1 Corinthians 1:30). And the Bible states clearly Christ as embodying her. "All the treasures of wisdom [*sophia*] and knowledge are hidden in him (Colossians 2:3).

Depersonalizing or neutralizing the feminine attributes of God as seen in Lady Wisdom or *sophia* has denied women the credibility (and opportunity) to realize their God-given image from within. A woman's ability to be credible and wise has everything to do with embracing God's wisdom – *sophia* – and nothing to do with the color of her hair or what kind of mood she's in. Stripping God's image of Lady Wisdom has perhaps been the most devastating assault to the power of Christian women, the dumb-down of all dumb-downs. As Bible translations hide the

---

1. Jann Aldredge-Clanton, *In Whose Image? God and Gender* (New York: Crossroads Publishing, 1990), 34.

22

feminine power of Lady Wisdom, and *sophia*, the narrative of women is seen largely as a silent external image, a hair color, a *gluteus maximus*, an aerobics instructor, a crazy old lady. It's time we wise up to the dumb down and embody our feminine wisdom, maturity, and power, regardless of our hair color, hair texture, or sexual image, because our own Lady Wisdom is more valuable than silver or gold (hair or otherwise).

> How fortunate are those who discover Lady Wisdom
> > and those who understand *her ways*!
> For her worth is greater than the most expensive prize *you*
> > *could win.*
> > Her profit is greater than the finest thing *you could buy*.
> No gem is more precious than she is –
> > your *most extravagant* desire doesn't come close to her.
> She holds *the secret of a* long life in one hand
> > and riches and fame in her other hand.
> Her ways are pleasant;
> > all of her pathways are peaceful.
> She is like a tree that produces a satisfied life for anyone
> > who can wrap their arms around her;
> > happiness waits for any who hold her tightly.
> > > (Proverbs 3:13–18, The Voice)

4

HUMAN RESOURCES

No-one would remember the Good Samaritan if he'd only had good intentions; he had money as well.

– Margaret Thatcher (1925–2013),
British prime minister 1979–1990

My fitness hobby started in the early 1990s when yoga pants looked more like a second skin of shiny spandex whose bright colors were still bleeding from the '80s. My hobby developed into a side hustle, teaching Hi-Lo aerobics, which moved into step aerobics, then kickboxing, Pilates, and yoga. For a mother of multiple young children, free day care at a gym goes a long way, so my side gig became my main gig. In those years I earned more money as a fitness professional, teaching classes and managing fitness programming at a gym, than I did as a professional clinician who would have needed to pay child care and clock into a clinic.

The work environment at a gym isn't quite as professional as a hospital or clinic. If ever there is a petri dish of sexist come-ons, it's a gym where management unashamedly judges which woman's backside is the hottest in yoga pants. Showing up to work in spandex brought on its own set of sexism. Keeping a cordial demeanor of "thanks for the compliment, but I'm here to workout" helped to fend off sexual innuendos. Spending every other year baring my pregnant belly also helped to send that message.

Since my managerial duties at the gym mostly involved the fitness instructors and programming, much of the job could be done at home or at the gym on my own schedule. As the programs grew, so did my influence, overseeing the exercise programs. In the early 2000s email marketing was proving effective. I was organized and collected members' email addresses as they attended the programs I oversaw. Most of the participants were women, and I communicated with them regularly to let them know about classes and programs offered. The management began to feel my influence with their members was a threat to the business. They pressed me for the email list, and I didn't hand it over.

During our months of discussion about the email list, I received a bit of intimidation from them. One manager threatened to fire me. Another – one of the world's strongest men, really – was trying to intimidate me with his machismo. I remained calm and polite; I *was* the yoga instructor, after all! At 125 pounds in my yoga pants, I stood my ground while facing twice my weight in muscle. When he was flying off the handle, accusing me of trying to steal his members, I stayed eyeball to eyeball with him and reminded him that I worked at his gym, not someone else's. Changing gyms in the fitness industry is a little tricky; and, fortunately for them, I didn't want to start my own gym.

We negotiated a better financial opportunity, even better than owning my own spot. We agreed, in writing, that I could use the square footage and equipment in their gym, free of charge, to train and run additional up-sell fitness programs, in addition to teaching my regular classes and managing the programs. It was a win-win deal for both of us because management got the email list they wanted, and I made 100 percent profit at their facility and still got my free day care!

Women face a unique set of challenges in the workplace.

Being proactive about making money not only pays bills but is upheld by Scripture as a spiritual issue in the parable of the valuable coins in Matthew 25:14–30. In this passage Jesus connects faith to our responsibility in multiplying the talents God gives us. The meaning of a talent is widely discussed, and it can mean many things; but in this instance Jesus used money as the example. We learn from the parable that when we don't use our God-given talents – whether that means money, skills, or influence – we can lose them. And a person who does not utilize his or her talent is a "worthless servant" (verse 30). In Jesus's parable the master honored the servants who were proactive to grow their talents, and he condemned the passivity of servant who buried his talent and was avoiding conflict. In fact, Jesus communicates punitive consequences for being passive.

Equating faith with earning money is a menacing teaching. Many believe money is evil, or they are victims of widespread social injustices that deny them economic opportunity, including women.[1] In the United States women earn an estimated 82 percent of what men earn for doing the same job.[2] Despite the obstacles, Christian women are called to produce fruit, just same as men, and are warned of condemnation when we bury our gifts. Unearthing the buried talents of women is an untapped opportunity of many churches. By teaching women how they deserve, and can negotiate, better business and wages, the church becomes a part of growing their talents, which is bound to reciprocate. Conversely, when churches dissuade women from pursing economic opportunity, the leadership is condemnable.

1. World Economic Forum, *The Global Gender Gap Report 2017.* Insight Report (Geneva, Switzerland: World Economic Forum) http://www3.weforum.org/docs /WEF_GGGR_2017.pdf.
2. Nikki Graf, Anna Brown, and Eileen Patten, "The Narrowing, but Persistent, Gender Gap in Pay," Fact Tank, *Pew Research Center*, April 9, 2018, http://www .pewresearch.org/fact-tank/2018/04/09/gender-pay-gap-facts/.

The Bible is very clear about church leadership being judged more strictly than those who sit in the pews (James 3:1). Church leaders who bury women's God-given talent – whether the talent is used inside or outside of church leadership – should really heed these warnings.[3]

I work in healthcare and fitness spaces, and I love to serve and help people become healthier; however, as much as this helps people, I cannot afford to do it for free. I've come to realize that if I do not charge enough money, I am limiting my resources to help more people in the future, denying my affluence in the same way the servant buried his talent. The parable of the valuable coins is a stark motivator for me to push for the raise, charge what I'm worth, and sell the book!

Advocating for myself has not come without conflict or uneasiness. With my boss at the gym, I had to curb my communications, navigate the verbal and nonverbal threats, and endure the once-over looks before we talked. I refrained from meeting with him privately during our bumpy negotiations, because I knew he had anger management issues, and I didn't want the potential verbal abuse. (For the record, cell phone videos are a great defense here.) Before and after that time, I met with him alone in his office as needed. Despite his unashamed affinity for women's backsides, he was never inappropriate with me, nor did he consider me some sort of female threat in spandex as I met with him privately wearing my yoga pants. We kept to our work and that was it.

In 2017 the Christian blogosphere reevaluated the "Billy Graham rule" when a prominent politician admitted to practicing it. The rule advocates that married Christian men not meet alone with women, other than their wives, to avoid temptation, gossip, or false accusations. It's also touted as a rule to keep women

3. Gilbert Bilezikian, *Beyond Sex Roles* (Grand Rapids, MI: Baker Academic, 2006), 140.

safe. The criticism on the Internet was that this rule misuses power, blocking women from promotional opportunity because it segregates them from accessing the power held by their male bosses.[4] It's clear to see how a woman would miss opportunity if she is restricted from meeting with her boss. My friend – a talented, degreed musician – once told me she was denied the position of music director at church because the pastor did not feel comfortable meeting directly with her as a single woman. He hired a less qualified man, and our worship suffered. She rightfully left that church, by the way.

My overall sentiment is that the Billy Graham rule lowers the Christian standard in the workplace by excusing men and women from developing personal virtues in the area of professional relationship. Legalistic rules do not create moral character, and the Billy Graham rule sees men as horny animals and women as morally dangerous. There are better ways to promote a safe and fair work environment for both women and men. Meeting in view of others, such as in office spaces with windows or leaving the door open, meeting in public, inviting a third person when appropriate, distributing e-mail recaps of meetings, keeping a work diary, and not micromanaging are only a few options. Staying focused on work is always the best option for everyone.

Women and men can hold private meetings without sexual distractions. I know this because many of us do. Throughout my professional career, which spans hospitals, clinics, university, and the office, I have met privately with many male bosses and coworkers without incident. At the gym my own intuition guided me to refrain from meeting privately with the personal trainer who had a sofa in his office, or the manager who watched porn on his

---

4. Katelyn Beaty, "A Christian Case Against the Pence Rule" *New York Times*, November 15, 2017, https://www.nytimes.com/2017/11/15/opinion/pence-rule-christian-graham.html.

computer. In high school and college, I did endure workplace sexual harassment and assault at my part-time jobs in which I held little professional power.

My first job was at a burger joint. I was sixteen, but my age didn't detour a manager from offering me alcohol and pot and asking me out on a regular basis. When I refused, my cash drawer would frequently be twenty dollars short. I was never fired, so I'm guessing the owner suspected I was being framed.

One Sunday afternoon, when I was in college, I was working at my job as a restaurant server, and I was assaulted in the deep freeze by a cook who exposed himself and refused to let me out. I hollered and with force yelled "No!" at him, but nobody came. He smiled wryly and moved towards me, insisting I give him a kiss. I gave him the peck on the cheek, so I wouldn't have to continue feeling his penis on my leg. I regret that I was more concerned about getting my slice of *a la mode* pie out hot with the ice cream cold, and keeping the fast pace of Sunday afternoon business rather than protecting myself with both hands.

A decade later, while I was working at the gym, I observed the front desk manager frequently groping a young female employee he had hired. Feeling that I was in a position of power to help her, I reported it to the owner, and he responded by firing the young female. It wasn't exactly the response I was hoping for. To the owner his manager was the more valuable talent, and the lower-level female employee was more easily replaced. Women who work low paying jobs often find themselves preyed upon.

In *Settle for More*, former corporate attorney and national news anchor Megyn Kelly describes the sexual harassment she endured when meeting privately with male bosses. Her testimony brought down one of television's most influential moguls and laid significant groundwork for the #MeToo movement. Kelly shares some very practical advice to document all incidences of sexual harassment and sexual assault, whether you do or do not report it. Placing the documentation on file with an attorney as soon as it happens is the best practice if you can afford it. At minimum a copy of the documentation should be shared with a trusted individual who can serve as a witness if needed.[5] Keeping a detailed work diary is a practical way for *any* woman – local waitress or national broadcaster – to protect and grow her professional power and keep track of situations that have made her uncomfortable.

As humans made in God's image, we have all been endowed with unique gifts; however, women's gifts are not always valued and therefore not invested in. The Bible lists many types of gifts: teaching, preaching, helping, administration, faith, healing, prophecy, and more. The gifts are never listed as gender specific, and all are said to be empowered by the same Spirit:

> And serve each other according to the gift each person has received, as good managers of God's diverse gifts
>
> (1 Peter 4:10)

> All these things are produced by the one and same Spirit who gives what he wants to each person.   (1 Corinthians 12:11)

Since the Spirit does not discern gifts by gender, it seems to me that interfering with women being able to use their gifts is an insult to the Holy Spirit, something Jesus considered a heavy misdeed. When women are not trusted to hold power, are paid less for their talents, prohibited from engaging in workplace meetings, or are not mentored or invested in because they are female, it's a violation of our call to multiply our human resources. It's unfair, yes; but, as women, we cannot afford to sit back and blame the system or sexism. We must not avoid conflict as the worthless

---

5. Megyn Kelly, *Settle For More* (New York: HarperCollins, 2016), 299–314.

servant did, but we must be proactive and assertive to multiply our talents. We are called to use our gifts to build affluence.

While I was going through my negotiations at the gym, there were many days I just wanted to quit. My mom gave me one of my greatest anecdotes: "Trust is better than like." There are many likable people who are not worthy of trust. I didn't necessarily like my bosses, but I trusted them to fulfill our contract. It's fair to say they didn't always like me either, but we were satisfied working together because we trusted each other. We worked in fitness to multiply the power of our clients as we spurred each other on to build our own. Trust is better than like; and often the people who grow our talents the most are those who painfully provoke us. "As iron sharpens iron" (Proverbs 27:17), these people are not always the ones we like, but they're the ones we must trust.

In the same way that iron sharpens iron,
    a person sharpens the character of his friend.
                    (Proverbs 27:17, The Voice)

5

PROMISE OR PROPERTY?

Virtue can only flourish among equals.

– Mary Wollstonecraft,
British writer 1759–1797

As a girl I never dreamed of my wedding day. In fact, marriage wasn't something I aspired to. My dreams were about growing up and being free of my parents. Really, I just wanted to be safe. Living in the chaos of my parents' marriage, their representation of the institution gave me a sour taste of holy matrimony. My younger brother has never married, though I eventually did. And for the record, I'm glad I did!

If I could do my wedding over, I would change a few things. Being escorted down the aisle by my dad would be the first. It's not that I want to dishonor my dad's memory; I want to honor myself. My husband stood at the altar with his brothers all tuxedoed up as groomsmen, with no parents necessary. Ceremonially, he could stand alone. As a female, I did not stand alone, because in tradition a bride is considered property of her dad, being handed over as property of her husband.

On my wedding day, my dad walked me slowly down the aisle so all the witnesses could ogle joyfully my ornamental wedding attire. It was a large wedding, and I remember smiling at each guest. I wanted to remember. Dad was crying like a child. When the time came our officiant (my older brother) asked, "Who gives this woman," and Dad could barely talk. His tears that day were a mixture of joy and bitterness. I had seen Dad cry before, but this was different. I wasn't sure he was going to make it. It felt more like I was the one walking him down the aisle, and I remember thinking I could have made easier by walking on my own.

Dad was always a bit unstable and unpredictable with his emotions. His passionate range was wide and wild. He and Mom had been divorced more than ten years when I married, and he was still stalking her. Dad called Mom each day and drove by her house at least once a week. He would not give up on the idea that Mom was *his*. Though legally their marriage was no more, *till death do us part* was still valid for Dad, and I often wondered if it would be him who brought that on for both of them. Bringing Mom and Dad together, especially under the circumstances of my wedding, was risky because they could have erupted into a violent argument. As part of the unofficial wedding party assignment, I asked my brother-in-law to be a special usher to my dad. No tuxedo necessary, just keep him pacified. My younger brother kept watch over Mom, maintaining his lifetime post of peacemaker between Mom and Dad.

As my husband-to-be and I were preparing for our big day, we decided our theme scripture would be, "We were glad to share not only God's good news with you but also our very lives because we cared for you so much" (1 Thessalonians 2:8). We put this passage on the front of the printed program and planned to center our vows around it. In the year 2001, which should have been a time of progression towards egalitarian marriage, we were told by my brother, the officiant, that Ephesians 5:23–25 must be shared at the wedding because it laid the foundation for biblical marriage: "A husband is the head of his wife like Christ is head of the church, that is, the savior of the body. So wives submit to their husbands in everything like the church submits to Christ. As for husbands, love your wives just like Christ loved the church and gave himself for her".

He said men are bullheaded and need five verses from God to love their wives (verses 25–30), and women only need one (verse 24) to understand that her submission is what makes a marriage work. For two becoming one, this seemed to divide instead of unite. I was ripe from graduate school, and my brother had been married for more than ten years. I assumed he knew better than I. I was ready to be married and didn't want to make a big stir about Bible scriptures. Besides, I had come from a fractured family. What did I know about marriage?

Just a few years prior I had plunged into a fresh start with "true" Christianity. I was a year from ending my seven-year college career, and I was starting to think about including marriage in the rest of my life, even though I didn't have a serious boyfriend. My older brother and his wife appeared happy, so I asked him what he recommended to have a good marriage. Their marriage was the brightest light I saw, so I wanted what he had. He was emphatic to share how his marriage would be over by now without the "kingdom" (his church) helping him to live in biblical marriage. I wanted to have a different marriage from my parents, whose misery spread like poison ivy. As far as marriage went, it seemed reasonable to do it "biblically," though I was blindsided by the stringent marriage regulations this "kingdom" would hold over me.

When the discussion about wedding vows took place, I was conditioned to not question the leaders in the "kingdom" because they were the leaders (*and clearly didn't want me to be a Berean, even though they said they did*). I didn't know a ton about the

Bible, although I had read it two or three times by that stage in my life. What my brother and the rest of the leaders (including women) never discussed was how *their* preferred wedding scripture is framed by other scriptures that involve Paul's teaching of mutuality. Paul applied Christ's law to marriage when he wrote, "Submit to *each other* out of respect for Christ" (Ephesians 5:21, italics mine).

Paul wrote these marriage instructions to the Ephesians because they were in a quandary of how to practice Christ's new law *and* adhere to the Roman household codes. The laws of the Roman Empire ordered hierarchy within the home, classifying women, children, and slaves as property of the man of the house, or *paterfamilias*. The *paterfamilias* was like a god, and everything was his world or property. Paul understood marriage to be a potentially intimate relationship and elevated Christian marriage to be based on love, not authority. He did this while continuing to recognize Roman law, knowing that most of his listeners were bound to it. Most of us aren't accustomed to the law dictating how we live in our homes, but household laws were a reality for the early Christians. The idea of women as submissive property stems from Roman law, not Jesus, and is the hallmark of patriarchy.[1] In his letter to the Ephesians, Paul elevated women's status in marriage, giving instruction to these specific people at their specific time in history on how to both uphold the commandment of Jesus – "Love each other. Just as I have loved you" (John 13:34) – and Roman household law, which ordered the submission of wives to their husbands.

The scriptures my brother held prescriptive to marriage were written in the context of women being property. Even as

---

1. Gordon D. Fee, "The Cultural Context of Ephesians 5:18–6:9: Is there a divinely ordained hierarchy in the life of the church and home that is based on gender alone?" *Priscilla Papers* 16:1 (Winter 2002): 3–8.

a preacher he did not understand how ancient Roman property laws that first-century Christians struggled with were not commands for my post-millennial Christian marriage...*I forgive you, bro!* Patriarchal marriage is a hierarchy where man assumes government over woman *as if biology could determine nonbiological realms.* Its traditions exploit women's nuptial promises of love and commitment by teaching their requirement to surrender power.

Many churches continue to uphold patriarchal marriage as God's standard, even though Scripture teaches mutual submission. The teachings in Ephesian 5 actually became significant in redefining adultery. I was shocked to learn that according to patriarchal law, adultery was not a moral offense but a property offense. It was impossible for a man to commit adultery unless he slept with another man's wife. An unmarried woman having sex, a prostitute, was not committing a crime against her husband and was therefore fulfilling an accepted service, however there were social consequences of her being branded unmarriable, used.[2]

In the patriarchal system women were legal property – like land – to be acquired and fertilized, not humans created in God's image. Men were permitted to accrue all the property they could afford, which made polygamy acceptable. Polygamy is *never* documented as a moral offense in the Old Testament, and we read about "honorable" men interacting sexually with prostitutes and possessing multiple wives and concubines without moral condemnation. Jacob, Gideon, and David are only a few of these offenders. While wives had some legal protection under Hebrew

---

2. Thomas A.J. McGinn, "Concubinage and the Lex Iulia on Adultery," *Transactions of the American Philological Association (1974–)* 121 (1991): 338–342. In the Bible we see the prostitute in Proverbs 5 is married and therefore condemned as an adulteress. In Genesis 12 Sarai is taken into Pharaoh's household as a potential wife but is not condemned. Tradition exonerates this because she is doing this as property of her husband Abraham.

and Roman household law, concubines had none and could legally be pimped out.

Nothing in the Bible outlaws polygamy; in fact, the Roman government outlawed it, not the church.[3]

In the late nineteenth century, suffragists worked tirelessly to expose the double standard in "Christian marriage," holding men to fidelity to elevate the legal status of women and slaves. Marriage is both a legal contract and covenant. It important to thread out of Scripture what are legal definitions pertinent to Bible times and what is hallmark to the covenant. Only in more recent history has legislation promoted a woman from being property into being a legal entity in marriage. It wasn't until 1993 that all American wives were protected by criminal rape laws in marriage; prior to that time marital rape was considered an oxymoron, as if sex was a wife's duty and a husband's right.[4] Traditional Christian teachings of wifely submission (as property) blinded many from seeing how a woman could be raped in marriage. Promoting mutuality in marriage is essential to honoring humanity in women.

When I married my husband, we were both working professionals. As a teenager I dreamed of earning a master's degree, not being a bride. After I earned my degrees, I didn't need to marry but wanted to be with the man who felt like home to me; he still feels that way. Like many educated women, my objectives to marry were shaped less about being provided for and more about emotional fulfillment. Jesus spoke briefly about marriage and quoted from Genesis 2:24: "And the two will be one flesh. So they are no longer two but one flesh" (Mark 10:8). Jesus declared the Genesis model of oneness for marriage, not the patriarchal model.

---

3. Wilda C. Gafney, *Womanist Midrash: A Reintroduction to the Women of the Torah and the Throne* (Louisville: Westminster John Knox Press, 2017), 28.
4. Jill Elaine Hasday, "Contest and Consent: A Legal History of Marital Rape," 88 California Law Review 1373 (2000).

The Genesis model is the unity of two equals; the patriarchal model executes oneness by man assuming a legal coverture or authority over a woman and the woman's identity being assumed into his.[5]

When I was planning my wedding, I was eager as a "baby Christian" to follow the ways of God. I had no idea my brother's teaching on marriage would later be held as a litmus test of my faith by leaders of the church. The overarching message I received about marriage was that my promise was expected to be a commitment to obedience to my husband – that was how I was to love him. I saw this teaching to be harmful to the men and women who defended it because it held the marriage as more sanctimonious than the women.

I can't remember a time when my husband has asserted his "authority" over me. In fact, he often put up a bumper to protect me when our prior church family was telling him to "get me in line." My husband and I each wield our power in marriage; that's not to say we haven't clashed. We are still figuring it out, trying to be one. I'm grateful to be married to a man who has always wanted me to be me, not to be folded into him. I'm encouraged to see more Christian egalitarian marriages these days. As for the legalities, I'm even hearing of couples bucking tradition and participating in the biblical practice of taking the wife's name (Ezra 2:61). If I were to go back and do it again, I would shape the vows around an entirely different scripture, one that centers on our promise and not my being property, a scripture honoring us both as "one."

Two are better than one because they have a good return for their hard work. If either should fall, one can pick up the

_____

5. Emily and George Walther, "Celebrating Our Partnership," *Priscilla Papers* 5, no. 4 (Fall 1991): 12–17.

other. But how miserable are those who fall and don't have a companion to help them up! Also, if two lie down together, they can stay warm. But how can anyone stay warm alone?

(Ecclesiastes 4:9–11).

6

THE MOTHER OF ALL COMMANDS

No laborer in the world is expected to work for
room, board, and love – except the housewife.

– Letty Cottin Pogrebin (1939–),
American author and social activist

iving near your in-laws is a fast-track way to understanding
your husband. It's like personal training for explaining him.
There's a regular grind of having your mother-in-law around
because she likely has different expectations for her son, which
may not always align with her daughter-in-law's. The proximity
begets a relational tug-of-war. Which woman will be "*the* woman"
in his life? The obvious answer is the wife; however, the wife can
be challenged to influence her husband when his old ways are validated regularly by his mom. I know this from experience. Overall,
I believe my proximity to my in-laws has been positive. However,
the experience unearthed the spectrum of conflicting values of
our families – important stuff, such as how (or if) to fold socks.
Living near my in-laws also was a catalyst for tough conversations
that dealt with what each of us considered "women's work."

Every family has their own set of ideas for what's "women's
work" and what's "men's work." When a man marries a carbon
copy of his mom, this isn't a big issue. When it comes to topics of

"women's work," my husband married the antithesis of his mom. My mother-in-law, – who I have called "Mom" for more than 18 years – believes it is a woman's role to serve up dinner to her husband each night. She refuses all evening social activity, so she can quietly participate in the sacred duty of serving a hot plate of food to her husband. As a general practice I make sure food is available – leftovers or spaghetti ingredients to throw together – but I frequently leave my family "on their own." While I, too, enjoy a freshly cooked hot meal, I work and often want to hit the gym in the evenings, not to mention the Mom/Dad taxi service we operate each evening; our appetites don't take precedence over my health and wellbeing. When I do serve dinner, it's buffet style. I don't set the table, and I expect the eaters to help clean up afterwards. I cook healthy, spicy, exotic ethnic recipes – like Thai chicken and kabobs – and I use chili peppers in my chili (because you're *supposed* to). I promptly let my eaters know they are cooking (of course, something healthy) the next day if they complain (*Yes, I'm like that!*). You see, I'm not the cook because I am a woman but because I am the better cook who spices things up (and keeps our waistlines at a healthy ratio with our heights)! My mother-in-law doesn't like spicy food; she is sedentary and carries candy in her purse. Her favorite colors are blues; I like reds and pinks. "Mom" is frugal and believes a wife should do all the housework; we have paid housekeepers. I don't like clutter, and she has kept magazines from 1975. This can go on and on.

To compound the differences even more, my mother-in-law is Catholic, and I'm Protestant. Of her four daughters-in-law, I'm the only one who was not born in the Catholic Church. My in-laws haven't been pushy with their Catholicism, though my Coptic baptism *is* recognized as valid by the Catholic Church. My Catholic-approved infant baptism also saves our children from otherwise being considered bastards in the eyes of God. *Whew!* Many of our family gatherings revolve around a religious holiday or Mass. My attendance of Mass has declined over the years; however, I know the Catholic liturgy because it is the same as the Lutheran liturgy I grew up with. My in-laws don't recognize our adult baptisms but have been supportive of us raising our children in church...even if it's a Protestant one.

If there is anything my mother-in-law holds closer than Catholicism, it is the belief that a woman's place is in the home with her children. Her expectations of "woman's work" was held by my husband too (*go figure*), and it hamstringed my confidence in being a working mom. With my in-law in constant proximity I felt immense pressure to conform to his family's beliefs of how a wife and mother should be. Before motherhood it was always my intention to continue working as an occupational therapist after having kids, even if part-time. Early in motherhood I worked two days a week at an outpatient clinic. As I had multiple children, that became more difficult. By the time I had my third and fourth child, I mostly stopped working because of childcare costs.

The opportunity for women to earn a paycheck is the opportunity for each one to develop a financial footprint. If I add up the income I didn't earn during my years as a young mom, it would be anywhere from five hundred thousand to a million dollars – depending on how much I worked. I'm all for making sacrifices for my kids; the problem is that as Mom, I was expected to make all the professional and financial sacrifices, and my husband was expected to make little to none. My Social Security pales compared to my husband's, and I missed out on the early years to invest, and those were recession years so my portfolio would have greatly amassed by now.

It's arguable that marriage and motherhood turned me into a domestic slave as I worked without pay. I became financially dependent as I shouldered most of the caregiving responsibilities. This spilled over into our relationship because I didn't feel free to make demands in our marriage, since he held most of the financial power. I remember feeling as if I was being held hostage by his family's ideals of "women's work" and was at his mercy. I spent lots of time with my mother-in-law and she shared with me how she was denied having a car or spending money early in her years of motherhood. It wasn't like she didn't suffer too; she just didn't believe that as a mother she had the right or power to remove that thorn. She would say how great her son was because he changed diapers for our children, while my father-in-law used to made fun of him – in our home – for doing so. My father-in-law once admitted to me he never changed a diaper – five kids and not one diaper. Couple my in-laws convictions of "women's work" with our church teaching traditional gender roles, and I was doomed to not have a voice on whether I wanted to work outside the home.

My mom had a full-time career until she retired. Despite her career, she bought into the traditional views of "woman's work." She didn't say much when I called crying about spending my life cleaning up after my family. If she did, she shamed my tears with her martyr's tone, "Well, I *had* to work because I had kids and didn't have someone (*like my husband*)." It was as though she was asking why I wasn't grateful I had a husband who could support me. Nobody asked why he wasn't supporting my working or why I wasn't so grateful my husband could afford to keep me at home as his domestic servant. When I lamented to my sister, she blew like a volcano because she couldn't have kids and thought my attitude was self-centered. She was hurting too, and I don't understand her pain, but why couldn't we both hurt? I longed for a woman mentor to encourage me in pursuing professional and financial goals. And what about God's will? What was God's will for my life and education?

After years of asking this question – because what I was taught seemed to conflict with my Spirit – I learned it was never God's plan for the sweat of women to be compensated less than the sweat of men. God had a plan for women to work *and* be a mom. Before the drama in the garden of Eden, God gave the very first social command for society:[1] "This is the reason that a man leaves his father and mother and embraces his wife, and they become one flesh" (Genesis 2:24).

The first two words of this command are, "man leaves."[2] Instead, the patriarchs eventually coerced women to leave,[3] and man stayed with his family to create family lines.[4] When men started coercing women to leave, the social acceptance of polygamy (multiple wives) became common for marriage. It's difficult to imagine polygamy as an accepted practice if men did not have turf where they could store up women. The first social command was God's provision to protect women from the domestic exploitation and neglect of patriarchy. Jesus lent significance to this lost command with his parable in Matthew 25 where the bridegroom went to live at the bride's house. The hearers of Jesus would have understood their fault in not obeying

---

1. All prior commands had been given to Adam solely, since Eve was not yet created.

2. To be clear, this command doesn't use the masculine term *man* to encompass all people but clearly separates husband and wife with the corresponding Hebrew terms *ish* for husband and *isha* for wife. See Katharine C. Bushnell, *God's Word to Women* (Minneapolis: Christians For Biblical Equality, 2003), paragraph 44.

3. We see how Rebekah was part of a matriarchal home, citing her mother's house and having voice in her marriage. As women were taken from their parents' homes, they became domestic slaves robbed of legal rights (Bushnell, *God's Word to Women*, Lesson 18).

4. Abraham wanted his son protected from foreign gods; however, he made the decision to bring a wife back for Isaac independently *without* consulting God. Even though that was the case, God provided Abraham and Sarah a wife for their son. As a father of three religions where patriarchal values reign, I wonder how different our world would be if Abraham had trusted a sovereign God to provide a wife for Isaac instead of taking matters into his own power.

God's first command to society that protects and honors women: man leaves his father and mother.[5]

Women hold an unequal share of responsibility in reproduction and nursing babies. It makes us vulnerable. God knew women needed protection from becoming a domestic slave within the household of her husband's parents. A woman's parents are less likely to exploit their daughter's vulnerability and turn her into a domestic service station. If you've read any women's history, you can completely understand why God gave this command as society's first command.

God had a solution to prevent patriarchy: The man "leaves" his parents and "embraces his wife." This means a husband is to fold the socks his wife's way instead of his mom's way. It's easy to see how Jesus was irritated with his people's disobedience of this command. After being asked about the parameters of the law for man to divorce his wife, Jesus rebuffed with Genesis 2:24, letting them know they were already doing marriage all wrong, (*and women were to have power in marriage too*). Men designed the laws of patriarchy to favor men. The laws exploited women's vulnerabilities by forcing them to be property instead of managing property as an heir. Paul reiterates Jesus's sentiment in Ephesians 5, explaining how a husband should love his wife (*not exploit her in marriage by forcing her to give up turf*).

An abundance of historical evidence explains how women have lost social freedoms and legal rights from living in marriage and having children. Women have lost: access to power, full citizenship, education, owning and controlling finances, property,

---

5. Some scholars have debated the accuracy of this parable because tradition did not validate the wedding held in the home of the bride. Weddings were traditionally held at the groom's home. See Arland J. Hultgren, *The Parables of Jesus: A Commentary* (Grand Rapids, MI/Cambridge, U.K.: Wm. B. Eerdmans, 2000), 171–172.

divorce rights, custody of children, financial maintenance, and sexual freedom.[6] We want "godly" marriages; however, living according to the patriarchal model controls wives' bodies and directly disobeys God's first command to all humanity. It has not been until women were given legal protection that they were able to make financial decisions that would benefit them. Women need the legal protection and her family's support to manage finances and own property – not to be property. The lie of gender roles – men provide, women serve – needs to be thrown out of our law books and churches. There should never be rules to keep women oppressed in "women's work." Centuries of laws do *not* protect men from folding socks, sweeping the floor, doing laundry, or changing diapers.

When my children were young, not being supported to work outside of the home robbed me of financial self-reliance. It's a crack in our marriage we have not fully healed. How do you get over losing out on a million dollars? As my kids are now attending school, I am back to work as a home health occupational therapist. I love working and am often in homes of elderly persons who hold rigid views of "women's work" (especially if they grew up without electricity). It's interesting to see how the power dynamics change in marriages when the husband becomes ill and the wife has newfound power, or the wife becomes ill and the husband must step in as caregiver. I often counsel them on my "young" (and radical) – *to them I'm just a babe in my 40s* – ideas that there is no such thing as "women's work" and "men's work" but just "housework." Elderly men and women often feel very guilty for crossing the boundaries of gender roles because they have been taught these roles as gospel truth! I assure them that I go

---

6. Rosalind Miles, *Who Cooked the Last Supper? The Women's History of the World* (New York: Three Rivers Press, 2001), Kindle loc. 953.

to many homes, and it's okay; in fact, it's more important to do what needs to be done to take care of your spouse.

My husband and I have grown to realize that we cannot become one flesh when we have separate roles. We try not to have "women's work" and "men's work" in our home. I teach my boys to cook and my daughter to use a drill (and vice versa) and don't feel guilty being the one who hangs out in the garage. Author Sheryl Sandberg[7] helped me to find the confidence to challenge my husband on some of his traditional gender role beliefs that were hurtful to me. When he talked about me arranging childcare so I could work, I challenged him with, "Why is the childcare for me (and not us)?" My husband had always referred to the house cleaners as helping me, and I challenged him again, "Why is this only helping me and not you?"

For all the single ladies reading this, I advise marriage to be considered only with a guy who understands the heart of God and obeys the commands that honor the power of women in marriage. If a man believes he has government over his wife by virtue of maleness alone – because the Bible said so – then run. It's important to learn about what your guy considers "women's work." If he asks you if you can cook, just ask him if he can build a house, or least make sure he is willing to clean up after the meal and do dishes (in case he's an unhealthy cook who can't spice things up in the kitchen!). If he can cook, or build you a house, you may have a keeper, but only if he's willing to share the property equally with you and listen to you over your mother-in-law when it comes to "women's work"!

> The young woman ran and told her mother's household about these things. (Genesis 24:28, NIV)

---

7. Sheryl Sandberg, *Lean In: Women, Work, and the Will to Lead* (New York: Alfred A. Knopf, 2013).

7

WHAT'S HER NAME?

Trust your husband, adore your husband, and
get as much as you can in your own name.

– Joan Rivers (1933–2014),
American comedian

My maternal grandma was born in 1903. She joked about being a product of "hook or crook." Grandma's dad (my great-grandfather) was nearly a full-term babe in his mother's womb when he rode in vitro on horseback from Kentucky to Iowa. His mother and father made the trip overnight, fleeing their plantation to escape the Civil War. In case you're wondering, five generations ago, my maternal relatives were American slave owners. The secret's out now; and yes, I have benefited from the fact my ancestors had the affluence to educate and make social connections, which has trickled down to me. Grandma's dad was born safely in Iowa shortly after the trip. His family bought land, and he grew up there, safe from the war's aftermath. In Iowa he remained single until his forties, when he impregnated a hired girl in his mom's home. My great-grandmother was already engaged to another; however, she was forced to break the heart of her fiancé and marry her rapist, an aristocrat twice her age.

Later in her life Great-grandma inherited vast amount of Iowa soil. At that time in Iowa, a woman could own property; however, a husband had the right to assume that property because his wife was legally his property. Her rapist husband not only took her body but also took her land. That farmland is still a bitter pill in my mother's family, because family legend has it that my great-grandmother wanted my grandmother to inherit a portion. My rapist great-grandfather left *all* the land – which is now worth millions of dollars – to their oldest son. The story goes that he went into town with his son one day and had the deed changed. With the stroke of a pen, the women of my family were erased from property deeds because they, themselves, were property.

Property and inheritance rights are essential to women's power in society. Historically women have been denied property, money, and even a name. The norm of patriarchy was once to turn women into nonbeings. Follow the branches of a family tree far enough, and the women are made to disappear. The Bible shares a (mostly) patriarchal lineage record of Jesus that spans generations of men. The women who provided wombs and nurtured the generations are scarcely remembered. However five are mentioned – four of them by name – Tamar, Rahab, Ruth, and Mary. (Bathsheba is the fifth but not mentioned by name).[1]

Women were expected to surrender their belongings and

---

1. Five women are mentioned in Jesus' genealogy, which is found in Matthew 1. A note from The Voice Bible says this: "Some of the women in Jesus' line are given to show how God is gracious to everyone, even to prostitutes and adulterers. Because some of the women listed weren't Israelites, but were strangers and foreigners, they foreshadow all the foreigners God will adopt into His church through Jesus. Some of the children in God's family are conceived under strange circumstances (like Tamar's twins being conceived as she played the harlot, and like King Solomon being born to adulterous parents). Now that it has been established this is an unusual family, what happens next shouldn't be a surprise – the conception of a baby under very strange circumstances."

their name to their husband. The missing maternal ancestors of Jesus aren't the only victims of the scribes' erasers. In Hebrews 11:32, where is Deborah in the "hall of faith"? Why does Barak get literary credit for her military leadership? For background on this story, Deborah was the fourth judge (ruler of the people) of pre-monarchic Israel. In Judges 4 she is recorded as directing a successful military counter attack against Canaan with her military commander Barak (who refused to go alone).

What is the Samaritans woman's name? She engaged in the longest-recorded conversation with Jesus; she was an outsider, and she recognized his divine identity – not needing the resurrection for proof as the disciples did. She also led a Christian evangelical campaign by bringing her neighbors to meet Jesus, which makes her the world's first female Christian evangelist.

And as historian Rosalind Miles titled her women's history book and says, "Who cooked the last supper? If it had been a man, wouldn't he have a saint's day by now, with a fervent following of celebrity chefs?"[2] *Truth!*

As if Jesus didn't have sisters? Or stepsisters? Or female cousins?

The book of 2 John is written to a "lady chosen." This woman is unrecognizable as an actual person. Some scholars think it is possible that John was addressing a church, but no one knows for sure.[3]

Pontius Pilate's wife deserves a name other than "Pontius Pilate's wife"; she *did* interrupt her husband's execution trial

---

2. Miles, Kindle loc. 65.

3. Margaret Mowczko, "The Elder and the Lady: A look at the language of Second John," *Mutuality: Men and Women Serving and Leading as Equals* (Winter 2016): 12–13. http://www.cbeinternational.org/resources/article/mutuality/elder -and-lady-look-language-second-john.

of Jesus to warn him of her intuition that Jesus was an innocent man.

There's an unnamed prophetess in Isaiah 8:3 whose lips forebode Israel's future in the form of a baby boy.[4] Only a woman can do *that!* That too deserves a name!

And then there's Noah's wife and daughters-in-law, whose matriarchy saved all humanity (Genesis 7:7). In a day before birth control, he and his wife are not recorded as having daughters, *hmmm.*

What about David's mother? (1 Samuel 22:3–4; Psalm 86:16).

Or the queen of Sheba? (1 Kings 10:1–13; 2 Chronicles 9:1–9).

Did Adam and Eve have any daughters?

Many, many more women have been made to disappear. If they aren't erased, they are sometimes omitted via sex change! As late as the twentieth century we find Junia experiencing a literary sex change with the stroke of a pen. The writer added an "s" to the end of her name, which made her a man in the Erwin Nestle's edition of the Greek New Testament.[5] The significance of this one-letter-sex-change-operation is significant, as pastors and students and translators depend and trust composite Greek New Testaments and Hebrew Old Testaments. The stakes are high, omitting the only female apostle recorded in the New Testament because that can rob women of the biblical credibility to rightfully assume positions of church authority.[6]

Women who traveled with Jesus are also given literary sex changes. Though these women followed Jesus as his disciples,

---

4. Wilda C. Gafney, *Daughters of Miriam: Women Prophets in Ancient Israel* (Minneapolis: Fortress Press, 2008) 104.

5. Scot McKnight, *Junia Is Not Alone* (Englewood, CO: Patheos Press, 2011) Kindle loc. 112.

6. Nympha and the female apostle Junia's womanhood is unstated in Romans 16:7 and Colossians 4:15 of older English Bible translations.

studied with him (yes, Jesus taught women (Luke 8:21),[7] and supported his mission financially, they are denied full apostle status and are positioned as caring for his needs The needs of Jesus are not specified. These female followers of Jesus are denied honor that God in the flesh washed feet and cooked for his disciples. Have you ever seen a painting of Jesus washing women's feet? Female disciples are worthy.

While Scripture memorializes a handful of early Christian women by name, many preachers, missionaries, and Sunday school curricula gloss over recognition for their contributions. If Paul greeted Prisca, Mary, Junia, and Julia, (Romans 16:3, 6–7), shouldn't we greet them in our Bible study too? Perhaps we should investigate the hard work for which Tryphena of Rome, Mary and Persis are recognized (Romans 16:6, 12). Euodia and Syntyche are recognized by Paul as fellow workers (Philemon 4:2–3) and Junia as an apostle (Romans 16:7). Phoebe is a deaconess of the church in Cenchreae (Romans 16:1); have you ever heard of her? While she is titled by Paul as a deaconess, various Bible translations have reduced her title to servant, while preserving the deacon title for the men.[8]

As the Bible was translated into a multitude of languages, translations were made to fit within the sexist notions and prejudices of these cultures. In the late nineteenth century, at the height of imperial evangelism – colonials out in the world to save the "heathens" – the female medical missionary Katharine Bushnell discovered the Chinese Bible was translated without Euodia

---

7. Mary Magdalene, Joanna, Susanna, Mary of Clopas, Mary mother of James, and Salome are named women taught by Jesus. See Angela Ravin-Anderson, "They Had Followed Him from Galilee: The Female Disciples," *Priscilla Papers* 28, no. 2 (Spring 2014): 5–8. Mary of Bethany is also documented being taught by Jesus in Luke 10:39.
8. Linda Montgomery, "Our Sister, Pheobe," *Priscilla Papers* 7, no. 1 (Winter 1993): 3–4

and Syntych, two women who labored with Paul in Philippians 4:2–3. When she investigated it she discovered these women received literary sex changes in order to cater to the prejudice toward women in ministry in that area of the world.[9]

The tradition to make women disappear – whether from Bible translation, history books, inheritance rights, genealogies, property deeds, parables, political policy, church pulpits, or marriage – assumes that a woman's identity is to be folded into a man's and she has none of her own. Let's just be honest – that's not what most moms and dads want for their daughters.

How a woman sees herself starts at home. The efforts of parents in the Bible who elevated their daughters from property to protected class don't get mentioned in traditional theology either. After a celestial showdown between God and the Accuser, Job matures morally to elevate the legacy of his daughters. Not only are his three daughters named – Jemimah, Keziah, and Keren-happuch, which mean "dove," "cinnamon," and "jar of dark cosmetics" – he grants them an equal inheritance with their brothers (Job 42:14–15).[10] Job is proverbial to see how the honor of his daughters, for which there was no rule, was a higher moral calling than honoring the religious patriarchal traditions.[11] God, too, deviates from the patriarchy by not only sending women and favoring the youngest throughout Scripture, but by being with us, delivered by a woman without validated recognition to man (Isaiah 7:14).

I used to be unnerved when I would crack open the New Testament and read the sprinkling of women mentioned among

9. Kristin Kobes Du Mez, *A New Gospel for Women: Katharine Bushnell and the Challenge of Christian Feminism* (New York: Oxford Press), 39–40.

10. See the footnotes for verse 14 in the Common English Bible for the meanings of Job's daughters' names.

11. Ellen F. Davis, *Getting Involved With God: Rediscovering the Old Testament* (Lanham, MD: Rowman & Littlefield, 2001), 142–143.

the many names of men. These days, however, I get excited because I see women who overstepped the boundaries created to obliterate their existence. We, as women, are called to create our own lives (Genesis 1:28; Ephesians 2:10). The women named in Scripture understood their God-given power while their humanity was absent to the rest of the world. These women took ownership of their own bodies and legacies in their own ways through wielding power that was rightfully theirs.

My paternal grandma was a little woman who wore heavy amounts of Egyptian gold. In her day, an Egyptian woman's only ability to own property was in owning jewelry. Her family was upper-class and gifted her an Alexandria apartment, which had to be titled under her abusive husband's name. With women becoming a legally protected class outside of their husbands in twentieth-century Egypt, and America, my aunt now owns that apartment, which is basically a penthouse. I'm proud of my aunt for advocating for herself within the Egyptian legal system to have her name on that deed; it wasn't easy for her to accomplish.

To be named is to be granted power. We name our children and our pets; we give pet names to our lover and dote on our children with special names because they have special places in our lives. I like the idea of granting daughters a maternal family name they can keep as their own. A lady with whom I work out told me she is the sixth Elizabeth in her family; her daughter is the seventh. My mom combined her two first names to create my middle name Joleen. My daughter's middle name is also Joleen. My mom sometimes encourages me to join the Daughters of the American Revolution, as her family can be traced back to that colonial era. That hasn't been an interest of mine, but it may be in the future, so I may learn the names of the women before me.

When women are without names, they cannot be memorialized. Coveting women's names robs women to be recognized with power. For Christian women to understand our value to God and our world, outside the service of our flesh, we need fresh biblical optics. Searching for the missing women is wielding our power. Mentioning the forgotten to those with voice helps us to remember it was men who forgot the women's names, not God. While the names of biblical women have been assaulted, not all were obliterated. God does not allow the women to be forgotten. In fact, God makes an offer. In its conclusion, the Bible invites us to be named as heir in the commonwealth of God! We will be given a name that lives for an eternity. So let's make sure the names of women are recognized today, modeling a world where each woman will be a mainstay in the presence of God, and no one will ever again ask, "What's her name?"

> As for the one who conquers *through faithfulness even unto death*, I will plant that person as a pillar in the temple of My God, and that person will never have to leave *the presence of God. Moreover*, I will inscribe this person with the name of My God and the name of the city of My God, New Jerusalem – which descends out of heaven from My God – and My own new name." (Revelation 3:12 The Voice)

8

BE FRUITFUL

Joy, feeling one's own value, being appreciated and loved by others, feeling useful and capable of production are all factors of enormous value for the human soul.

– Maria Montessori (1870–1952),
Italian physician and educator

Pregnancy is a sure way to make your body public for discussion. I know firsthand there is a distinct difference in how people treat a pregnant woman, because I've spent more than three and a half years of my life pregnant. There's the stranger who tries to touch your belly or the public declarations of older women that "she's ready to go any day." *Umm, no, I have two more months.* Pregnant women are constantly expected to answer questions about their swelling body, by complete strangers or distant acquaintances, that non-pregnant people, or their partner, aren't subjected to. The standard probing inquiries for my first and second pregnancies were, "Is this your first baby?" or the more invasive, "Are you planning to breastfeed your baby?" During my third pregnancy I received ruder comments like "Do you know how that happens?" *Uhhh, I quit eating the watermelon seeds?* In my fourth pregnancy, people were just flat rude. My standard response became "How dare I have four kids," or "They even have the same dad!" The last one got laughs from the guys and pained looks from women. The world was okay with me having one or two kids; it let me squeeze out a third, but four was out of boundaries. I was not conforming to what was the 2.3, now 1.76, American norm so I had to defend my right to have four kids.[1] Church was somewhat the same; however, among the women, there was a sort of concession as if I was forging ahead of them. I was told by multiple women at church, "You're better than I," simply because I had more children.

Having a small army of children has long been considered a moral responsibility for Christian women whose faith is still within the soft bounds of patriarchy. Now let me say that I'm all about large families. I came from a blended family of four children, and my husband was one of five boys; I can't imagine our home to be anything but the party it is! Our family, however, is small compared to the Catholic families of my brothers-in-law. One brother-in-law has five kids and another has 10 children with their respective wives. I informed my husband promptly after child four that as much as he enjoys rivaling his younger brothers, we will not be competing in *that* contest!

The teaching that God instructs us to have as many babies as possible is inspired by a patriarchal value, not a biblical command. The basis comes from God's commands to be fruitful and multiply (Genesis 1:28; 9:1, 7; 35:11). Women carried the burden to fulfill this "command," and it was considered their duty to give men legitimate heirs. Children were considered an economic and tribal asset in agrarian society, and they were solely the property

---

1. T.J. Mathews and Brady E. Hamilton , "Total fertility Rates by State and race and Hispanic Origin: United States, 2017," *National Vital Statistics Reports* 68 no 1 (January 10, 2019): 5–6.

of men, not women.[2] Although children elevated a woman's status, the ancient conception of conception did not give them biological credit.

In Old Testament times, ideals of society revolved around agriculture. Sex education taught that a man's semen was seed and a woman's womb was soil. Each seed of man (sperm) was considered a tiny human carrying all the necessary components that would sprout in the soil of women, *just like a watermelon seed!* A woman was only a passive vessel to shelter and nurture the man's seed that it might germinate until born.[3] Despite the reference to women having a seed or offspring in Genesis 3:15, the religious system ordained this "conception of conception" for millennia. It not only influenced the legal system but pervaded modern scholarship. As late as the early twentieth century, textbooks had illustrations of what scientists "saw" when putting sperm under the microscope. Within the sperm drawing was a fetal positioned tiny human. The textbook term was *homunculus*, named after the "scientist" who saw his personal ideology as a prenatal babe when viewing sperm in the microscope.[4] The *homunculus myth* is now a textbook lesson in scientific objectivity!

As the Monty Python song goes, "Every sperm is sacred."[5] Throughout history, men were thought to have sacred sperm

---

2. Alvin J. Schmidt, *Veiled and Silenced: How Culture Shaped Sexist Theology* (Macon, GA: Mercer University Press), 35.

3. Schmidt, *Veiled and Silenced,* 117.

4. While the mainstream ancient Jewish narrative upheld women did not have seed, ancient writings confirm there were opposing, "feminist," narratives of men who claimed women had seed. See Edward Reichman, "The Rabbinic Conception of Conception: An Exercise in Fertility," *Tradition: A Journal of Orthodox Jewish Thought* 31, no. 1 (Fall 1996): 35–36.

5. Monty Python, "Every Sperm is Sacred," MetroLyrics, accessed July 26, 2018, http://www.metrolyrics.com/every-sperm-is-sacred-lyrics-monty-python.html.

because it was thought to be little humans.[6] "Spilling seed" became analogous to shedding blood of humans made in God's image.[7] Being fruitful was a moral obligation taught by religious authority, and women were expected to perform *mitzvah* or a mercenary act (sex) for the proper emission of his seed, never mind whether she was in the mood.[8]

At the time of Jesus, any man who did not obey the religious command "be fruitful and multiply" regarding procreation was thought to have renounced the essential purpose of creation. Men were to create more men to offer witness of God in creation.[9] Women's only way to be fruitful, or to witness, was through man's seed. The Bible never discusses sterility as the fault of man but always the "bad soil" of women. In that culture, a woman's only spiritual contribution was to help create more witnesses. To be barren was considered shameful and a curse from God. Polygamy was justified to ensure a man would create many legitimate heirs and witnesses.[10],[11]

In those days, women were expected to be faithful "baby machines." A woman's spirituality was defined by whether she had children, who she had children with, how many children she

---

6. Couple this life-carrying responsibility with God's command to be fruitful and multiply (Genesis 1:28; 9:1, 7; 35:11), and "spilling seed" or the "sin of Onan" (Genesis 38:8–10) became a wicked and deadly offense.

7. Teachers used Genesis 9:6–7 to teach spilling seed was like spilling blood. See Fred Rosner, "Contraception in Jewish Law," *Tradition: A Journal of Orthodox Jewish Thought* 12, no. 2, (Fall 1971): 94.

8. Rosner, 94–95.

9. David S. Shapiro, "Be Fruitful and Multiply," *Tradition: A Journal of Orthodox Jewish Thought* 13, no 4; 14, no. 1 (Spring–Summer, 1973), 62.

10. Schmidt, *Veiled And Silenced*, 117.

11. Abraham used Hagar when Sarah did not become pregnant; however, Hagar was not readily accepted into the family unit. Jacob made use of Rachel and Leah's maids after they were unable to bear children in Genesis 30, the beginnings of a polygamous family unit.

had, and if her children were boys or girls (girls were considered less valuable than boys). In my experience church environments today still seem to emancipate a woman with children as a fully qualified Christian woman. However, Jesus redefined what it means to be fruitful. "A certain woman in the crowd spoke up: 'Happy is the mother who gave birth to you and who nursed you.' But he said, 'Happy rather are those who hear God's word and put it into practice'" (Luke 11:27–28).

Women hold the potential to be fruitful for God in so many ways that are not directly related to her ability or desire to have children. Women must see their worth beyond their reproductive status, however. This is not always easy when ultraconservative Christian colleges and church staffs still view motherhood as part of a woman's job requirements. Motherhood is still exalted to such extent that Christian women with ambition or full-time jobs are criticized.[12] It's been my personal experience that the more a mother invests into her children – working in the home or even homeschooling – the larger her "badge of honor" in some Christian communities. This positivism isn't what Jesus taught.

Our badge of honor comes when we put God's word into practice. We each have a unique set of eyes to witness God, and individually capable hands to do the work God created us to do.

My sister struggled with infertility, and it has taken years for her to believe she is not deficient. We need to mature as Christians to validate women's power outside of motherhood, to heal the wound of being unable to have a child. My sister wanted a family and has created one through marrying a man who already had children. We often enjoy time with her children and grandchildren. Her career as a full-time administrator and educator has

---

12. Julie Ingersoll, *Evangelical Christian Women: War Stories in the Gender Battles* (New York and London: New York University Press, 2003), 78–79.

touched thousands of lives. One former student provided her and her husband a private place to live near the hospital while she battled cancer, and survived! Family isn't always a bloodline with a patriarchal name.

My former church recognized being "fruitful" as baptizing as many witnesses to Jesus as possible. It's a beautiful thing to baptize another witness of the Christ, however this definition of "fruitful" was held over our heads as the sole purpose of our existence. There was little room for individuals to share their talents and gifts. This made me see my work in occupational therapy as unfruitful because it didn't teach people directly about God. I regret buying into the baptism machine idea. I missed out on the joy my work brings me now. I did, though, find comfort in Colossians 3:23, which says, "Work willingly at whatever you do, as though you were working for the Lord rather than for people (Colossian 3:23 NLT). This scripture validated to me that my work is not in vain and I do not have to conform. I know I am talented in my understanding of the human body; and as a fitness and yoga instructor, I'm great at instructing people how to move. So I work to create stronger, healthier bodies in the clinic and in the classes I teach. I strive to do my best for the Lord.

Being fruitful may require us to move outside of the boundaries of expectations set for us. When I started teaching yoga, I received hate mail. Years later I made my class "Christian" and called it YOGATHEA®, and I was told how my yoga universalism had no place with Christianity. One person said it was from the bowels of hell! Another told me meditation was evil, *so why is it commanded in the Bible?* (See Psalms 19:14; 46:10 and others.) I don't believe in throwing pearls to pigs so I don't even try to explain to the naysayers. These days I hear more good about YOGATHEA®. People love the yoga and music and are moved by the meditation. My favorite part of YOGATHEA® is the meditation at the end where people lie in quiet. It gives me space to go deeper within myself and see more of who God created me to be. I've come up with some of my best ideas during meditation.

When I think of being fruitful in my life, I think of YOGATHEA® and my work as an occupational therapist to create healthier lives. Even with this book, I am writing to help women understand the power inherent in their female flesh. Most of my family, and even much of my church family, see my productivity as being a mother of four. Yes, I have children, and they are a fruit of my life; however that's something I've produced with my husband. To know my individual power in God I have come to know myself as fruitful, individually. And you can too!

Fruit is what we joyfully produce. Listening to patients share about their fruit reminds me of what's important; the women talk about what *they* did, not what someone told them to do. One of my favorite stories is the lady who started her liquor business during the prohibition, *and she was still running it at ninety-six, sort of!* Each woman has her own call to be fruitful, and that call isn't necessarily tied to having children. Some women are called to create beautiful homes and children; and yes, they can still be feminists. Other women *choose* not to have children, and that doesn't mean they're selfish. Human nature is timeless, so the temptation will always exist to rob women of their joy in producing fruit by telling us we're not worthy. Women deserve to produce fruit in conditions of "love, joy, peace, patience, kindness, goodness, faithfulness, gentleness, and self-control" (Galatians 5:22–23). So don't ask a pregnant woman questions you wouldn't ask a bald man wearing a suit. The fruit of her womb – and *any* woman's career and body – are none of your business. Your business is encouraging each woman in your life to find her joy in producing her fruit.

And so I *heartily* recommended *that you pursue* joy, for the best a person can do under the sun is to *enjoy life*. Eat, drink, and be happy. *If this is your attitude,* joy will carry you through the toil every day that God gives you under the sun.

(Ecclesiastes 8:15, The Voice)

9

A WARNING TO MANKIND

Try to be a rainbow in someone's cloud

– Maya Angelou (1928–2014),
American writer and civil rights activist

At the Christian Elementary School my brother and I attended, each Thursday we had chapel and learned that Jesus was coming back in the clouds. We neatly groomed children could barely see over the back of the pews as we looked up to the pulpit to hear the weather report. The daily lesson warned us if it was safe for us non-saved kids to play outside. If the clouds were out, Jesus could be coming back, and that meant we were in *big* trouble because he would be destroying the world. *Fear the clouds!* I always wondered why Jesus would want to ruin a perfectly beautiful day and destroy the entire world, including my banana curls that Mom so carefully crafted by brushing my wet hair around her finger each morning. I liked cloudy days just fine despite the weekly threat, and I even liked the rainy days. Why would Jesus want to suck up all the good fun of playing outside? A small prayer I uttered with my first-grade teacher in a back room during reading time, asking Jesus to save me, was enough for me to play outside on a cloudy day and not risk hell. No more apocalyptic fears of cloudy days. Problem solved.

My parents moved us to public school after being notified of my younger brother's "sin" of spilling chocolate milk. My new public elementary school allowed me to wear jeans, and I was unsure if that was okay, since jeans weren't allowed at the Christian school. Using moral authority to shame children (or adults) is never okay. It's called *spiritual abuse*. I know survivors of this kind of treatment who have left church to never look back, and I understand their reasoning all too well. The fundamental scare tactics that threatened me with hell made me conscious of how I present my faith to other people, including my own kids.

When my daughter was an infant, I laid her to sleep in a nursery decorated with a Noah's ark theme. It was all the baby nursery rage in the early 2000s. Perhaps I felt the biblical images of the boat and animals somehow put a blessing on my children. The cute wallpaper border displayed a cartoon of the ark, the rainbow, lots of animals, and happy, white Noah holding out an olive branch with the dove flying out. Interestingly, his wife didn't make the wallpaper. Years later, our family of six survived a tornado that passed over that room. The tornado destroyed my neighborhood. The Noah's ark wallpaper border fulfilled it's blessing for safety as the force of the tornado shook the upstairs as if a train was driving through it, while our family was huddled in the partial basement. The kids were asking if me if we were going to die. *Why didn't they ask their dad instead of me?* I answered with a calm, "I don't know if we are going to die today, honey" and finished the sentence off using my flesh to give a warm extended assuring snuggle. The body shelter my husband and I provided over the children turned more into a group hug as the house shook from a force stronger than anything we had ever experienced. We all survived, and somehow our house remained standing, but not without damage.

The next day the national networks brought out their news helicopters and broadcast the crumbled houses of my neighborhood that had been destroyed by the storm. Belongings were strewn throughout the yards. It's awkward to ask your neighbor if the slow cooker you found in your yard is theirs. It's also awkward to get a call from relatives across the United States saying they saw your damaged house on the news. Amazingly, nobody in our entire city died from that tornado. It was a miracle people survived being in houses that were lifted and moved to an entirely new address. Some homes were splintered into the winds. Until I survived a tornado I never knew trees and telephone poles could fall like dominoes and computer keyboards could fly like birds.

The power of nature can be fierce and deadly – within minutes it can rob us of our homes and freedom. Now get this straight: *nobody* was smiling after the destruction of our neighborhood *until* we made sure everyone we love was still alive. This included the neighbor's dog, who constantly barks to alert the entire neighborhood that he's alive (and able to bark). When we learned our family and neighbors (and yes the dogs) were still alive, we celebrated and made jokes, and my neighbor took a selfie with the uprooted tree that had fallen on her house. We cried together with people we didn't know. In our moment of shared humanity, the joy of my neighbor surviving felt like my joy and the sadness of my neighbors who lost their home, felt like my sadness. I was even sad for the annoying ten pounds of barking and jumping, who had momentarily disappeared but came back! I know the dog means a lot to his elderly owners. In our neighborhood's vulnerable moment, I learned why the Bible says, "Be happy with those who are happy, and cry with those who are crying" (Romans 12:15). We are to be with them in spirit, to be there. It's how we are called to share our faith. To otherwise say I was blessed felt as though I was deeming myself worthy of salvation and my neighbors deserving of the hell that ravaged their homes.

The Bible shares the story of the famous apocalyptic flood of Noah and his floating ark. Certainly Noah and his family were not celebrating, cracking jokes, or holding out the olive branch as they did in the wallpaper border. I suspect they peeked their heads out the window of the ark to see the dead bodies and carcasses of their neighbors and friends blanketing the muddy landscape from a flood that destroyed their entire civilization and the known world. I bet there were lots of maggots. I bet it smelled.

The sun does often shine bright and steady the day after a storm. However, it has occurred to me that we have taken the disaster of Noah's ark and turned it into kids' songs and cartoon characters, forgetting why the rains came down and floods came up. Was Noah "blessed" and the rest of the world condemned? We know God destroyed the "bad" people of the world through a flood and spared the only "blameless person" and his family (Genesis 6:9 NLT). We've candy-coated the wrath of God with cartoon Bibles, songs, and wallpaper borders; but our church narratives don't delve into why God felt compelled to destroy the world. Sunday school teachers many times do not teach the fact that Noah's ark sailed because of how vile and evil humanity had become, including the fact that sinful men robbed women of their power:

> Then the people began to multiply on the earth, and daughters were born to them. The sons of God *saw the beautiful women and took any they wanted as their wives...So the* LORD *was sorry he had ever made them and put them on the earth. It broke his heart.* And the LORD said, "I will wipe this human race I have created from the face of the earth.
>
> (Genesis 6:1–2, 6–7 NLT, emphasis mine)

Looking into the world of primitive tribal times, "took any they wanted as their wives" isn't getting on one knee and promising love and commitment to a woman for the rest of one's life. God didn't destroy the world because it was filled with chivalry and good manners. If that is the case, I shouldn't want to be a

Christian. When God considered evil humanity and felt compelled to destroy the world, God understood the trauma in the lives of these women. In this story, in the primitive and tribal world, taking "the beautiful women" is kidnapping, rape, abduction, and sex trafficking. The men forced these "beautiful women" into sexual slavery and stole their personal agency. [1] *Personal agency* is an ownership of power, to act on one's own will. Sexual assault robs victims of personal agency. So why aren't we Christians discussing how God destroyed the world because the "sons of god" stole the power of women?

The ancient *and* modern oral traditions dismiss the feelings and heart of women. To *our* shame we are also validating the ancient practice of "taking" women when we dismiss the narrative of the ancient women. We say the people were evil, and we sweep the sexual crimes under the apocalyptic rug. Have you ever heard a pastor discuss "sons of god" and their sins of sexual violence? The pain and trauma of these women has been ignored by the modern church because they were labeled as "wives."

When we are willing to see past the walls of sexism in our traditional Christian theology, we clearly see how these ancient "wives" were diminished in the biblical narrative of Noah. God does not forget the silenced voices and shattered stories of these women, we do. The transgressions against these ancient women who lived before the flood are offensive. The world is *never* right when the voice and role of women are reduced through massive scale sexual assault and rape. God cares about and remembers women, even when preachers, Sunday school teachers, and wall-paper designers reduce their story. Though the Bible was written

---

1. These women were considered "ownerless" items and were taken as legal property, "unmistakably" for sexual intercourse. See Meir Malul, *Knowledge, Control And Sex: Studies in Biblical Thought, Culture and Worldview* (Tel Aviv/Jaffa, Israel: Archaeological Center Publications, 2002), 206, 242.

from a male perspective – an ancient Jewish male perspective that often marginalized and sexualized women – we cannot justify their cultural blind spots so that we become our own blinders to women. It's time to interrupt the one-sided narrative. We can no longer silently consent to theology that steals the agency of biblical women, making everyone in church a silent bystander. The sexually entitled see silence as a nod; and it communicates to women, and the non-toxic men who care for them, that behaving as silent victims is acceptable. This is not the heart of God.

Sexual assault breaks God's heart. Rape culture in Noah's day was evidence of the vileness of humanity – a vileness that justified an apocalypse of wind and rain. Our sugared down theological diet frosts over the part of the story where women are treated as disposable commodities. During the time of Noah, rape culture infected society, as it still infects ours today. Imagine how different our girls would be treated in junior high schools or how much less the porn and sex industry would net if each time a kid heard the story of the great flood, he or she was reminded that the treatment of women only as sexual objects was one of the reasons God destroyed the world.

Sexual assault is a raging storm that terrorizes victims into a personal hell. Nearly 1 in 5 women in the United States has been raped at some time in her life.[2] Many of these women are sitting in churches looking for answers and feeling ignored. I have been warming church pews for decades and have *never* heard a sermon on the sin of sexual assault as an apocalyptic offense that contributed to making Noah's ark necessary. As long as our faith communities refrain from speaking out against the actions of these "sons of God," even in church, women will continue to

---

2. National Center for Injury Prevention and Control, Division of Violence Prevention, *Sexual Violence: Facts at a Glance*, Centers for Disease Control, 2012, https://www.cdc.gov/violenceprevention/pdf/sv-datasheet-a.pdf.

be seen and labeled by their female flesh alone. As postmillennial Christians, we have the power to disparage rape culture through changing how the story of Noah's ark is told. As women, we have the power to set this in motion.

Passing over the story of the women of Noah's day passes over the opportunity to teach both young men and women how to honor women. Assaulting the female flesh is assaulting God, because the female flesh was created in God's image. God dwells in women *and* men, which means we can all act godly. This means women were created with power, and we must wield that power! God has a heart that sees women *as more* than their female flesh and has already given a stern warning to mankind. Knowing God promised to never send another apocalyptic flood has further helped me understand God's grace – that my neighbor's pain is my pain, and we share our joy as well. Let's listen to the victims of sexual assault.

The church has an incredible opportunity to help survivors, and all women, realize and wield their power by reemphasizing the parts of the Bible that celebrate and value women. God proclaimed to Noah in the new covenant, "For in the divine image God made human beings" (Genesis 9:6 CEB).

And yes, in case you weren't sure, women are humans, created in God's image to wield God's power. The new covenant was sealed with a rainbow, and when sunlight breaks through the clouds, the rainbow appears. So in every storm or cloudy day, I no longer see potential for hell but potential to see God's value in every living thing (including the yappy dog). I'm still learning patience in waiting for the clouds to break as I mourn with those who mourn. The spectrum of human suffering and joy is vast, and when everyone is free to share their true colors through the rains, floods, winds, and perfectly sunny clear days of our lives, and little kids can play outside without fear of condemnation, we can shine together as a vibrant image of God's light. It's taken a few storms in my life to see this; but now, when I'm confronted with yet another threat of hell (they're always out there), I see the rainbow of promise emerging through the clouds instead.

When that rainbow appears in the clouds, I will see it and remember this eternal covenant I have made with all living creatures. (Genesis 9:16, The Voice)

10

GUYDOLATRY

*I think unconscious bias is one of
the hardest things to get at.*

– Ruth Bader Ginsburg (1933–)
associate justice for the
Supreme Court of the United States

How many ways can a girl dodge the question, "Where are you from?" *Ohio*. I never quite knew how to answer this because what people were really asking was, "Why do you look different?" My Egyptian dad's dark eyes and olive skin coupled with my mom's curly hair graced me with an exotic, hard to place Mediterranean look. My Midwest accent didn't reveal more than *Ohio*. If *Ohio* didn't suffice the unsolicited curiosity, which it usually didn't, I heard, "What's your ethnicity?" or "Where's your family from?" This feels a little bit like being asked by a stranger for your past medical history. As a girl I felt powerless by this question. If I didn't answer, I would seem suspicious. If I did, I would be considered different (*but that is why they asked*). What *were* they planning to do with this information – appease their own prepackaged ideology? This line of questioning has always made me feel judged and different, as if I didn't quite belong.

At the age of twenty-five I married into a more "American"

name and learned to straighten my hair with a flat iron, which seemed to fend off bloodline questions. Even as a professional adult, patients often assume the right to dig into the roots of my family tree. After September 11, 2001, each time I called my parents, there would be a click after about eight seconds into the call, and the line became more muted (which made talking with Mom especially challenging because she's hard of hearing). We joked about the lines being tapped, but it was really no joke to us. While we do not know for a fact if Mom's lines were tapped, we do know the clicking stopped only a few years back. It's difficult to understand systematic discrimination unless one has been a victim.

The traditional way to discriminate is by the flesh – race and gender. Looking different becomes justification for dividing people, which then brings about marginalization and unjust hierarchy. Cruelly, I learned this is exactly how the nation of Israel judged persons worthy of God in Bible times. The Israelites were "God's people." Since there was only one God, there was only "one" kind of person God dwelled in: Jewish men. Everyone else was "other."

To be "other" was to live alone outside the presence of God; it was the fate of the leper, the outcast thrown out from society. Woman was "other" but not cast from society because she was used for biological reproduction and to service "one." Slaves, who many times were foreign, also remained to serve the carnal desires of "one." This system of legal control over "others" developed an idolatry of powerful, privileged men.[1]

The problem with idols is they promote an image of power at the expense of others. These images stand to obstruct our vision of power in "others." One of the central messages in the ministry of Jesus was that all people had power; however, some Christians today still disguise worship of power as worship of Jesus. Jesus

---

1. Malul, *Knowledge, Control and Sex*, 16, 83.

is King; Jesus is coming back on a white horse (*to destroy the world*); Jesus is almighty. While all these attributes may be true, the weak and vulnerable parts of Jesus are either abandoned or assigned to "others" – the foreigner, refugee, eunuch, child, orphan, widow, woman – and machismo male images become our "one" image of power in God. If a woman or any "other" has power, it's often challenged for respect because it is thought to not rightly be theirs. Women and all "others" are robbed of their right to power. The idea of maleness as the only image of power is idolatry, or more specifically, *guydolatry*, as I call it. Many say, "Oh, we don't teach sexism (or idolatry) in our church"; all the while their teaching staff and boards are stacked with men.

When I was six years old, I worried the iron and bronze Hatshepsut and King Tut statues in our home were idols. Mom and Dad said they were fine, but I didn't believe them. I hid them to save our family from some curse from God. I was too embarrassed to tell Mom this when she pressed me about her missing home decor. Like people today, my misunderstood logic believed the bronze and gold that makes up an image was an idol. I didn't understand how the offense of idols is the judging who is and is not worthy to be an image of God's power. Idolatry lurks in our hearts when we can only recognize power in the "one" image.

Idols promote an ideal that benefits a small demographic while subordinating the rest.[2] The Bible's "one" Jewish man has evolved into today's privileged white man. Our social values have progressed from biblical values. For example, some Christians in earlier times used to attempt to justify slavery by using the Bible. However, in our time, slavery is a social structure universally rejected by Christian authority. These days, women *have* been elevated. Some Christians argue "biblical" justification for the

---

2. Andy Crouch, *Playing God: Redeeming the Gift of Power* (Downer's Grove, IL: InterVarsity Press, 2013), 99–100.

subordinate role of women, claiming her submission to man as God's "divine will,"[3] but that would be idolatry. Let me explain.

Throughout Bible times, women as "other" were expected to address their "one" husband as lord because men had ownership over women. The Hebrew word women used for their "lord" (husband) was *baal*, which signified legal control, to rule, to possess, to conquer, to control, to be master – all the not so great uses of power Jesus criticized (Luke 22:25). Although *baal* could roll off the tongue as a pet name, the term was actually a title of legal authority like senator, president, congressman, and so forth. It was expected for women to address the husband as lord, baal, of woman. It's no coincidence that the name *Baal* was also given to one of Israel's most pervasive idols. Israel created the idol's legal authority, which was not aligned with God's authority, because the idol worshipers were unwilling to see God outside of a "One" powerful being. Israel's golden calf *Baal* and husbands as *baal* are the same term![4]

The direct line between the authority of the golden calf and husband as *baal* illustrates clearly how idolatry of the husband has been indoctrinated into the Judeo-Christian tradition for thousands of years. While America touts the separation of church and state, our "Christian" nation's once legal doctrine of coverture – women's legal standing being relinquished to her husband upon marriage – reflects traditional Christian guydolatry.[5] There

---

3. Slavery is present throughout the Bible. Though the Bible regulates it, it does not legitimize slavery. See Kevin Giles, *The Trinity & Subordinationism: The Doctrine of God and the Contemporary Gender Debate*, (Madison, WI: InterVarsity Press, 2002), 251–258.

4. Malul, *Knowledge, Control and Sex*, 110–112, 159, 239–240, 364. Rabbinical sources indicate a sexual connotation to this authority; however, the occurrence is not accepted in the biblical Hebrew.

5. Hendrik Hartog, *Man and Wife in America: A History* (Cambridge, MA: Harvard University Press, 2009), 118–120.

are still churches in America that teach baal marriage, claiming the man has government or authority over woman. I was a part of one of those churches. Baal marriage promotes cherry-picked scriptures to justify their imbalanced and idolatrous model. At a point of their understanding, women are responsible for promoting guydolatry as well and should not always be considered a victim when they defend men as "God's designed leaders." When my husband and I realized the idolatry in the doctrine of marriage taught to us, we stopped attending church until we could find a less idolatrous environment. I'm forever grateful to my husband for his humility to recognize this and move to make us blameless. As we've cut the spousal line of command, we're uniting as equals, not by me relinquishing my power. The power imbalance robbed our marriage of intimacy, just as it harmed ancient Israel's intimacy with God.

When we investigate the Old Testament, elimination of idol worship and women wielding power in society are directly correlated. Two biblical time periods, 1580–1085 BC and 663–525 BC, we read about women exercising freedom and wielding power. It is no coincidence that in these time periods Israel's leaders were eliminating idol worship. When the Baals and Asherah poles were erected, women were reduced to the status of being sub-human. [6] The attitudes and lives of the women in the Baal-free eras are quite inspiring, yet rarely spoken of from the pulpit. I struggle to bring my daughter and sons to a church that rarely speaks of powerful biblical women. While I appreciate the emphasis on egalitarian marriage, and the ministering to children and teens,

---

6. From Ruth and Naomi traveling alone safely as single women, to Deborah exercising authority as a tribal leader or judge, to scholar and prophetess Huldah, who was advisor to the king. Miriam also led millions of Israelites in a song of worship and victory across the divided Red Sea. See Schmidt, *Veiled and Silenced*, 77–78.

I don't want to discredit or disrespect church authority, so I am gentle in pointing out the one-sidedness to my children and those who speak in church. Our children need to hear how women, too, wielded God's power if they are going to eliminate guydolatry in this next millennium. It is my job, my daughter's job, and everyone else's job to destroy the guydolatrous image of Baal, who is still worshiped in our churches when biblical women's powerful stories are muted or minimized.

Idols are powerful because they are largely unrecognized, since they don't replace God altogether.[7] Idols stand as an obstruction to seeing the full image of God. According to Rabbi Herzl Hefter, "the ultimate object of worship remains God. The problem is that only an aspect of [God's] 'personality' is being adored".[8] The alluring temptation of idols reduces a sovereign God into the worshiper's images of power. It imagines God as a fixed image of power, which is only one facet of God. The facet of God's masculinity and power is what guydolatry sees, which reduces our relationship with God to a measure of obedience. Guydolatry obstructs God's power in women and is a tradition with deep roots in pulpits, legal benches, and the hearts of Christians. Living according to the Bible sounds noble, but with improper teaching and an improper understanding, it can often mean living within the oppressive prejudices of ancient peoples' legal systems, instead of being Christlike.

Understanding the mass atrocity of how people have been oppressed in Christianity through the ages has been challenging for my faith. It helps me to remember God stresses that creation

---

7. Moses was at Sinai, and the calf was formed initially to take his place in leading the people to God, not to replace God. Later, in Jewish history the idol did seem to usurp God.

8. Herzl Hefter, "Idolatry: A Prohibition for Our Time," *Tradition* 42, no. 1 (Spring 2009): 16.

was given to *all* peoples of the earth. "Don't look to the skies, to the sun or the moon or the stars, all the heavenly bodies, and be led astray, worshipping and serving them. The LORD your God has granted these things to *all the nations* who live under heaven" (Deuteronomy 4:19, italics mine).

When I feel defeated by sexism or the patriarchy that marginalizes so many, I remember the blessings of God are for me too. Sexist practices that marginalize or segregate women from power are idolatrous. This includes withholding women from being an image of power to serve the community, the church, and bear the image of God. The first creation story in Genesis 1 defines God's nature to be plural, able to create both male *and* female in God's image: [9]

> God created humanity in God's own image,
>> in the divine image God created them,
>>> male and female God created them.
>>>> (Genesis 1:27)

Theologians and church fathers have passed down the message to our churches that women are inferior to men because women are not created in a powerful image of God. The view that women are inferior and undeserving defies what is taught in Genesis and denies women the full image of God. [10] Denying women's humanity and divine nature in God's image is denying God, and it is idolatry.

Imago Dei ("image of God") teaches female and male were created in God's image. Reading the creation narratives, we see

---

9. For a full discussion on God in the image of both sexes, see Gilbert Bilezikian, *Beyond Sex Roles: What the Bible Says about a Woman's Place in Church and Family,* 3rd ed., (Grand Rapids, MI: Baker Academic, 2006), 17–21.
10. Jann Aldredge-Clanton, *In Whose Image? God and Gender* (New York: Crossroads Publishing, 1990), 21–22.

man not only needed woman but all of creation needed woman to reflect the fullness of God. God is the ground of our being,[11] and it's time to start owning that ground as women. Women bear the image of God *and* power of God. It is inherent within us. Owning the fact that women are created in the image of God is the first step to removing the detestable guydolatry in our Christian tradition. So long as religion teaches a male-only image of God, women will be conditioned to fear men and the power of women will be a battleground of men's faith. As we learn to see men and women as equals – equals bearing the image and power of God – we will find the power of God to create a better world together.

> Of what value is an idol carved by a craftsman?
>   Or an image that teaches lies?
> For the one who makes it trusts in his own creation;
>   he makes idols that cannot speak.
>
> (Habakkuk 2:18, NIV)

---

11. Thank you, theologian Paul Tillich for coining "ground of being."

PART 2

BODY LANGUAGE

You've always had the power my dear,
you just had to learn it for yourself.

– Glinda the Good Witch
from *The Wizard of Oz*

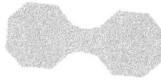

II

MISS BRANDED

Conversation between Adam and Eve
must have been difficult at times, because
they had nobody to talk about.

– Agnes Repplier (1855–1950),
American essayist

College was a time when I learned to stand alone as a woman. Away from my parents, and without a boyfriend, I developed autonomy to create my own brand of womanhood. I had boyfriends in high school, but I was tired of them, no longer wanting to be *his*. The single life brought the increased pressure of dealing with unwelcome advances. Guys didn't sling "slut" at me when I had a boyfriend, but if I rejected them while "on the market" – as if I were a piece of meat – that was "slut" worthy. Enjoying anything physical with a guy who didn't "own" me as *his*, or wasn't trying to woo me as *his*, also risked slut-shaming. Being *his* was in some ways easier because the world wanted my body labeled that way.

Nothing sparks gossip like the body of a young, single woman; just being "on the market" makes her fodder for judgment. Despite the liberating qualities of education, I still bumped into sexist expectations for my female flesh: Who are you dating?

Are you safe living alone? When are you getting married? It was clear the expectation for my life was to be associated with a man. It seemed as if there was always someone trying to set me up. It was an exciting time but also a painful time of developing into a woman. I received a lot of attention from older men (who could legally prey on me), and nobody had taught me how to rebuff or deal with their sophisticated advances. I bumped into a few married ones and was fortunately smart enough to sniff out that they had a wife. *Rejected!* In college everyone is broke, so dates with college guys were VHS and pizza with the beverage of your choice (I hear that's "Netflix and chill" these days). I quickly learned to keep my dates and time with guys to public locations because they often made uncomfortable advances towards me in private. In my new world of dating, I had no idea whether men liked me or just what my body could do for them. I watched lots of women fall prey to being *his*. Some fell for the married guy; others hooked up on Saturday (and cried in the dorm on Sunday). A few women boasted of their experiences and rated them publicly for the rest of us. Many just kept steady boyfriends so they didn't have to deal with it.

The old double standard was that women were sluts and men were studs. If a "hookup" *did* happen, the woman got labeled and man got high fives. If a woman had too many hookups, her flesh was branded a "slut." I don't remember *her* name, whether she was a biology or education major, if she swam or was in drama club; I just remember that she was a slut – *and yes shame on me*. We all know her, the one to whom the label stuck, the one whose name and value are stripped from our memories, the one who's flesh is branded. We tell a narrative of her life that veils the essence of who a woman is and the creative works she can produce. Her brand of womanhood is permanently burned into the worthiness of her female flesh.

Our next generation may be lacking in vocabulary as they

communicate with emojis and hashtags, but they haven't failed to generate a new label to stick onto bodies of girls and women. *THOT (That Ho Over There)* is the new "slut," the label most girls and women nowadays attempt to avoid. THOT joins the cannonry of labels reserved for the sexual expressions the female body can elicit. The sexual labels have branded almost every generation of women, and they become especially derogatory when the women's flesh is not *his*.

The Bible	1920s My Grandma's Generation[1]	1990s, My Generation	2019, My Daughter's Generation
"Virgin" (available)	"Tart" (temptress)	"Loose" (loose morals [not vaginas!])	"Virgin" (*the new derogatory "too-good"*)
"Prostitute" or "Harlot" (sells sex)	"Slag" (trashy)	"Easy" (to get sex from)	"Pure" (*the religious "too-good"*)
"Concubine" (sexual slave)	"Flapper" (wears short hair and skirts)	"Knocked up" (pregnant on accident	"Baby-Momma" (*got pregnant, got dumped*)
"Widow" (her husband died)	"Tramp" (slut disguised as a lady)	"Lady of the Night" (trades sex favors for money)	"Ho" (*the new whore*)
"Wife" (married)	"Hussy" (saucy and imprudent)	"Too-good" (*She has standards above mine*)	"THOT" (*the new slut*)
	"Floozy"	"Prude" (*more standards... dude's sob story doesn't work with her*)	
	"Broad" (makes herself seen)	"Whore" (had *to be given money before she finally put out sex*)	
	"Whore" (any woman from prostitute to one showing too much skin)	"Bangable" (acceptable for sex)	
		"Frigid" (*not interested in sexual pursuits*)	
		"Slut" (*any female participating in activity not pertaining to homemaking skills or prayer!*)	

Since Bible times, women have been labeled, and even shamed, for their sexual expression – as if what she does with

_____

1. I found it interesting that many sexual labels for women arose in the 1920's when women were asserting power. The labels from the late 1950's and early 1960's, my mom's generation, were carry overs from the 1920's.

her body is everyone's business – while men are excused with "boys will be boys." By the time I was in my early twenties, I had a few decaying stories that weren't quite yet skeletons. Some of my experiences left me feeling discarded like yesterday's dirty rags. It wasn't that anyone was calling me these names, or that I was socially rejected, I *felt* those labels in my heart and was self-accusing. I looked to a Christian brand of womanhood. I was shown through repentance and baptism I would be washed clean. I still believe that, but in addition to being washed clean I was branded *His*, and not really set free (2 Corinthians 3:17, John 8:36). According to how that particular church taught the Bible, God saw men as leaders of women, so women not led by a man were, by silent default, unwholesome. There were women in leadership; however, they were wives, daughters, or girlfriends of the real leaders; they were *his*. I was smart enough to realize the bias in this "leadership" but understood I, too, held a soft amount of power as *his* sister, my brother in ministry.

After graduate school, and a couple years of sexist church indoctrination, I "assented" to marriage with a man I met there. Once again, I was officially branded *his*. My identity became folded into my husband's. There was the name change, and my "Mrs." title told the world of my officially changed sexual availability. I had no idea that the challenges to navigate sexist doctrine would be much more difficult because of my direct relationship with my husband. With marriage came a different set of expectations for my body...bearing *his* children.

Ladies, try attending a new church and not revealing your marital or motherhood status, it's nearly impossible. Last year I was placed into a new women's small group at our new church. Immediately the women wanted to know my marital and motherhood status (what my body was doing for a man). The truth is, though, if my four kids weren't *his* in marriage, I would be regarded a charity case, despite my ability to care for them emotionally and financially on my own. It still feels awkward that we judge a woman's life according to the men (or absence of men) in it. It's as if our womanhood is not only branded *his*, but our value in the world of Christianity is in direct correlation to how many rug rats we've produced with *him*. Unmarried women – especially divorced women – who are defining their womanhood without being *his* are treated as suspicious. Singles and single moms go into separate "reject" categories in church. In the single mom category, the more kids you have the worse. *How dare you have a family that's not his!* Just as the Pharisees had their "clean" and "unclean" categories for flesh, the Christian brand has "approved" and "unapproved" categories for female flesh.

Arguably the most controversial and slut shamed woman in Christianity is Eve. We don't know whether to classify her approved or unapproved, *his* or her own. Eve swallowed the forbidden fruit, which forced the rest of the world to digest its pulp. This "pandora theology" – blaming a woman as a source of evil – has saturated our interpretation of Scripture since it became popular in Greek mythology.[2] Looking closely at the Bible, I was shocked after many years of Bible reading (and Bible thumping) to discover Eve was misbranded. If we read the text literally, Adam was kicked out of the garden, not Eve.

> The LORD God made garments of skin for Adam and his wife and clothed them. And the LORD God said, "The man has now become like one of us, knowing good and evil. He must not be allowed to reach out his hand and take also from the tree of life and eat, and live forever." So the LORD God banished him from the Garden of Eden to work the ground from which

---

2. The spread of Hellenism, largely associated with misogyny, is attributed to seeing Eve as Pandora, a Greek mythology character from 800 BC who brought evil into the world. See William E. Phipps, "Eve and Pandora Contrasted," *Theology Today* 45, no. 1 (April 1988): 34–37.

he had been taken. After he drove the man out, he placed on the east side of the Garden of Eden cherubim and a flaming sword flashing back and forth to guard the way to the tree of life. (Genesis 3:21–24, NIV)

Rub your eyes and tell me, just where did God expel Eve from Eden?

Looking in the New Testament, I discovered Paul declares that "one" was responsible for the fall. In Romans 5, the Bible holds Adam responsible for sin eight times, not Eve.[3]

Since my childhood, all my religious training presented the image of Eve as the guilty one, Adam's downfall. She was called "Devil's Gateway" and "Evil Temptress" through apple-picking jokes and sermons. The tradition of Eve's disparity was used as praxis to brand all female flesh guilty. The Eve-shamers have even transformed her supposed culpability into a prescription for women to be governed under men, to be *his*.[4] This manipulative theology upholds the "she's a slut, he's a stud" double standard as a Christian staple, punishing Eve and all women who chose to be with a man. Like a "knocked-up" teenage girl, Eve gets the wrath, and Adam is treated like an anonymous MIA sperm donor. In pandora theology, Adam dodges responsibility and Eve gets the blame; this is reflective of blaming women for unplanned outcomes of sexual expression. Both the man and woman crossed the line, but it's a fault line for women – the "girls fault line." Women are blamed for crossing a line that boys cross freely. Eve,

---

3. It's not arguable here that "man" meant "mankind" or all people (women, children, elderly, etc.), because when the Bible is inclusive of all humanity it uses the Greek term *anthropos* which is *not* used in Romans 5:12, 14–19. See Bushnell, *God's Word to Women*, par. 91–92).

4. For a full discussion, read Gilbert Bilezikian, *Beyond Sex Roles: What the Bible Says about a Woman's Place in Church and Family* 3rd ed. (Grand Rapids, MI: Baker Academic, 2006), 104–106.

of course, sinned, as did Adam, but the Bible doesn't hold her responsible as it does Adam.

Reading closely the account of Adam and Eve as primitive humans, we see that Adam was created before Eve and was the only human to receive God's instructions about the tree. We can say this made Adam responsible for the instruction. "Eat your fill from all of the garden's trees; but don't eat from the tree of the knowledge of good and evil, because on the day you eat from it, you will die!" (Genesis 2:16–17).

Immediately in verse 18 God sees it is not good for man to be alone and creates a parade of animals that Adam names but do not suffice until woman is created later. Eve never received the instruction from God, and only Adam had information about the tree of knowledge of good and evil. In fact, there is no direct interaction between God and Eve until God is cleaning up the fruit incident. If Adam remembered, he likely warned her because she did verbalize to Satan what God had said. When God blew the whistle in Eden, we see Adam blaming the woman, *and* God, assuming everyone else is wrong but him. Conveniently, he offers up his wife for punishment: "The woman you gave me, she gave me some fruit from the tree, and I ate" (3:12). Eve blames the serpent: "The snake tricked me, and I ate" (verse 13).

We've all heard the "they tricked me" excuse from kids. While the child may be telling the truth about being tricked, there is also a measure of responsibility and consequence required so that the kid doesn't make the "childish" mistake again. Adam and Eve were both guilty here; however the Bible seems to handle Eve with "kid gloves."

Adam received the eviction notice from paradise.[5] "The LORD God sent him out of the garden of Eden to farm the fertile land from which he was taken. He drove out the human [Adam]. To

---

5. Because Eve rightly blamed the serpent.

the east of the garden of Eden, he stationed winged creatures wielding flaming swords to guard the way to the tree of life" (Genesis 3:32–34).

Outside of Genesis, there are two biblical references to Eve (2 Corinthians 11:3; 1 Timothy 2:14), and neither holds her ultimately responsible. Paul describes Eve as "extra" deceived, and the significance of this is that it exonerates Eve from the weight of the world's sin.[6] In this logic, the woman Eve was out of her league, as a young child would be with a molester. Reading deeper into Scripture, the Bible *specifically* names Adam culpable twice: "In Adam all die" (1 Corinthians 15:22) and "Death reigned from Adam" (Romans 5:14). Ouch!

So, all *do not* die in Eve, we live! In Genesis 3:20, Eve is "the mother of everyone who lives"![7] The name "Eve" means life. If Eve was life separate from Adam, then she didn't belong to him. Tradition likes to assume Eve as Adam's (*his*), upholding them as a prototype for conjugal relationship. The relational words "husband" (Genesis 3:6) and "wife" are not original to the Hebrew text but in fact words inserted from translators,[8] and many scholars do not believe Adam and Eve to be actual people.[9] The story of Adam and Eve is timeless midrash[10] portraying our human capacity to

---

6. *Ēpatēthē* and *exapatētheisa* are essentially the same Greek word with different conjugations for "deceived"; however the prefix "exa" describes a condition of thoroughly or completely deceived (See Bushnell, par. 91).
7. Later in the text her son dies, so she becomes the mother of the dead too, giving life to the "father of murder."(See Wilda C. Gafney, *Womanist Midrash*, 26–27).
8. Gafney, 22–23.
9. C. John Collins, "Adam and Eve as Historical People, and Why It Matters," *Perspectives on Science and Christian Faith* 62, no. 3 (September 2010): 147+. https://www.asa3.org/ASA/PSCF/2010/PSCF9–10Collins.pdf.
10. *Midrash* is an ancient Jewish literary form that combines both history and pastoral poetry, or elaborations of imagery, to teach a moral lesson. Midrash is not exclusively history to document names and dates; facts were often

sin, and we all know both men and women sin. Human nakedness is on full display in the story of Adam and Eve; but tradition sizes up Eve's nakedness as more condemnable than Adam's, while the Bible ultimately holds Adam more responsible. As the Adam and Eve account is still upheld as a standard for marriage, in my own experience of marriage, I've found that fixing the blame is damaging. We've found fixing the *problem* to be much more effective in our relationship; it doesn't always matter how much of whose fault it was.

Branding Eve as "guilty" is baked into the story of our world religions. Her misbranded image of cooked-up falsehoods is used to brand women as sexual objects that can become *his* – owned under the moral authority of man. It made us "other" than human in Scripture, assigning labels of sexual expression. This view has harmed women throughout history and does yet today by robbing us of the inherent goodness and power created in our female flesh. It has even sadistically justified the punishment and suffering of women. The accepted falsehood is that women are deserving of sexual labels like "slut," and her sexual expression should be labeled everybody's business to know, because the Bible says so. But labels are for objects, not for people. Sexualizing women leads to abuse. The next time you hear someone label a woman, with a sexual label reserved for women speak up and speak out because labeling her is an attempt to remove her from her human existence and make her an object of flesh. And the next time you hear an Eve-bashing joke, call out the person who is telling it, especially if it's a pastor, because it's not funny and is subtly calling all women "evil" and *his.*

---

elaborated into imagery to make a point. Midrash was the ancient Jewish standard for interpreting Scripture. See David Stern, *Midrash and Theory: Ancient Jewish Exegesis and Contemporary Literary Studies* (Evanston, IL: Northwestern University Press, 1996), 15–26, 51–52, 77.

Christians are, of course, free to read and interpret Scripture as we see fit, so if Christians choose to read Scripture *literally*, they need to remove the focus on Eve's unworthiness enough to ask why she left her God in the garden and why she preferred to follow into Adam's story instead of remaining the central figure of God's story in Eden. To say it was her place to follow Adam is to say a woman's place is with man and not God.

I am more than *his*. God created my female flesh *good* and separate from man or *him*. I am an individual, and to understand the goodness and power in my female flesh I had to understand the slut-shaming of Eve and sexualization of the other women of the Bible. It has been wrongly assumed women are created morally inferior to men and therefore a consumable. I had to understand how this biased judgment of my sexual expression expects my female flesh to be branded as *his*. If women are to feel *good* in our flesh, we must uphold a faith to see each woman worthy beneath the sexualized labels and brands that get seared into our identities.

The first word of the Bible is translated as "the beginning" but accurately means "a beginning."[11] Each woman has a beginning, created as her own being. We are given a beginning each day, but die only once. So dare to feel good in your flesh, find your power within it, within you. Reject the labels and believe that God declares *all* creation good, including the woman.

> Then God surveyed everything He had made, savoring *its beauty and appreciating* its goodness.
>
> (Genesis 1:31, The Voice)

---

11. Gafney, *Womanist Midrash*, 19.

12

SHE KNOWS IT

*Our school education ignores, in a thousand
ways, the rules of healthy development*

– Elizabeth Blackwell (1821–1910)
British physician, first woman to receive a
medical degree in the United States

As a curious ten-year-old Bible reader, a year between pretending to believe in Santa Claus and wearing a training bra, the passage of Genesis 4:1, among other scriptures made me very scared of men knowing me because it might get me pregnant: "The man Adam knew his wife Eve intimately. She became pregnant and gave birth to Cain, and said, 'I have given life to a man with the LORD's help'" (Genesis 4:1). According to my understanding of the Bible, Eve *and* the Virgin Mary got pregnant without sex, so my logical mind reasoned it could happen to me. Since natural law didn't apply when it came to the Bible, I was not going to allow a man to "know" me and get me pregnant. I stayed away from my older brother and dad because they were men and knew me. No hugs, no snuggles, no "let's go for a bike ride." I understood those supernatural swimmers were lurking out there in toilet seats, swimming pools, and the chair at the doctor's office. A girl never could be too safe, and God wasn't one to mess with.

Becoming pregnant outside of marriage was a big no-no in my family's expectations of my body. My mom had a shotgun wedding and climbed her way out of the "girl's fault line"; and to protect me, the pressure to avoid pregnancy outside of marriage was high. As a girl who didn't know many facts about sexual reproduction, I hated when my belly would hang out. I remember lying prone on the floor, hoping it would put my tummy back in so I wouldn't be pregnant. Mom eventually explained to me that it took more than a man "knowing" me to get pregnant. Mom hadn't read the Bible, however, so I wasn't real sure about her explanation. It seemed, *excessive.* Certainly people everywhere weren't doing *that!...Especially her and Dad! Eww!*

What I did *not* know in my naive logical strategy to avoid getting pregnant was that much of the Bible was written in literary form, as poetry. The Bible is full of stories written with ancient language and symbolisms that don't fit into the context of our modern imagery. It obviously takes more than a man knowing his wife "intimately" to get her pregnant. So let's talk sex!

As an adult Bible reader, I learned the verbs for *sex* and *knowledge* in Genesis 4:1 are similar.[1] In Genesis 4:1 Adam is the stud impregnating Eve, knowing all that is going on. Eve is passive. As the passive agent of the active verb Eve seems to have no power in sex. Sex was the one-person act of Adam, and Eve is an unknowing sex object. This narrative has set the stage for

---

1. We see this linguistic relationship in modern phrases like "carnal knowledge" or "Adam knew his wife." *Yādaʿ* is the Hebrew word for the copulation, "knew." Reading Genesis 4:1 literally, I was right to be afraid of supernatural sperm because the verb conjugation of *Yādaʿ* is male or masculine, attributing Adam the "knowledge," while the verb object is female, who is the recipient of Adam's knowledge. Malul, *Knowledge, Control and Sex,* 233–234.

all women to be considered passive sexual agents. Adam and Eve's sexuality is held up as the Christian model; however, Eve's passivity has left generations of women feeling insecure about embracing their active sexual desires or seeking sexual pleasure. It's as if anything outside of being a passive agent for a husband to impregnate is unacceptable sexual behavior for a Christian woman. As a girl growing into womanhood, the conversations I had about sex with adults centered around avoiding or achieving pregnancy. Nobody ever told me about female pleasure or passion in sex – that was taboo.

When it comes to sexual pleasure, we all have heard that boys get it and girls give it. So what about the girls getting something other than pregnant? Was the sexual appetite created only for men? Of course not! *Duh!* The sexual appetites of women and men are an incredible gift, like fire. Responsible human sexuality provides light and keeps us warm. Sex and fire have kept humans alive; but when misused, sex and fire destroy, ravish, and burn. With all my female sexual passion talk, I do believe God advocates a loving and committed marriage of mutuality to be the merited environment for sex to honor and respect the flames of sexual passion.

I felt the threat of that fire at age ten and was already suppressing my being a sexual being. My Christian world had taught me that I was created as a passive agent for man, not as a woman who had been given the potential to experience God's pleasure through healthy and honorable sexual behavior. If there was any burning passion in my female body, it was clear that was sinful. I still wonder how different my life would have been without all the shaming and expectations for my body. When we teach women to be passive sexual agents, it teaches them to become sexual objects for a man, which makes them vulnerable and perpetuates fear. Sects of Christians give men a godlike role over women in the sexual relationship, emphasizing the passive model of female sexuality in Genesis 4:1.[2] This teaching is antithetical to God's warning to humanity, destroying the world because of rape-marriages. In America, sects advocate to control women not only with theology but also in legal policy of sex education.

In my Illinois public school sex education class, we studied our eggs and learned to fear they could be impregnated at *any time* in our cycle. Never did we study the feel-good parts of our bodies or how to say yes or no; nothing about female erogenous zones, the clitoris, or the electrifying female orgasm. Girls were circumcised in this abstinence-only education, and I had no idea until well into my 30s that female erection was even a thing my flesh could achieve. Neglecting to discuss the entirety of female genitalia made me wonder if those parts of my body – clitoris, labia majora, labia minora, the clitoral hood, or the mons pubis, collectively the external vulva – were dirty or wrong. My sex education discussed the vagina, the part of a female's body which primarily pleasures men, while glossing over women's external genitalia or vulva, the parts essential to pleasure. Unsanctioned to feel pleasure, I learned from sex education to prevent pregnancy but mostly heard *don't*.

My sex education in the 1980s began the era of a federally mandated abstinence only until marriage (AOUM) curriculum that schooled girls to believe their bodies were passive.[3] The

---

2. Sects of Christians who teach women to be passive agents uphold what's called *complementary theology*, meaning that women were created as a complement to men. Egalitarian theology teaches that God created men and women as equals with interchangeable roles and responsibilities. Some say their relationship is complementary but have decided the roles and responsibilities themselves in an egalitarian manner; this is often referred to as a soft complementarian relationship.

3. Peggy Orenstein, *Girls & Sex: Navigating the Complicated New Landscape* (New York: HarperCollins, 2017), 52.

presumption in AOUM programs was, if girls know the truth about their bodies, they will explore sex outside of marriage *and might even enjoy it (gasp)*. AOUM curriculum hinges sexual activity around pregnancy risks, making vaginal intercourse central while ignoring the risks and benefits of all other sexual activity. It was a scare tactic, and I remember being told that taking my clothes off could get me pregnant, so I imagined the little swimmers swimming my vagina to get me pregnant! AOUM has been connected to an increase of teenagers participating in alternative sexual activity because they don't consider sex to be anything but vaginal intercourse. Teenagers were taught to avoid pregnancy, and they responded in doing "everything but" (vaginal intercourse), which became "everything butt." Increased anal sex, oral sex, and not using condoms is directly tied to abstinence only programs.[4] The AOUM expired and evolved into "virginity pledge" subculture. Neither curriculum discussed sexual consent or female pleasure, and both are related to risky sexual behaviors.[5,6]

Considerable evidence has shown that Comprehensive Sex Education (CSE) has led to more favorable effects in reducing

---

4. Sloan Caldwell, "Let's Talk About Sex: The Failure of Abstinence-Only Policies in America's Public Schools," *senior thesis, 2015)*, 1035, Claremont McKenna College: 25–26, http://scholarship.claremont.edu/cmc_theses/1035.
5. John S. Santelli et al., "Abstinence-Only-Until-Marriage: An Updated Review of U.S. Policies and Programs and Their Impact," *Journal of Adolescent Health* 61, no. 3, (2017): 273–280, https://doi.org/10.1016/j.jadohealth.2017.05.031.
6. Sex education has political significance again in the U.S. (See The Editorial Board, "The New Era of Abstinence," *The New York Times*, May 5, 2018, https://www.nytimes.com/2018/05/05/opinion/sunday/the-new-era-of-abstinence.html). AOUM is making a resurgence, rebranded as "sex risk avoidance" (SRA) programs. These SRA programs withhold potentially lifesaving information and promote dangerous stereotypes and inequality. See also Jesseca Boyer, "New Name, Same Harm: Rebranding of Federal Abstinence-Only Programs," Guttmacher Institute, February 28, 2018, https://www.guttmacher.org/gpr/2018/02/new-name-same-harm-rebranding-federal-abstinence-only-programs.

sexual activity among teens.[7] CSE gives comprehensive information on safe sexual behavior, including contraception, consent, and avoiding sexually transmitted infections, while distributing accurate information for healthy development in all areas of sexual development – openness on consent, honesty about risks, decision-making, and communication in relationships, and so forth.[8] CSE has proven more effective in delaying sexual activity in teenagers and preventing pregnancy, sexual violence, and diseases. It also does not shame teenagers for being curious or having questions about sex or criminalize teenage girls for being sexual beings.

In college I was baptized into a purity culture church. I took a vow of abstinence at baptism. This subjected me to the religious warning labels such as "fallen," "impure," "used," and "chewed up (*like used bubble gum*)" to hinge my salvation on avoiding *any* sort of sexual activity outside of marriage. "Worldly" labels such as "cunt," "crotch," or "twat" had already given me a squeamish idealization about my genitals. These shameful influences on me segued into an inhibition to voice my sexual desires to my husband. I became passive, as I was taught to be; though I knew the accurate anatomical language for my body, I lacked confidence to use to use it for my pleasure. I still am inhibited from initiating sexual activity, because there's still a voice in me that says I'm not supposed to be sexual. My husband and I have been married

7. H.B. Chin et al., "The Effectiveness of Group-Based Comprehensive Risk-Reduction and Abstinence Education Interventions to Prevent or Reduce the Risk of Adolescent Pregnancy, Human Immunodeficiency Virus, and Sexually Transmitted Infections," *American Journal of Preventive Medicine* 42, no. 3, (March, 2012): 272–294.

8. Society for Adolescent Health and Medicine, "Abstinence-Only-Until-Marriage Policies and Programs: An Updated Position Paper of the Society for Adolescent Health and Medicine," *The Society for Adolescent Health and Medicine* 61, no. 3 (September 2017): 400–403.

eighteen years, and it's still challenging for me to ask for sex or describe what I want sexually because I feel ashamed. I must remind myself I am worthy of sexual pleasure to speak up (and I'm doing absolutely nothing wrong).

Women have power in voicing their sexual desires and consent. Wielding this power in my marriage has helped my husband and me grow in our sexual relationship, but not without marital bumps along the way. I have gradually come to realize that I will never have equality in the public sphere if I don't have equality in the private sphere of my own bedroom.

God created women as active sexual beings, and research is showing our equal, active nature in our female reproductive cells. Our ova have been traditionally described as a periodically released nest of eggs that passively wait to be conquered by a sperm competition. Rather than a sperm race to win the right of impregnating, research is showing how women's macroscopic ova actively select which microscopic sperm to consume that it may evolve.[9] *Of course they do! We women knew that!* So teach your daughters how their eggs will compel millions of tiny little fellas into competition to be chosen and devoured by her!

The truth may set a girl free, but it also makes her safe. As we teach our girls to rightly wield power in their sexuality, they become more reliant on themselves to select partners, use protection, and have the vocabulary to confidently voice consent or dissent and specifics about their own bodies and desires. The #Metoo (and #Churchtoo) sexual harassment revelations have brought to light how passive we have taught women and girls to be. Teaching girls to be sweet and passive teaches them to be silent. As one rape victim put it, "I lay there trapped by

_____

9. Carrie Arnold, "Females' Eggs May Actively Select Certain Sperm," *The Atlantic*, November 25, 2017, https://www.theatlantic.com/science/archive/2017/11/choosy-eggs/546062/.

politeness."[10] We can no longer afford to lie to girls by telling them they are immoral for possessing sexual power, experiencing sexual pleasure, or having questions. We must stop shaming women for being sexual beings. Even if we shame with silence.

What we teach ten-year-old girls about their developing sexuality weighs immensely on their ability to feel the goodness of God in their bodies and their ability to trust God. When religion teaches *her* desires are of less value than *his* in marriage, girls and women rightfully lose trust in the church. When girls and women are honored as equals, having been created in the image of God, they are not seen as passive or become prey by being trapped into being passive agents. Even as we teach skills to communicate consent, consent is the "low bar"[11] for a woman to find pleasure in her sexual relationship.

In contrast to other Bible translations, The Voice Bible translation portrays Eve as an active agent in the sexual experience: "Now Adam and Eve discovered the pleasures of lovemaking" (Genesis 4:1). How beautiful is that? *Thank you!*

All women are active sexual agents and need to have that carnal knowledge not only from sex education but from the Bible. I hope to see more Genesis translations honoring Eve as an active sexual agent. It may just influence how people "[discover] the pleasures of lovemaking."

> **Her:** You, my love, are so handsome! A pleasure *to behold*!
> Our bed is *a lush*, green *field*,
> The beams of our house are *majestic* cedars,
> and the rafters are *tall* pines.
>
> (Song of Songs 1:16–17, The Voice)

---

10. Jessica Bennett and Daniel Jones, "45 Stories of Sex and Consent on Campus," *The New York Times*, May 10, 2018.
11. Orenstein, *Girls & Sex*, 243.

13

BEATING THE OBSTACLE COURSE

*My style has stayed pretty consistent over
the years. I always wear what I like and
what is appropriate for the occasion.*

– Melania Trump (1970–),
First Lady of the United States of America

The year between the end of my elementary school and junior high school years, I ignored my parents' instructions and bared the landscape of my freshly developed female curves in a two-piece swimsuit at the public pool. This was before the days of worrying about cellulite, or even knowing what cellulite was, and I wanted a better tan. My skin has always been a fair olive tone, burnable from Mom's Scandinavian whiteness, but able to hold a base tan for the entire winter with Dad's Middle Eastern brown.

As a family we rarely swam; Mom refused to be seen in a swimsuit, and I'm pretty sure she tried to save the world from being exposed to Dad in swim garb. I have clear memories of his Mediterranean boy-short speedos being worn with an oxford shirt, black knee-high socks, and a fedora hat. He looked like he was in his underwear. *Go Dad!*

Mom and Dad were clueless on swimwear fashion, my need for a tan, or anything else, Mom purchased the synthetic fire-engine red two-piece the year prior for me to wear as a base layer underneath a two-piece belly dancing costume. I picked out the loud, and very ethnic, red and gold costume in a busy and dusty Cairo market crawling with cats and people as a souvenir from Egypt. The costume hung in my closet to wait ten months for Halloween, while I developed a bra size during that time.

The following spring, after trick-or-treating as Cleopatra, I still had the bright red two-piece swimsuit (that was *only* supposed to be worn for Halloween) and received my first taste of how my more womanly body signaled power when secretly wearing it to the public pool. My exposed flesh controlled the gaze of two older – and more powerful – guys who were probably all of fifteen years old. Hah! It was an empowering feeling strong enough for me to remember today as my body felt a surge of fresh energy and my heart thumped heavier. Just the sight of me consumed their attention, and they conveniently and leisurely sat at their table and watched my every move as if I were eye candy. Too innocent to understand sexual attention, but skilled in maintaining poise in a swimsuit, I loosely used my pageants skills to move. I had been trained in being looked at and judged.

The key to winning pageants is to relax and let your personality shine through your polished appearance. I remember giving a wave and smile, though it probably looked natural, and they probably didn't care. Then I remember feeling like I could vomit. Being judged by these guys felt much different from being judged on the pageant stage. It wasn't as if there were prizes at stake, or that I was bringing voice to a just cause. They weren't about to award me a TV, bike, or trip to Hawaii for my poised presentation of smile. This prize, whatever it was, felt a little sickening. I kept up the show, though, because I did not understand that how I felt inside my body was more important than how I looked. I had already swallowed the belief that my primary obligation in life was to look good.

The guys had excitedly waved back but didn't wave me over. They just watched me as if they knew something I didn't. Wherever I went, their eyes and attention and conversation went too. I went about my swimming and playing, doing crazy jumps with my younger brother as if my athletic ability to do toe-touch jumps and cannonballs into the pool while drenching him would impress the guys. I could feel them watching me as I played. Whenever I looked their way they gave a crooked smile, sliding their gaze elsewhere but keeping me in their peripheral vision. I wondered why they didn't come play with us, but I was aware that it was some sort of social faux pas to ask them. In that moment, with all their staring, I knew I had control of them even though I didn't understand exactly why.

As an eleven-year-old girl on the margins of my childhood world, I was beginning to play with the sexual signals between men and women. Though I knew nearly nothing of sexual relationships, I still somehow knew the script that said I was expected to perform. My naturally curly hair often frizzes after being in a pool, so I kept it wet with my dives in the water. Coming up face-first, using both hands to slick my wet hair back behind my ears, made me feel like a model. At that time in my life, my image of female power was models with hot bodies, so that's what I pretended to be. Vicariously, I was experiencing my sexuality through an image of another woman rather than through myself.

As I dissociated the experience in my body and put it into the appearance of a model's hair, I was learning to self-objectify my own body as a collection of parts created for someone else's pleasure. I learned to fuss about my abs, my thighs, or how my posterior side appeared, while neglecting how those parts of my body really felt. I did not know how to feel good in my flesh because I reduced myself to my appearance.

Looking good is not a feeling, though I use to think it was. I claimed feeling "hot" or "sexy" or "tight." "Sexy" is not sexual satisfaction. I was really saying I thought I looked good. I felt "hot," like a model, that day at the pool, but my flesh felt a little queasy. My feelings had much more to do with their male gaze than with my confidence in my body. Women perform for men at the expense of their own desires, and I'm first in line to confess my guilt in this area.

I remember the two guys at the pool were tall with broad shoulders, and the one had clear smooth skin with visible muscular abs. He looked hot in his sunglasses, spiked wet hair, and smooth caramel chest. That day, I realized I liked looking at them too, at least more than at the pimply, shorter, sunburned junior-high-aged boys in my life. Early in sexual development, girls are shamed for being "boy crazy" when they express desire, while boys get a free pass with the standard "boys will be boys." The Christian social script demonizes and suppresses female desire, blaming the entire sin of humanity on the wrongly labeled "temptress" Eve, whose mistake fictitiously punishes all women. The result is girls and women are conditioned in religious circles to feel shameful of their bodies. And worse, girls are conditioned to take the fault for male gaze, as if she is controlling his ocular muscles and the imagination of his brain. The desires of boys and men are to be controlled by moral women with a dress code even though Jesus said to handle this differently. "Every man who looks at a woman lustfully has already committed adultery in his heart. And if your right eye causes you to fall into sin, tear it out and throw it away" (Matthew 5:28–29). Jesus *never* held women responsible for a man's lust. A man's lust is something in his imagination and not in the flirting, behaviors, appearance, or clothing choices of a woman. With these violent remedies of amputation for lust, I'm thinking Jesus believed men *could* control their lust (*just as he was able to, even alone with a sexually expressive woman [John 8:9–11]*).

Jesus makes the point that we are to separate ourselves

from whatever causes us to sin, not declare its superintendence. Church youth group swimming parties will enforce no-midriff swimsuit regulations for girls to safeguard the boys' purity without consideration of a girl's sexual desires. It's as if only boys are deserving to have libido. Are girls' bodies dangerous? Some say yes, claiming boys are different from girls. To that I say I love looking at a good bicep as do many other women and men, *which doesn't necessarily make me a predator or make men homosexual.* The double-sided deal of biased dress codes not only makes young men vulnerable but completely ignores female desires. The female body is considered tempting and in need of covering because the men were trying to "protect" themselves from lustful desires. This is only one example of how churches reinforce the "girl's fault line" excusing males of culpability as if a female's clothing choices are solely responsible for what goes on in the imaginations of boys and men. So why aren't we covering the boys' midriffs? Their shoulders? Their arms? We could do this, but it would then be shaming the bodies of boys.

Biased dress code assumes my daughter's female flesh is dangerous to boys, while assuming my son's body is neutral. Only boys are protected from being overwhelmed by the image of another's body, and there is no regard for girls who may become excited, overwhelmed, or even tempted by the sight of a lean six-pack on the front of boys, flexing to dive in. These dress codes frame female desire as abnormal while normalizing male sexual desire to see girls' bodies as objects. The result is, girls become ashamed of their bodies and pretend to be someone else or merely an appearance because they, too, have come to see themselves as objects and not human with desire.

The miniskirts, swimsuits, and "acceptable" lines of sexual expressed desire are always changing. What hasn't changed is the honor and worthiness inherent in all flesh. Churches would better serve young persons (and adult persons) by teaching honorable strategies to navigate their sexual desires as bearers of God's image. Modesty is in order for everyone, both male and female, but modesty should not be confused with a dress code.

Prior to marriage I was chided for a bra strap that fell off my shoulder, gym shorts, and my bright lipstick. I cared for my church brothers but not enough to give up lipstick for them (Sorry, guys). I did, however, make sure to bring extra clothes to wear to church instead of bebopping in with my gym shorts after a workout. I secretly rolled my eyes about the bra strap; I thought about just not wearing one but decided to save that goal for retirement. Shaming kids and unmarried adults for having sexual desires just inspires shame, secrecy, dissension and dissociation. Covering the entire bodies of women excuses men from exercising self-control. It's idolatrous for men's unchecked sexual desires to have a godlike authority over women's clothing choices. We are Christians, not the Taliban.

The day I wore the red two-piece suit to the pool I discovered the image of my body had the power to dominate the thoughts and gaze of two older boys. These hot young men would not have been overwhelmed by my bikini body if they had chosen to see me as human and not as a sex object – I *did* have more body parts covered than they. It's laughable to accuse my eleven-year-old self of trying to seduce these boys at the public swimming pool that day. I think, as any other young person, I was trying to be seen, and the world was most willing to see me as a sexual object. So how about seeing women as humans created in the image of God and not sexual objects? That seems to be a better way to avoid being overpowered by the image of a junior-high girl in a two-piece bathing suit (if you're really that afraid of her and not just trying to control the appearance of her body).

It's been my observation that women too are intimidated by the body of a young girl and often cast the most shame onto their bodies. I can still hear my mom telling me to close my legs.

It's not what she said but the distress in how she said it that sticks with me; her tone made me feel as if I was doing something bad. I see women inspect the bikini bodies on tabloid covers or serve as a bathing suit judge of other women on the beach. I haven't decided if this keeps them from gawking at men or helps them feel morally superior in their own bodies, which isn't usually a beach body.

The sexual attention and judgment women receive can be an obstacle course. Beating the course enables girls and women to seize power outside the image of their flesh. Sexual attention isn't inherently a bad thing; I know a few disabled and aging women who yearn for such attention. The line between noticing a good bicep and lust is indistinct and different for each individual, as are appropriate clothing choices for each environment. Outside of the obstacle course is virtue, and feminine virtue isn't a wardrobe but a mindset about how we use our bodies and determine God's will within our flesh. And when we're focused on finding and doing God's will, our flesh isn't so preoccupied with appearances, ourselves or others.

> So, brothers and sisters, because of God's mercies, I encourage you to present your bodies as a living sacrifice that is holy and pleasing to God. This is your appropriate priestly service. Don't be conformed to the patterns of this world, but be transformed by the renewing of your minds so that you can figure out what God's will is – what is good and pleasing and mature.
>
> Because of the grace that God gave me, I can say to each one of you: don't think of yourself more highly than you ought to think. Instead, be reasonable since God has measured out a portion of faith to each one of you.   (Romans 12:1–3)

14

A NEW LABEL

You are never too lost that God cannot reach you.

– Annie Lobert (1967–),
founder of Hookers for Jesus

W hen I was in college I went to a Janet Jackson concert in Cincinnati. My friend happened to score front-row tickets through her brother who had connections. At the concert I met a guy who claimed to have connections with Prince and could get me tickets for the next day. He, of course, invited me home with him and I, of course, knew better and politely refused, feigning that I needed to drive back to Indianapolis with my friend that night. We exchanged phone numbers (I still don't know why I did that; succumbing to pressure to be polite, I suppose). He wanted to fly me out to Cincinnati to see a Prince concert the next day. My gut told me that was not a good deal. The guy called, and called, and called my dorm phone leaving message, after message, after message on my answering machine that he was at the Indianapolis airport and ready to pick me up. Thank God this was before the days of cell phones. My roommate was fearful for me, and rightfully so. She told me to *not* call him back, and of course I didn't. Thanks, Alley, for watching my back. I know that wasn't my only time bypassing abduction into sexual-slavery.

In a world where millions of women are for sale as disposable commodities of female flesh, the "profession" is often called the oldest in the world. Just as the story of Noah's ark becomes a nursery theme, there is also a fairy tale that glamorizes women in the sex industry, telling an illusionary story that these women are doing sex work of their own free will, that they are not being exploited and the money is all theirs. Think, for example, about the movie *Pretty Woman*. As in all fairytales, the *Pretty Woman* fantasy ends with "happily ever after," justifying and normalizing the buying of female flesh as a commodity: "*She needs the money*"; "*She chose to work this job*"; "*She gets to have her hair and nails done.*" This story is fiction.

My high school classmate had an older sister who "moved away" with her boyfriend after graduation. She was murdered at age nineteen. Word was she was "selling it," although that has never been confirmed. Many sex workers are coerced with the heartstrings of a boyfriend turned pimp or the peer pressure of "friends" who gang-rape to "break her" into the job.[1] Others are lured from their homes with promises of work. Some are young girls taken against their will and are trafficked into sexual slavery to start their adult life on the wrong side of the law. As my friend's sister had vision for her life, moving away, God has greater vision for women beyond being disposable. Most women don't up and decide to sell their flesh in the sex industry. I believe this is why God remembers the women whose flesh is for sale. Scripture is not short on warnings to men who use prostitutes, and it doesn't hold back condemning Israel comparably as one engaged in

---

1. To learn more about how women are initiated into prostitution I recommend reading *Fallen: Out of the Sex Industry and into the Arms of the Savior* by Annie Lobert.

prostitution (Hosea 4:13–14; Proverbs 6:25–27; Proverbs 29:3; 1 Corinthians 6:15–16). Interestingly, when God addresses the women who were prostitutes, the tone is clothed in grace, not contempt. This dichotomy seems to be a non-accidental grace, perhaps because God knows prostitution is riddled with subjugation and trafficking of women whose personal agency has been stolen and exploited? I believe the large-scale commerce of the female flesh is an assault on all women. Our image is created in God's image, and God is not for sale.

In Luke 7 Jesus attended a party with a "sinful woman" who some scholars believe to be a *hetaerae*, or prostitute.[2] When I read about ancient Greco-Roman culture, I was shocked to learn that proper hospitality at the time of Jesus *expected* hosts to provide women as entertainment for guests. Though the Pharisees were Jewish and didn't necessarily follow Greco-Roman customs, prostitutes provided what was considered a legitimate service to *any* man, religious, married, or unmarried. There's lots of debate on who the sinful woman was; at minimum being a foreigner would have made her sinful in the eyes of the Pharisees. I did some research on sex workers and learned there were various types of sex workers in Jesus day. *Hetaerae* were the highest ranking prostitutes. These women were educated and often used for intellectual and sexual stimulation. They were kept outside of the home of their owner and had free reign of the city, like a "high-class" mistress. As a *hetaerae*, the "sinful woman" would have been in a select class of women with financial resources to independently purchase perfume, and then dispose of it at

---

2. The idea is widely accepted that "sinful" woman at least made this woman a non-Jew. For a little background from my reading up on this, *heteraes* were educated prostitutes of the Roman-Greco world who entertained high-status men. The entertainment custom was like an oriental *geisha* providing stimulating conversation and sexual favors. See William W. Sanger, *The History of Prostitution* (New York: Eugenics Publishing Company, 1939), 54.

a dinner party. *Auletrides* were exotic dancers and flute players, more overtly seductive in their service, popular in dicey house parties. *Dicteriades* were street walker or brothel sex workers; sometimes wives and concubines broke the law to make money on the side as an *auletride*. The lowest rank of sex worker was a *concubine*, a slave expected to provide sexual service to and for their rich male owner, or "master."[3]

Prostitution was legal and regulated; men could hire women for sex. The religious double standard made it impossible for *any man* to commit adultery or be sexually immoral with a woman, so long that the woman didn't belong to another man.[4] There's lots of speculation about the sinful woman's intentions in approaching Jesus, including the symbolism of her loose hair.[5] The Bible, however, only says she was a "sinful woman," which means she could be *any* woman. For all we know she could have murdered someone, been a swindler, or involved in espionage for the Roman government. She, too, may have been in the business of selling other women's flesh. The Bible doesn't connect her sin to her financial ability to purchase an alabaster flask of perfume, nor does it clarify what she was doing at that

---

3. Sanger 26–37.

4. The woman providing a sexual service was considered sinful because she was not marital property of a man, not because of the sex. The man only became sinful when he violated another man's female property, which included wives and concubines. See Schmidt, *Veiled and Silenced*, 112.

5. The loose hair in ancient Greco-Roman culture was a sign of a sexually available woman and was considered sexually scandalous to let loose at a party of men. Unmarried women wore loose hair as did prostitutes who were working. Grieving women also wore their hair loose, and it is a documented first-century practice of women who were baptized. Charles H. Cosgrove, "A Woman's Unbound Hair in the Greco-Roman World, with Special Reference to the Story of the 'Sinful Woman' in Luke 7:36–50," *Journal of Biblical Literature* 124, no. 4 (Winter 2005): 27–28, 32. https://www.jstor.org/stable/30041064?seq=1#page_scan_tab_contents.

dinner party. I personally find it unbelievable that she barged into a private dinner party.

In this Bible story, Simon the Pharisee was hosting his dinner party with Jesus as his guest. Jesus was at the table and was approached by the sinful woman; however she wasn't interested in making money or turning a trick from Jesus.

> She brought perfumed oil in a vase made of alabaster. Standing behind him at his feet and crying, she began to wet his feet with her tears. She wiped them with her hair, kissed them, and poured the oil on them. When the Pharisee who had invited Jesus saw what was happening, he said to himself, If this man were a prophet, he would know what kind of woman is touching him. He would know that she is a sinner.   (verses 37–39)

Instead of taking or receiving from Jesus, as so many did, and do, this woman gave. She gave what power she had: perfume of her financial resources, tender kisses, and tears from her heart. She gave the full-heart expression of her story. Every story starts with a feeling, a desire to share and give.

Feelings are communicated through emotional expressions and then formed into words (if we work at it and develop them that far). Sometimes the feelings are too deep for words, and the story can only be heard through primitive emotional expressions, such as smiling, hugging, and tears; and then there's all the body language, the guarded posture, jaw clenching, and carrying the weight of the world on one's shoulders. Our flesh cannot hide our story. Jesus was willing to listen to this woman's emotional expression, a story where her words could not yet organize the mess in her heart. Her flesh told her story through tears and desperation from her life.[6] Jesus treasured hearing and feeling

---

6. It's nice to think she got to go home and keep her money; however, women

her story above feeling her body. He gave her peace (verse 50). Don't we wish all men were like Jesus?

As a woman I want to be more than a label, and I want to be felt as more than my female flesh. The sinful woman's abundant outpouring of tears and wealth were her *full* story. It takes a lot of courage to expose the truth in our heart and allow another to feel us, especially when they can take advantage of our vulnerability. The truth is, when our story is felt, we become human. Jesus helped this woman feel humanity in womanhood. He felt her beyond her sinful flesh. While she was still on her knees, Jesus stood up for her. As he demonstrated, it was okay and right to stop a table full of male religious leaders and listen to a sinful woman fully express how she felt about her world. He made them listen to a disposable woman.

When Jesus listened to the sinful woman's story, he opened the space for each woman to be heard at the table of religious authority. Rising out of the ashes of her destroyed humanity, this amazing woman could feel again, and she still swallows us in two thousand years later. She challenges us to see *all* women worthy of space to share their story and be heard at the place where religious authority fellowships and share in ceremony. Sex worker, drug addicts, women who have accused a man (whether falsely or not), women who have harmed their children. It sounds so cliché, but it is true: Jesus does not care about the labels on our female flesh, if women are married, single, divorced, slut, virgin, modest, deflowered, impure, baby mama, bad mom, tattooed, hairy, wrinkled, black, brown, Aryan, Jewish, skinny, chubby, scarred, blemished, boyish, sick, or covered in cellulite and fat rolls.

The labels applied to our flesh cover our hearts, smothering the "springs of true life" (Proverbs 4:23) flowing from the sacred

---

in the United States could not individually have a bank account until the 1960s, so I doubt the ancient Near Eastern women had pecuniary autonomy.

organ that makes us *all* human. Our heart pumps life into the veins of our stories. Our heartfelt stories are worthy to be felt at the table and are sacred to anoint the very feet of Jesus in remembrance and celebration of our shared humanity. Jesus reminds us, it's not the religious rituals that make us clean, but the cleansing of our hearts (Matthew 23:25–26). Stories of Jesus are stories for all humans because they invite us to share our heart and humanity, and we are still honored with a space at the table to fully share our part of Jesus story, no matter how repulsive the story.

Each story is a part of God's greater story. If the female flesh is reduced to being a playmate or just something to feel or shame, women will not own their stories. If they cannot own their story, they are not free. In Luke 7:44 Jesus scolds the religious leader with his timeless question, "Do you see this woman?" He forced them to recognize their exploitation of her. The church has long denied the experiences of women, which teaches women cannot be believed or trust their own experience. It's time for women and victims to be heard at the table. As the church is under fire in #Metoo (#Churchtoo) allegations, we must listen to each woman and victim as Jesus listened to the sinful woman.[7]

Religious hostility towards women's sexual history communicates there will be no place for women to be heard. No room for forgiveness. Jesus had many words for the men who looked down upon the sinful woman but only words of forgiveness for the unnamed woman herself. His view should be a guide to addressing sexual sin as a church. According to research, pornography is a past or present struggle for over half of youth and senior pastors. Over half of Christian men ages 18–24 seek porn

---

7. Dr. Christy Sim provides an up-to-date resource for church leadership and clergy on how to listen to women who claim to be survivors of sexual assault, in *Survivor Care: What Religious Professionals Need to Know About Healing Trauma* (Nashville: Foundery Books, 2018).

out regularly, but only 21 percent of those who wanted to stop reported having someone to help them.[8] It's difficult to procure data on Christian men who use prostitutes. It's easy to blame and shame sinful women and ignore the responsibility of men who finance the sex industry, men who may be sitting next to us in church. And there should be room at the table for those men who want out of their shameful warp of sexual addictions. Ironically, curbing the sexual exploitation of women is shared goal of both conservative Christians and feminists who have yet to form a coalition to create real change. I would be thrilled to see some cooperation there as a byproduct of this work.

Feeling a women's story is feeling her power. When a woman's story is heard – from the woman – she becomes the author; she finds her author-ity, her power. Jesus didn't "save" this woman by bringing her home as a prince rescues a helpless princess. He told her to go; she could be her own woman in peace. As Jesus honored her gratefulness and commended her faith, he also gave the religious leaders an opportunity to do likewise. The same invitation is extended to us today. I'm inspired by the woman's pursuit of honor; if she could attain it, certainly *all* women can. In honor of her pursuit, Jesus removed the "sinful" label from her flesh. We can only hope she used her power to write a new label.

From his fullness we have all received grace upon grace.

(John 1:16)

---

8. Barna Group and Josh McDowell Ministry, *The Porn Phenomenon* (2016), 6, 110.

15

INTIMATE JUSTICE

We must send a message across the world that there is no disgrace in being a survivor of sexual violence – the shame is on the aggressor.

– **Angelina Jolie (1975–)**,
American actress and
survivor of sexual assault

t was just another Saturday night of cruising country roads, drinking beer, and making out by moonlight. It was only 9:45 p.m. and my curfew was 11 p.m. There was plenty of time. My boyfriend (*yes, the awful one*) and I had mastered the art of having sex on the hood of his car. We had our places where trees or cornfields blocked the sideshow. It was always his car. I used to think he was being generous by burning his gas, but now I think he was really looking to gain turf.

There was a light rain that night, but he had towels to wipe off the droplets. He could keep most of his clothes on; I decided the moisture would get my shorts too dirty, so I left them on the passenger seat instead of hanging around my ankle. We did our usual routine of car-top positions. He was seated on the hood with his feet on the gravel road; my feet were on the bumper. I straddled his lap with my back toward him. He missed.

He acted as if it were some sort of delicious accident, holding me tighter and pumping harder exclaiming how great I felt. I was seventeen and didn't know I was being raped. I believed the more I pleased him the better. He gets it, I give it. I went along, uttering the obligatory pants and moans. My sperm-toilet acting job lasted approximately three and a half minutes. The next day I was numb and had loose bowels. I wondered if the uncontrollable flow of clear fluid coming from my violated orifice would stop. I had no idea if I was hurt, but I wasn't about to mention my sodomy to anyone who could help me.

It all happened so fast. I was unprepared. My sex education only discussed *never* getting pregnant outside marriage (which meant *never* doing it). My parents *never* discussed sex, however they somehow communicated clearly to me to *never* get pregnant outside of marriage. Church taught me to *never* have sex outside of marriage or I would *never* be accepted by God. I mostly heard *never, never, never* get pregnant outside of marriage. Nobody taught me about sexual intimacy or agency.

If you would have asked my high school senior self about rape, I would have given some story about abduction by a stranger from a dark alley who restrains the innocent woman inside a creepy utility van without windows. I believed I couldn't be raped by someone I had consensual sex with. In my mind, because I had gone "all the way" there was nothing left, so everything was yes. It was all or nothing thinking, black or white, nobody talked about the "fifty shades of grey"[1] or "fifty shades of rape"[2] back then.

If you ever want to get mansplained with the Bible, start talking about intimate justice or "Intimate Partner Sexual Violence" to the "Christians" who believe a woman's God-designed role is to

---

1. E.L. James, *Fifty Shades of Grey* (New York: Vintage Books, 2012).
2. Ruth A. Tucker, *Black and White Bible, Black and Blue Wife: My Story of Finding Hope after Domestic Abuse* (Grand Rapids, MI: Zondervan, 2016), 129.

serve and obey men. These *guydolaters* refuse to acknowledge how their complementarian theology – God-designed specific gender roles for church and family government – paves a freeway to domestic abuse and sexual assault. When writing my rape story, I briefly mulled the idea to ask my husband if he minded my telling it. What I quickly realized is that it's my body and my story, not my husband's. I share my body with my husband, but it is not his. My ultraconservative Christian upbringing taught me that my body belonged to men, first my father, and then my husband. It also taught me that shameful experiences of my body were reflective and shaming to these men. Fortunately, my husband has agency that doesn't believe my experiences disgrace him.

My Christian world taught me to (or not to) give myself away: all I could do was give. It *never* taught me to wield power through agency. In "giving" my agency, it was assumed he was "getting." He gets it, I give it; that was the lie I believed. When I gave, I became his; and as his, he became entitled to my body (any part of my body at any time because it was his). This dangerous teaching was all hidden in the faulty theological foundation that I was created for his pleasure and benefit. This lie gave *him* power to define the story of my body. My desire was supposed to be for *him* and *his* pleasure, so never mind my pleasure. The teachers of this false doctrine misuse Genesis 3:16, "You will desire your husband, / but he will rule over you."

Many complementary Christians will use spaghetti logic to claim "he will rule over you" as God's prescription. But from the other side of their mouths they'll argue that death was never God's prescriptive design.[3] These were part of the same curse. Advocating a male role to govern women *is* upholding the curse of death as God's design.[4] People who say men are designed to

---

3. "To the soil you will return" (Genesis 3:19b).

4. Gilbert Bilezikian, *Beyond Sex Roles*, 41.

rule over women because of the fall, are misinterpreting Scripture. Claiming men have governing power over women is failing to understand that God gave free will to humanity, and women have a choice. I was astonished *and* delighted to discover the curse in Genesis 3:16, as stated in the original Hebrew, is *contingent* on a woman's choice to have a man in their life. In short, translators took out an "if," as if a woman were without the power to turn her desire toward or away from men. As Eve had a choice to choose God or Adam, she also had choice in choosing to desire Adam. Go figure! Who would have guessed a woman may not desire a man! (*Big eye roll on that one.*)

The word for "desire" (sometimes translated "lust") is more accurately translated as "choice." A more authentic translation of Genesis 3:16 gives women agency and choice.

> "[if] your turning is toward your husband, he will rule over
> you" or
> "[if] your alliance is toward your husband, he will rule over
> you" or
> "[if] your power is aligned with your husband, he will rule
> over you"

The choice for Eve here was to choose between God and man. Male translators felt they were enough to be god for women and stripped them of a choice. We like to hold up our Bibles as "God's Word," however, we must acknowledge that what we are holding up is a translation. Centuries of male translators saw women as passive objects of female flesh, so they naturally translated women to be passive in their prose[5],[6].

---

5. The word for Eve's "desire," sometimes translated "lust" is misleading and arguably inaccurate. In the original Hebrew Bible texts of Genesis 3:16 is *tᵉšûqâ*. *Tᵉšûqâ* means "turning," such as power to turn or turning one's alliance or influence to wield power. Prior to 1528 *tᵉšûqâ* was translated as "turning," "alliance,"

As Genesis 3:16 currently reads, if I happen to desire my husband (which I believe is a good thing), I am inherently succumbed into government by him. Or, if *any* woman turns her alliance or power, desire for relationship – toward her husband or man, the man would rule her. This writes the desire of the female flesh to be an imprisoning impulse. The key to understanding this scripture is to see women with the personal power to choose. I am free to desire my husband (again a good thing), *and* I may choose to keep my power aligned with God. I simply need to align my desires (or power) with God over my husband. Reading into the original Hebrew, women have the power to choose who and what empowers or owns our female flesh. We have choice to give and get, not just give.

---

and "power" in *all* ancient biblical texts. In 1380 a skeptical Latin translator violated Hebrew grammatical rules to change "turning" into "desire." Because of his bias towards women, he could not believe that Eve could have "power" to wield (yes, history knows his name, but I'm purposefully not including it). A simple future tense verb became a volitional statement and swindled Eve out of her innate ability to choose to turn or wield her power or alliance toward God or her husband (Bushnell, *God's Word to Women,* Lesson 18). In the grammatical rules of Hebrew, future tense is not obligatory unless the context dictates. This rule was duped but not without critical scholarly commentary of the day. Richard Simon wrote in the journal *Biographie Universelle,* criticizing the first Latin translator to make this sexist change, "[Biased translator] has too much neglected the ancient versions of Scripture." Despite the alarm, seven short years later, [Biased translator's] Latin Bible was used to translate the Coverdale's English Bible. These linguistic manipulations of Scripture eventually seeped its way into the English King James, and the Scripture became a prescriptive prophecy for all women, with or without a husband. Women were robbed of their matter of choice, ability to wield power, by a Bible translator inferring his presupposing views about the female flesh by making a Hebrew grammatical error. Eve's confounded "lust" made its way into following English translations up to our current day Bibles (Bushnell, *God's Word to Women*), LESSON NUMBER 18–19

6. *The Malleus Maleficarum,* a Christian treatise on witchcraft, was written shortly after the 1380 linguistic robbing of Eve's agency. *Malleus Maleficarum* was written by a Catholic priest and used as courtroom manual to eliminate

When I believed my role as female was to "give" it, I *never* learned intimacy. I was uncomfortable telling my boyfriend what I liked sexually. He often shamed my female body as gross, which assaulted my self-worth. He made me feel undeserving of pleasure, and I doubt he would have honored my requests. I'm not sure how he would have responded if I would have told him to stop his sexual assault. Deep down I was afraid he would drive off and leave me naked in the woods. When I look back, it was he who suggested I leave my shorts in the car that night.

Teaching mutuality as a standard for relationships empowers women to protect themselves from "Intimate Partner Sexual Violence" and domestic abuse (which are statistically linked[7]). Like my dad, some Christian men will justify abuse to keep women in their "God-designed role." The teaching that God created men and women as equals is called egalitarian theology.[8] Promoting egalitarian theology in our churches will help eliminate guydolatry and promote intimacy in marriages. Intimacy is only possible between equals.

It was 9:45 p.m., and my husband and I got to bed in plenty of time. He was sensitively caressing me as he does. His hand moved around my backside, his fingers sliding along my crack. And I froze. Then I started to shake. Of the hundreds, if not thousands

---

women as witches. It was undisputedly an era of misogyny and bias towards women having power (Schmidt, *Veiled and Silenced*, 51–59).

7. "Most research supports the claim that sexual assault is common in physically abusive relationships. McFarlane and Malecha found that 68 percent of the abused women reported having been sexually assaulted by their intimate partners. Sexual assault occurred repeatedly within these intimate relationships – almost 80 percent of sexually assaulted women reported more than one incident of forced sex." J McFarlane et al, "Intimate partner sexual assault against women: frequency, health consequences, and treatment outcomes," *American Journal of Obstetrics and Gynecology,* 105(1), (January 2005): 99–108.

8. You may find more information and resources on egalitarian theology from Christians for Biblical Equality (CBE) at www.cbeinternational.org.

of times we've made love, this hadn't happened before, *ever*. My mind was flashing back to the rape I survived decades ago. My husband honors my stories to be mine (not his), so he didn't press me for details. He quietly held me and listened to whatever I shared, which was mostly shaking and sobbing. We didn't get to our lovemaking that night but made a greater kind of love. It was one of more intimate evenings he and I have shared.

Finding power in intimacy requires vulnerability, which must be met with acceptance. Being seen in our weakness can be incredibly painful yet liberating. If you've had an unjust sexual experience, I encourage you to share it. If you don't have anyone you trust, get on my website www.yogathea.com and share it with me anonymously. By sharing you begin the journey to understanding the power and worth inherent in our bodies. That understanding gives us the confidence to be seen in our weakness and a hope for intimate justice.

Here's what I want: Let justice thunder down like a
    waterfall;
let righteousness flow like a *mighty* river that never runs dry.
    (Amos 5:24, The Voice)

16

GREAT SEXPECTATIONS!

*No woman gets an orgasm from
shining the kitchen floor.*

– Betty Friedan (1921–2006),
leading woman's activist
and author of *Feminine Mystique*

After our 11 a.m. wedding, banquet lunch, and afternoon of dancing, my husband and I drove to the Canterbury Hotel, hopped in bed, and stayed there all evening. It didn't occur to us to eat dinner. The next morning we caught a plane to Costa Rica; and by the time we landed, thirty-six hours after our wedding, we were famished. The restaurants had closed, and our last substantial meal was the BBQ chicken we had eaten hurriedly at our reception *(yes, we served BBQ chicken!)*. He was tired, and I was awake, so we had our first marital bump over sex on the second night of our marriage.

Some couples have regular marital bumps over money or kids; my husband and I bump over sex. I often feel guilty and defensive about my body being higher maintenance or more difficult to please. While he can respond in a moment, I take longer. For years it took a fight breaking out between us for me to understand my feelings, and then our fight destroyed the mood or any possibility of us being satisfied. Sexual passion mixed with expectations can be explosive. Compile years of marriage to the equation, and it feels like unearthing a land mine. More often than speaking up, I've suffered silently to avoid starting another fight, staying up to watch a movie or read a book alone.

Avoiding vulnerable conversations with my husband about our sex life has brought me years of silent suffering, which I have become an expert in masking. Sometimes I escaped with pseudo-fantasy. During sexual activity I have pretend to be another woman (one who knew what she was doing). Other times I've sang a sexy song in my head and conjured up images. These imaginative strategies ultimately dissociated my sexual experience from my authentic feelings, which have not always been erotic. There's an overabundance of resources out there to take us into sexual fantasy lands, but I've tried to avoid those because I believe they are like eating fast food on the fly instead of preparing for a healthy sexual diet. My husband and I can study all the sexual techniques that stimulate pleasure and have some fun trying them out; however, technique can never replace good old-fashioned intimacy.

Sharing desire is a fundamental component of intimacy but is still difficult. If we've learned anything, we've both come to understand that when it comes to sex, "Ladies first" is just good manners. Even after years and years of marriage, the topic of sexual satisfaction can make us feel like failures. I'm grateful he wants to please me and I hope he knows I want to please him. I want to be encouraging, and not accusing, but I don't want to be left burning and acting out some sort of lie. I get embarrassed to ask, to explain my desire, my body. My female body is like an oven; it can take a while to warm up, but once I'm hot the heat can last for days. To have a satisfying sex life, I need consistency to keep those flames of passion burning. Off and on is difficult for me, while maintaining a steady temperature is much easier.

Sex is *never* a one and done experience for my body. It needs a steady, nourishing diet, not quick bites with a fanciful feast on holidays.

Having four kids and many responsibilities, our busy schedules are now the greatest threat to our sex life. Reigniting the flame after a drought – say a busy week or time away – can be lots of work. When this happens, I go back to feeling guilty because I can't perform or be ready. Once again, I must voice my desires, share my vulnerability. There are also nights and seasons of life when I haven't been in the mood. I'm glad my husband honors my desire to sleep rather than pushing me to have sex when I'm half asleep. When my libido has been stronger, my body not satisfied, or not being in the mood, have made me feel ashamed because they were all breaks from the traditional sex roles we were taught in church.

We married in a church that taught complementary theology – men and women are created with different sex roles. They upheld the traditional idea that men were to be pursuers of women. These biblical manhood and womanhood teachings implied it was my duty to be ready for him, whether I was in the mood or not (so he isn't tempted to cheat, *as if he is unable to say no or control his flesh*). I heard church leaders at marriage retreats pull out scriptures such as 1 Corinthians 7:4, which states a wife's body belongs to her husband, and preach about sexually submissive wives, while completely ignoring the rest of the verse about the husband belonging to wife. This teaching made me feel that something was wrong with me when I was in the mood and he wasn't. I was ashamed to have desire, because *nobody* taught about female desire. *Nobody* told me I had the power to voice my opinions to shape our sexual relationship, so I felt guilty doing so. My job was simply to satisfy him and his desire and make sure he didn't stray. Looking back, I cringe about the damage this puritanical teaching did (and does) and how it robbed us of intimacy.

Meeting each other as equals has been a fundamental compo-nent of intimacy between us. If there is a power imbalance in the relationship, the survival needs of the least powerful will coerce their behavior. I know this firsthand, because during the spell of my life when I worked in the home as caregiver to our young children, I was dependent on my husband's income (as were our children), and I was more guarded in our sexual relationship. I didn't feel safe to share everything I felt because it might anger him, and he could wound me, and our children, financially if I wounded his ego. It's mutuality, not respect that has brought us greater intimacy.

My husband is a gracious man and has *never* accused me of not fulfilling "wifely duties." I believe his respect for me has nurtured intimacy and vulnerability between us, especially when I have loathed myself over sexual tussles. We haven't always gotten it right, but we're both willing to try, most of the time. At times, he has given up heart. At other times, I have. During these droughts, we have gone through the motions of our relationship, but hav-en't engaged our hearts. Our sex life has seemed to reflect our emotional willingness to participate in the relationship. How we act and feel outside of the bedroom sets a template for intimacy in the bedroom.

Someone once said the brain is the biggest sex organ of the body, so how I feel, think, expect, and experience sexual activity is what makes it fresh, exciting, satisfying, and comforting. Only as I have learned how to use my body for *my* sexual pleasure have I been able to feel worthy and secure to honestly share what I desire and enjoy (and my distastes). This has required both my husband and me to learn about my female body. My general knowledge is that most men know what's under the hood of a car more so than what's under the hood of a clitoris, but I also think this is true for women. Women know more about how to look good than how to keep their sexual engine humming to feel good.

In my younger years I confused looking good with feeling good. It was a lie I swallowed, and I really want my daughter and the next generation of women to own their desire over being desirable, because I know how this has stunted my sexual maturation to seek sexual satisfaction. As I age, I'm learning to reject the script that equates successful sex to my looking good, but I have missed out on what could have been many good years. Pleasure cannot be measured in appearance. I still spend copious amounts of time picking out preferred clothing or cosmetics – to appear just right – but only a fraction of that time communicating what pleases me. I'm not sure I always even notice what makes me feel good in my own skin. I've exercised for most of my life; however, it was only when I started to practice yoga that I began to slow down and focus on how I felt in my body and not just keeping my butt into size 4 pants.

Participating in healthy practices that connect us to our bodies and bring us pleasure is important for women. Obviously not all women exercise or are involved in a sexual relationship, at least with another person, and there *are* other ways to be present in our flesh (*ahem, yoga and meditation*). It has been my observation that when women are present and comfortable in their flesh, they are more willing to participate in sexual intimacy.

There is nothing like sexual intimacy that bubbles up the questions: Am I worthy to receive pleasure? Am I worthy to ask? Am I more than an object created for service? Am I more than something to be had? What do I desire?

Rather than asking ourselves what makes us feel good in our skin, the world (and church) has man-made answers scripted for women as a moral code. Reading the Bible independently I found there's a bit of erotica within its pages. In Song of Songs we find female sexual desire on full display! What I love about the Shulamite woman is how she boldly shares her sexual desires *without* the gaze of her lover. She feels an uncontested worthiness of her passion and acts to attain sexual pleasure in her flesh:

> My insides began to throb for him.
> I leaped from my bed to let my love in.
> My hands were dripping *sweet* myrrh,
> My fingers were coated with myrrh,
> as I reached for the handles of the lock.
>
> (Song of Songs 5:4b–5, The Voice).

If this woman is finger painting with myrrh, I want to color my world the way she did. Alone, she's unashamed to relish her sexual desires. She aches in desire. She opens the lock. *She's vivacious in her sexual experience!* No fast-food sex for her. This woman has great *sexpectations*!

There is a common thread of harmful sexpectations for women that connects modern pornography and teachings of the "Council on Biblical Manhood and Womanhood," an organization that influences churches across the world. Both frame men as superior or dominating figures over a woman. Both relinquish women's pain and suffering as normative, which strip women of pleasurable sexpectations. Both require women to be submissive to survive.[1] If women are "drinking the Kool-Aid" of complementary theology, pain and suffering will be considered normative to their sexual experiences – whether sexual, emotional, or both.[2] Some teach

1. A study revealed 88 percent of scenes in the fifty most rented porn videos included violence towards women. See Gail Dines, *Pornland: How Porn Has Hijacked Our Sexuality* (Boston, MA: Beacon Press, 2011).
2. Larry Solomon, "Why A Wife Should Endure Painful Sex with Her Husband," Biblical Gender Roles, December 20, 2018, https://biblicalgenderroles.com/2018/12/20/why-a-wife-should-endure-painful-sex-with-her-husband/

women to tolerate abuse, even if just for a time, to preserve the marriage.[3] Women are made to feel unworthy and even immoral to seek sexual pleasure, unable to look their partners in the eye as an intimate equal.

After leaving a church that subscribed to CBMW roles, I experience more pleasure in our sexual relationship. A mentoring couple (one of the good ones) from that church wisely shared how our relationship was fun stuff to work on. I still remember that and try to practice the "fun" when bringing up our seventeen-year-old issue that hamstrings our sex life every so often. It should be fun to work towards experiencing more pleasure in sex! I wish it hadn't taken me so many years to feel deserving of it, but I'm glad I found the space and partner to do so. I hope we continue to grow to feel we deserve more with each other!

An endless supply of books and resources exists to help couples with sex issues. It's embarrassing to sit on a sofa with your husband and talk with a licensed therapist about sex issues; however, it is totally worth it. My understanding of extramarital affairs is that they are rooted in the inability or unwillingness to communicate sexpectations.[4] Working through our issues is fun (when they are resolved, anyway), and sharing how I *really* feel proved to be less painful than suffering the dissonance between us. It has taken a skilled professional help me realize this.

Learning about your body is essential to sexual satisfaction and gynecological health. Sixty-five percent of women beat around

---

3. John Piper, "John Piper: Does a Woman Submit to Abuse?" YouTube video, https://www.youtube.com/watch?v=3OkUPc2NLrM&fbclid=IwAR3f3NBXRKx 378aJILOoztHrJJN2vZbbJzPTt3PBylpm6Mp6tbi6eUsxebo.
4. Karin Jones, "What Sleeping With Married Men Taught Me About Infidelity," *New York Times*, April 6, 2018, https://www.nytimes.com/2018/04/06/style /modern-love-sleeping-with-married-men-infidelity.html.

the bush (pun intended) to use the words "vagina" or "vulva."[5] The vulva's cornucopia is essential to orgasm and pleasure so reducing female sexual anatomy to "vagina" or "down there" communicates that a woman's sexual pleasure is not important. Overcoming my embarrassment and shame, and religiously indoctrinated inferiority, to enlighten my husband about what pleasures my flesh has been fruitful to our sex life. Vagueness is a killer to sexual empowerment, so as I mature I explore and edify my evolving preferences.

If I had to do it over, I would still wait until marriage to have sex, but would have followed the biblical example of the Shulamite woman to heighten my ability in experiencing pleasure. I believe our abstinence prior to marriage built a foundation of trust and gave us space to know each other, even though it made the bedroom more awkward. I would have sought counseling earlier in our marriage and rooted myself in a church that taught egalitarian theology, despite having to leave many good friends. It's still my belief that a committed marriage of two mutual persons is the safest place to nurture sexual intimacy. However, when complementarian teachings – man over woman – are present in the marriage, hierarchy will seep into the bedroom and crush intimacy because the relationship's foundation becomes about power over the woman's body and not espousing equality. In Genesis 18:12 Sarah is recorded as laughing at God for the idea of her having the "pleasure" of creating a child. Scholars cite her rhetorical question as wetness, explicit to female pleasure.[6] All women, even "old-lady" Sarah, can experience pleasure. Only among equals are women able to seek great sexpectations! And

---

5. The Eve Appeal, "Why 'vagina' should be part of every young woman's vocabulary," *The Eve Appeal*, July, 2016, https://eveappeal.org.uk/wp-content/uploads/2016/07/The-Eve-Appeal-Vagina-Dialogues.pdf.
6. Gaffney. *Womanist Midrash*, 36.

great sexpectations is our most intimate expression of power God does not want us to submit.

> **Her** (*to him*): Kiss me with the *sweet* kisses of your lips,
>   for your love delights me more than wine.
>
> (Song of Solomon 1:2 The Voice)

17

SPACE TO BE

*I no longer want to live someone else's idea of
what and who I should be...I'm going to be me.*

– **Diana (1961–1997),**
Princess of Wales[1]

At least once a day I would stand in front of the toilet and force myself to vomit. I made myself do it off and on for more than ten years until, after a while, I couldn't stop doing it. I started in high school and kept my daily regimen going through grad school. Vomiting was like using the toilet in a non-traditional way. It became to me as common as doing my hair or brushing my teeth, and I brushed my teeth several times a day to protect my tooth enamel from stomach acid and my breath from hurting someone. In my early years I used my right index and middle fingers to stimulate a gag, but eventually I could perform the purge without them. I aimed and ejected, quietly and quickly. It only took a little glottal coordination and a cough-like maneuver. Not too many people knew; and the ones who did

---

1. Princess Diana shocked the world by sharing publicly her private turmoil of bulimia.

had no clue what to do about it, as I kept a perma-smile, as every good American teenage girl is supposed to do.

Once, my sister and sister-in-law confronted me on the drive home about an after-dinner purge at a restaurant. I was in high school, and they rightfully spoke to me about their concern. The intervention must have been my sister-in-law's idea because she whipped out her wallet-sized Bible and read Luke 14:26–33 to me. With a soft, "caring" voice she warned of God's army coming against me. She said we all carry a painful cross and should do so by surrendering to God instead of vomiting in the toilet. I listened to her from her backseat-bully pulpit, and as she spoke holy words of armies and battles, I heard "You're worthless, and God is against you." I think my sister-in-law believed she did something righteous with her Bible threat that made me cry. I was sobbing and couldn't really blow her off with a smile or an "I'm okay." My sister smoothed the awkward moment out a little and gave me a hug. My sister is twelve years older than me and has always been a mom-like-big-sis to me...and she did change my diapers.

The Bible intervention didn't scare me out of vomiting, but it did cause me to think about how shameful I was. God was against me! Eating disorders are rooted in a deep belief of being unworthy, and her use of Scripture only confirmed my unworthiness and lack of power against the forces that were coming to overtake me. I had already puked in the restaurant bathroom that night and brushed my teeth. After the Bible intervention, I went home and puked again – this time without getting caught.

Society often blames eating disorders on beauty culture, as if a lifetime of picking up a magazine with 2-D photoshopped images of "perfect" women permanently body-shames young preteen girls into an eating disorder. This superficial theory portrays girls and women as stupid, selfish, and frivolous, as if we are all dying to become an ideal standard of beauty. Yes, I'll be the first to say our fashion editors and movie directors can do more to help women have healthier self-images by showcasing women of all ages, shapes, and sizes; but blaming beauty culture excuses everyone and everything else for refusing to accept girls and women as rightful proprietors of power. We are beings who instinctively want to be fulfilled through wielding our power in the world, but we struggle to get there because of the prevalent message that we are unworthy.

In the awkward space between being a girl and a woman, I wanted to grow up and be something; but at every turn my world only had a space for me to be an image and not a real player. It said my body was not really my own, but something to please others, so I wasn't allowed to feel at home in my flesh. Being a female was work – work to please, work to prove myself, work to manicure every inch of my body for someone else's pleasure. The judges were everywhere, and no matter how I presented myself it was never quite enough. The world loved the image of a passive woman, not an assertive girl-becoming-woman such as me. A woman who took power risked being unloved but could earn acceptance through a fitting appearance, which was restricted and narrow. So I denied and starved myself in order to squeeze into the thin boundaries that allowed me to earn power and be loved.

A huge piece of fiction out in the world tells women we will be happy if we portray the ideal image. The demon whispers to every woman that she should "slim down," "shrink," "self-deny," "submit," "smile"; "be good enough," "pure enough," "nice enough," "sexy enough," "not too sexy" – enough, enough, enough! The goal is always just out of reach. Trying to become the ever-moving image of acceptable womanhood is exhausting. It's work! For me, Christianity upheld benevolent sexism; the media upheld sexual objectification; and my school shared a message of equality, while demonstrating the opposite, as men served as superintendents and principals with their flocks of female teachers under their authority. In a world where women struggled to hold power, and the purchase of women's bodies was as normal as folks breaking the speed limit, I couldn't see a space for my power, so I constricted it. As my sister-in-law said, there was an army coming for me, and it felt as if my female body was the battleground.

As crazy as it sounds, anorexia and bulimia gave me hope, because it gave me power over my body in a world vying to reduce me to an image of a happy, young lady who was becoming a fine woman. I had internalized the sexism but couldn't digest it. Vomiting became my violent revolt. Calorie control was my power to order the emotional chaos. My heart starved to be loved for who I was, to reveal my power. I wanted to be accepted and respected as a being and not a standard. On the outside I met the standards, as I smiled and pretended to be happy, and all the while I was dying inside. My secret life of anorexia-bulimia was hardly a quest to meet beauty standards; it was a rebellion against feeling powerless because the world had taught me I was undeserving to have both power and love.

The peak of my disease was in graduate school. The control I cherished whirled into a cyclone of binging and purging, storming every area of my life. Bags of candy, cartons of ice cream, and entire pizzas macerated and spewed. I began having blood sugar problems, which still haunt me to this day. One evening I was lying on my sofa, half blacked out and too tired to move. I rubbed my hand over my belly and felt the bones protruding from my hips. I hid my malnourishment, wearing two or three layers of clothes, with long sleeves and long pants because my legs and arms were too thin. I hadn't had a menstrual period in almost a year. My complexion was a grayish color, and I was too afraid to look at my unclothed body in the mirror. It was almost Christmas, and I had spent the fall semester dissecting a cadaver in gross anatomy. Spending such intimate time with a dead person – we named the cadaver "Eleanor" – made me not want to die. I remember holding "Eleanor's" preserved pancreas in my hands and knowing mine was in bad shape. As I incised her esophagus, I wondered if my esophagus still had its mucosa layer or if it had eroded from years of exposure to stomach acid. I understand discussing a dead body is graphic; but when we discuss eating disorders, we must discuss death because eating disorders are the deadliest of all mental disorders.[2] In the United States someone dies from an eating disorder every sixty-two minutes. Eating disorders are also widespread and estimated to have their tentacles in 20 million women and 10 million men in the United States alone.[3] We're just people, dying to influence the world. Eating disorders are not about becoming a size 0 or meeting beauty standards; they are about finding space to freely express oneself and one's power: They are an internal battle to find the space to hold power in this world.

Let me interject this: People respond to stress in different ways. It's hurtful to tell a person who struggles to eat that he or she is lucky or "I wish I had that problem." Some people overeat in times of stress, and some binge eat. I entertain my demon on a deadly diet of coffee and water. Food disorders have a wide spectrum and manifest themselves in different ways. Overeating and stress eating are also ways to control space in the world. Obesity is prevalent in nearly 40 percent of American adults and

---

2. Jon Arcelus, Alex J. Mitchell, Jackie Wales and Soren Nielsen"Mortality Rates in Patients with Anorexia Nervosa and Other Eating Disorders: A Meta-analysis of 36 Studies," *Archives of General Psychiatry* 68 (7) (July 2011): 724–31.

3. Eating Disorder Coalition for Research, Policy, and Action, "Facts About Eating Disorders: What the Research Shows," (2016), accessed September 21, 2018, http://eatingdisorderscoalition.org.s208556.gridserver.com/couch/uploads/file/fact-sheet_2016.pdf.

20 percent of our youth.[4] Both restrictive eating disorders and obesity – or "overnourishment," as I document in my medical charts – are rooted in feeling undeserving to enjoy the fruits of this world. As the overeater hoards food within the body, and the anorexic restricts, both use food to control the emotional response to a world that requires so much to do yet rewards so little for being.

Any person with a food disorder had heard the judgmental Christian teaching that our bodies are temples (and therefore we should treat them better!). One of the most important, life-saving messages of Christianity is the belief God dwells among and within each of us, but it should never be used as condescending teaching. The moral of this teaching is that God creates space for each kind of person to be. There's an old Jewish Shacharit – daily prayer – that has been used for thousands of years and was practiced in the time of Jesus. According to my Jewish neighbor, it's still in circulation today, uttered daily by Orthodox rabbis, thanking God they were not created a Gentile, a poor or ignorant slave, or a woman.[5] Although Christ challenged these notions, many of the early Jewish-Christians were still uttering this morning prayer. The apostle Paul challenged this Shacharit

---

4. Craig M. Hales, Margaret D. Carroll, Cheryl D. Fryar, and Cynthia L. Ogden, "Prevalence of Obesity Among Adults and Youth: United States 2015–2016," National Center for Health Statistics (NCHS) Data Brief, no. 288 (October 2017), Centers for Disease Control and Prevention (CDC), https://www.cdc.gov/nchs /data/databriefs/db288.pdf.

5. "Blessed be he that did not make me a gentile; blessed be he that did not make me a poor [ignorant slave]; blessed be he that did not create me a woman." –Traditional Jewish *Shacharit*. According to the ancient writings, this prayer has been attributed to be coined from Greek philosophers that made their way into Jewish liturgy. See Ruth Langer, trans., "Liturgy: Daily Prayers: 'Who has not made me a gentile.'" Boston College Center for Christian Jewish Learning, https://www.bc.edu/content/dam/files/research_sites/cjl/texts/cjrelations /resources/sourcebook/shelo_asani_goy.htm.

directly in his letter to the Galatians: "There is neither Jew nor Greek; there is neither slave nor free; nor is there male and female, for you are all one in Christ Jesus" (Galatians 3:28). All are one in Christ. Paul understood that the new church would not achieve its potential with hierarchal teachings that marginalized people from the power of Christ. All people have proportionate access to God, and all are meant to hold God's power.[6] I'm sure this was a highly controversial subject, because Jewish men were considered the rightful holders of power in faith, as often men, specifically white men, are today. Paul was creating space for all people in Christianity. Enshrining racism, classism, and sexism is unacceptable in Christianity. There is one life in Christ, one vast space for every person to be.

Our collective faith has not entirely accepted this truth of Christianity. Some Christians still set aside specific standards for women, denying us the space to be powerful *and* loved. As I spent years starving to relish in the fruit of a world that reduced me to an image, I still must manage my eating disorder by finding space to be me, space to wield my power. I stopped the bulimia years ago, but I still struggle with constricting myself. I keep a healthy weight when I surround myself with people who love me in my power and do not find my power offensive. I make sure my environment allows me to exercise power, and that has meant distancing myself from some Christians, so their oppressive teachings on womanhood do not throw me back into the prison of my eating disorder. I'm still learning to use my power as Jesus so beautifully

---

6. Galatians 3:28 directly challenged the Jewish temple segregation laws that privileged only Jewish men to stand in the space where God was thought to reside. The temple curtain that allowed entry into the very presence of God was torn from top to bottom at the time of the crucifixion – from the top there was no longer a gatekeeper needed in order to enter the presence God. See Letha Dawson Scanzoni and Nancy A. Hardesty, *All We're Meant To Be: Biblical Feminism for Today*, 3rd edition (Grand Rapids, MI: William B. Eerdman's, 1992), 321.

modeled, making space for all persons to be empowered and loved. Even as I age, I hold out faith to create a world that has room for all women to nourish great power through love.

Let them see the full extent of Your power that is at work in those of us who believe, and may it be done according to Your might and power. (Ephesians 1:19a, The Voice)

18

HOT LIKE ME

*The path to coming up with better solutions
for women is slowed down because
no-one wants to talk about it.*

— **Kiran Gandhi**[1] (1989–),
American music producer, activist,
and free-flowing marathoner

During each of my pregnancies I taught fitness classes, in spandex, even within twenty-four hours of giving birth. When I was pregnant with my youngest son, I did the moves teaching Zumba®. My fitness and yoga classes were the most popular when I was pregnant, especially the Zumba® class. I think it gave women permission to use their bodies. Women often told me after class that they saw me shaking it pregnant and thought, if a pregnant woman can do this, then I can too! During the Zumba® craze, several conservative Christian women

---

1. Kiran Gandhi ran the London Marathon in 2015 without menstruation products. She let her period flow to bring awareness to women throughout the world who are disenfranchised because of their periods. You may read her commentary on that here: https://www.independent.co.uk/voices /comment/heres-why-i-ran-the-london-marathon-on-the-first-day-of-my -period-and-chose-not-to-wear-a-tampon-10455176.html.

confided in me about their moral dilemma of doing Zumba®; it was a great opportunity to deconstruct teachings that made these women feel shameful in their bodies. "Working it" in a fitness class is a whole lot different than working it to seduce a man. I encouraged them by saying that we were not seducing any men while doing Zumba®, and Latin dance is not a crime. These women found the kind of yoga pants they felt comfortable in and joined the class. We had nightclub-type lighting, sound, and fun. It really was a party with many, many different types of women expressing celebration through their different bodies. It was freeing for me, being pregnant, to do dance moves on a stage in front of scores of women (and the men who dared to peep in the back and risk having attention drawn to them by being invited into class over my headset microphone! I sent away more than one hackled gym-gawker because he wasn't "strong enough to dance with us"!) My body was different – bigger with my baby bump – I could do moves like no one else, really! When the music played, I showed off my pregnant hips, shaking them with my arms in the air. I was fully into it, the music and moves awaking my new flesh within me.

Pregnancy is an accomplishment, but it is often treated as an illness or something shameful to hide. I've heard story after story from my female patients, still incensed sixty-five years later that they were forced to quit their teaching or nursing positions because their pregnancies were considered an ailment.[2] As feminists have made significant gains to create egalitarian work and academic environments for women, they, too, have hidden

---

2. The Pregnancy Discrimination Act was passed by the United States Congress in 1978 as an amendment to the Civil Rights Act to protect women from workplace discrimination because of pregnancy. See Ellen Carol Dubois and Lynn Dumenil, *Through Women's Eyes: An American History with Documents* (Boston, MA: Bedford/St. Martin's , 2005), 628.

pregnancy and motherhood. Feminist theory all but avoids discussions of pregnancy and motherhood, as if they are social diseases or oppression.[3] Many women's magazines with long histories of promoting sexy women have had long-standing policies to not cover pregnancy or motherhood issues. It's as if we are either a mother or a "liberated" woman, but not both.

In the Bible's shortest parable, Jesus shared about the kingdom of heaven as something in the hands of women. "The kingdom of heaven is like yeast, which a woman took and hid in a bushel of wheat flour until the yeast had worked its way through all the dough" (Matthew 13:33). Yeast is a fungus, so the kingdom of heaven is a fungus? What preacher gives a sermon on that? Baking bread was also considered to be "women's work," and they usually don't give sermons on that either.

But here it is, the kingdom of heaven is an active agent managed by a woman. The smallest of germs processed in the hands of women is likened to heaven. Similarly, women grow children, working our yeast through the dough as they mature. We mold and shape them by women. As a woman forms her children as bread, it's significant to connect how Jesus calls his very self the bread of life (John 6:35, 48, 51). As bread sustains life and is the staple in the Christian observance of Communion, "living bread" feeds us eternal life.

Women also shed blood for the renewal of life, every month, through menstruation. Our bodies embody the sacraments to create life. We break our bodies and shed our blood to give life.

---

3. Andrea O'Reilly "Ain't I a Feminist?: Matricentric Feminism, Feminist Mamas, and Why Mothers Need a Feminist Movement/Theory of Their Own," MOM Art Annex: Exhibition & Education Center, accessed October 8, 2018, https://mommuseum.org/aint-i-a-feminist-matricentric-feminism-feminist-mamas-and-why-mothers-need-a-feminist-movementtheory-of-their-own/.

Women are the handlers of life and creation. *That* is beautiful *and* sexy, not something to be hidden in shame.

Rather than celebrating the magnificence of women's bodies, the power of our bodies are often discussed in terms of morality. Women are judged on whether we are worthy to embody the splendor of creation, and that judgment comes under a microscope when a woman is pregnant. People feel entitled to know every detail of a pregnant woman's life before praising her. Single women feel this the most. Here is a public service announcement: congratulations and encouragement are the only appropriate responses to a pregnant woman, assuming you are 100% positive she is pregnant. It's no one's business if the pregnancy is her first, or fifth, whether she has a job outside the home, or who the dad is. It's also nobody's business how she looks if she decides to bare her belly on a beach. Spending so many years moving in spandex and pregnant in front of a crowd, I started to see how women looked to me for how to move while pregnant. My love for dancing and athletics did not go away just because I was pregnant. Many older women asked me about what the doctor said about me doing burpees and yoga. The doctor told me if I did it before I was pregnant, I should continue, so long as there is not any pain or discomfort. I've spent years pregnant, and it took years for me to finally believe I was a sexy creator of life when pregnant and not a fat "beached whale." Knowing this, I signed up for karaoke at a Christian women's conference and hammed it out singing the Pussycat Dolls R & B hit "Don't Cha (Wish Your Girlfriend Was Hot Like Me)." My middle-age backup dancers followed my exaggerated pregnant Zumba® moves and wondered if all the belly rubs, booty rubs, and slapping the floor was legal. Several hundred women in the room followed my moves, dancing along with me, and none of them had a dry eye. We had all laughed ourselves to tears, and it was cleansing;

because, in that moment, we Christian women had smashed the modesty and morality rules for our female bodies and owned our bodies as our own.

Even if a woman doesn't participate in the biological process of breaking her body and shedding her blood for new life, or is beyond those years, women are bonded by the shedding of blood for the renewal of life, menstruation. Menstruation should be upheld as an honorable rite of passage for our girls, not a dread. Our very existence as humans is dependent on this distinguishing process of women, yet it's treated as secret or taboo, and even dirty or "unclean." The products we use are called "sanitary napkins" or "feminine hygiene products," which implies unsanitary. Why can't we just call them menstrual products? If you visit the Indiana State House and my friends' gym you will find complementary menstrual products in the women's restrooms; and they don't expect women to bring in their own toilet paper either. I was socialized to be ashamed, and even fearful, of my period. While it is none of anybody's business if a woman is menstruating, or if a preteen has started her period, in my mom's effort to protect my privacy she expected me to hide clean wrappers in the trash as if they were damaging evidence. Boyfriends called me gross or disgusting and even treated me as if I were a different person while menstruating. Ladies, if a man makes you feel less or gross because of your period, or any part of your body, you can choose to believe him or to find your power in the blood.

Jokes about premenstrual syndrome, PMS, are still socially acceptable, and not funny. Period. They're an excuse to dismiss or withhold respect and validation for an assertive or emotional woman. I'm grateful to my husband, who has loved me the same, regardless of whether I am shedding blood. Women deserve to be embraced, no matter the time of month. The theological teaching that menstruation is "the curse" from Eve's sin assaults the dignity of women and isn't even biblical.[4] Ancient Hebrew traditions disenfranchised women as unclean, however Jesus shattered this notion by interrupting a mission with a synagogue leader and stopping a crowd to affirm to a woman she was worthy of his power, even when bleeding: "Then he said to her, "Daughter, your faith has healed you. Go in peace" (Luke 8:48 NIV).

Jesus never said you are now clean because she was never "unclean." Jesus demonstrated that even a bleeding woman's faith can seize the power of God, as a daughter, not an outcast. For the record, ladies, your menstruation is *not* a curse, and your body is clean (unless you don't bathe). As with any other body function, menstruation is not unsanitary when managed with the necessary products, but not everyone believes menstruation products are necessary. My home state of Indiana taxes menstruation products as optional consumables, while exempting men's prescription erectile dysfunction medications, pixie sticks, and barbecue potato chips as "necessary."[5] Menstruation products should at least be tax-free and available. Always. When I give to a shelter

---

4. The idea that menstruation is a curse of Eve came from medieval theology. See Charles T. Wood, "The Doctor's Dilemma: Sin, Salvation, and the Menstrual Cycle in Medieval Thought" *Speculum* 56, no. 4 (1981): 713. The Bible only mentions pain in childbirth as the woman's consequence for sin in Genesis 3:16a and does not include menstruation. To say menstruation was a curse from God for sin is to consider apes and chimpanzees human because they menstruate too! The only biblical scholarship on menstruation as "the curse of Eve" is the history of its misogyny and superstition.

5. Because of how Indiana defines candy, Pixie Stix do not get taxed; they default into a nontaxable food category. Chips are taxable depending on where they are purchased, which tends to hurt the financially insecure residents who may not have direct access to a grocery store that sells prepared items. Exempting feminine menstruation products has been discussed in Indiana legislature; however, it was turned down because it was considered prejudicial towards women. All prescription medications are tax exempt in Indiana; however, over-the-counter medications such as Estroven, used for menopausal symptoms, are taxable. For more details on our screwy sales tax laws, see State of Indiana

or food bank, I almost always donate menstruation products. Women across the globe miss school and work because they do not have the necessary items to manage their menstruation. Some women are even temporarily banished to life-threatening environments outside of their homes because of the superstitions of menstruating women being toxic. Recently The New York Times has reported multiple deaths of women and children in western Nepal, where women are banished to the elements and other harsh conditions – including attacks by animals and sexual assault – in *chhaupadi* huts because the community believes its women are unclean when they menstruate.[6] Less than a week ago, as I write this, another woman and her two sons died from smoke inhalation as they tried to keep warm on the mountain's wintry night.[7] While the Nepali government has recently outlawed *chhaupadi*, religious beliefs reinforce that it is "protecting the purity of the community."[8] As a woman I've had a difficult time reconciling these similar ideas and traditions found in the Old Testament. These "unclean" Hebrew women certainly faced similar circumstances to modern day Nepali women when they were banished from the camp.

When my children were young, I often thought how being away while menstruating would give me peace and quiet, time to

Department of Revenue "Information Bulletin #29: Sales Tax, April 2016), https://www.in.gov/dor/files/sib29.pdf.

6. Jeffrey Gettleman, "Where a Taboo Is Leading to the Deaths of Young Girls" *The New York Times*, June 19, 2018, https://www.nytimes.com/2018/06/19/world/asia/nepal-women-menstruation-period.html.

Bhadra Sharma and Jeffrey Gettleman, "In Rural Nepal, Menstruation Taboo Claims Another Victim," *The New York Times*, January 10, 2019, https://www.nytimes.com/2018/01/10/world/asia/nepal-woman-menstruation.html.

7. Binaj Gurubacharya, "Woman, 2 Sons Die in Nepal Town in Suspected Menstrual Exile," *The Associated Press*, January 10, 2019, https://www.apnews.com/3c78299490694b7cb09ecfaef3638bc7.

8. Gettleman June 19, 2018.

think and meditate. Perhaps when the Bible ordered menstruating women out of the camp, God was giving them a deserved break from children and family, a few days off each month to celebrate the life-giving process of shedding blood with other women? How we think of women's menstruation should distinguish us with the honor of shedding blood for the renewal of life, not shame.

As women hide menstruation, we also hide the distinguishing biological functions of motherhood. When my children were young, public toilets became my "office space" to complete my motherly duties. At church, I nursed while seated on the toilet in the women's restroom because there just wasn't space for us in the auditorium with small cramped seating. Besides, I didn't want to nurse a baby in front of a man seated thirty-six inches behind me with an aerial view. When I returned to work part-time in the outpatient clinic in 2003, after having my first child, I was expected to pump milk on my own time. So, again, I sat on the toilet with the *wiing-wahh-wiing-wahh* sound of the breast pump filtering through the two sheets of drywall, with my male coworker eating lunch at his desk on the other side. A colleague told me years later that she, too, was told by the hospital she worked for to clock out and pump, but she pushed back saying they did not expect their other employees to clock out for bathroom breaks. She also was backed by new laws, which required employers to allow women reasonable time for breaks to pump breast milk while at work. Breastfeeding is often even seen as immoral or lewd when others can see a woman breastfeeding her child. This summer, patrons at a public pool called the police simply because seeing "too much" of a woman's body functioning as a mother was vile for them. Nobody called the cops on all the topless men exposing their nipples that day while all women were reported keeping their nipples covered, including the nursing mom.[9]

---

9. Yoo, Sharon, "Police Called on Moms Who Were Breastfeeding Their Kids

Women's bodies create the blood and the bread for new life. Our bodies do this in perfect biological rhythms, and even when our female bodies don't work so perfectly, Jesus still validates the shamed woman as worthy to carry God's power! Whether dancing pregnant, purchasing menstruation products, breastfeeding a baby in a bikini, or just letting it flow, the bodies of women hold a piece of heaven, and heaven is not vile. Hiding the functions of our bodies that are the sustenance of life is not what Jesus advocated for; he paused his business with the religious leader and stopped a crowd so he could hear a woman talk about her physical issue. It's because women make the kingdom of God grow, and that's something to stop and talk about and show off to the entire world!

> Your sprouts are an orchard of pomegranates and exotic
>   fruits –
>   with henna and nard,
> With nard and saffron,
>   calamus and cinnamon –
> With rows of frankincense trees
>   and myrrh and aloes and all the finest spices.
>   (Song of Solomon 4:13–14, The Voice)

---

at the Pool," *USA Today*, July 24, 2018, https://www.usatoday.com/story/news/nation-now/2018/07/24/police-call-breastfeeding-mom-minn-pool-leads-nurse/824931002/.

19

DELIVERING LIFE

Imagine what might happen if women emerged from their labor beds with a renewed sense of the strength and power of their bodies, and of their capacity for ecstasy through giving birth.

– Christiane Northrup, MD (1949–),
American women's health author

D elivering my first child was one of the scariest things I've ever done. I walked into the labor room, knowing I would leave a different person. However, I didn't understand that babies are easier to care for inside the womb than out, so I easily agreed to inducing labor with my overdue child. The Pitocin started at 7 p.m., and I was holding my son by 10:00 p.m. The IV was like a ball and chain. I didn't know if I could stand or walk, so I played cards with my husband and groaned every few minutes, until it became writhing and I accused him of cheating. When it was time to push, the doctor plopped down between my legs and performed an episiotomy, without my consent, which allowed the baby to come out in two easy pushes.

He was headed for vacation the next day, hence the "let's get the baby out" offer. Afterward, Doc seemed more impressed by my husband's composure than my two rookie pushes that felt like a bowel movement. Evidently dads often become frantic, and even queasy, in the delivery room; my husband looked on without a word or blink. The doctor repeated enthusiastically, "You're the best dad I've ever had…and it was your first time!" *Uh, what about me?!* I had just delivered my first child in two pushes (and then a third for the placenta) and my husband was reaping the compliments. Now I've heard many delivery stories and I understand mine were relatively easy compared to many though not without difficulty. Each woman who gives life to a child deserves honor because delivering life is the vital work of God!

The Bible tells story after story of God delivering life, including the hallmark deliverance of the Hebrew people in the book of Exodus. God opens the waters of the Red Sea to birth them into new life from slavery. Most people skip the first chapter about two midwives who serve courageously as Israel's first deliverers after defying Pharaoh, who recruited them to the politically unpopular work of genocide and gendercide:

> The king of Egypt said to the Hebrew midwives, whose names were Shiphrah and Puah, "When you are helping the Hebrew women during childbirth on the delivery stool, if you see that the baby is a boy, kill him; but if it is a girl, let her live." The midwives, feared God and did not do what the king of Egypt had told them to do; they let the boys live. The king of Egypt summoned the midwives and asked them, "Why have you done this? Why have you let the boys live?"
>
> The midwives answered Pharaoh, "Hebrew women are not like Egyptian women; they are vigorous and give birth before the midwives arrive." (Exodus 1:15–19, NIV)

That these two women's names survived the millennia of oral tradition and male-translation is almost as much of a miracle as the fact that they survived after lying to Pharaoh's face when he asked them why the baby boys were surviving. For all the power

Pharaoh had, he certainly never mustered the courage to witness the delivery of a child. If he had, he would have immediately known Shiphrah and Puah were feeding him a line about the vigor of Hebrew women. Pharaoh underestimated the power of the midwives, Hebrew girls, and Egyptian women. Shiphrah and Puah had witnessed God's power in the delivery of new life, and *that* gave them the courage to deliver the Hebrew people. They didn't need coaxing or a flaring sign – as Moses did – to face power.

The delivery of my second child gave me more agency. Three weeks before my due date, my water broke around midnight. I didn't have a hospital bag packed, and I needed a shower. At the hospital, the nurses were ready to hook me up to the Pitocin again, and I flatly told them I was not spreading my legs until I had a shower. After some discussion, we agreed a nurse could supervise my shower in the event the baby would fall out. I showered in a seated position and obediently got into bed for the IV and pain. By 6:30 a.m. I was begging for an epidural, and the nurses were telling me not to push because the doctor wasn't there yet. The doctor arrived, caught my baby, and handed to her to me. Afterward I pondered why I waited for him and endured that excruciating urge to push.

With pregnancy and delivery, I felt as if everything I did was judged as a moral decision. Drinking coffee, sunbathing without sunscreen, or taking a Tylenol became ethical. It's infantizing to be told, by nearly anybody anywhere, what I should and should not eat, drink, lift, do, wear, and feel. What we expect of pregnant women isn't natural, but we judge them on whether they are *natural* enough. People really don't want a natural woman but somehow want us to glide *naturally* through pregnancy *and* delivery without the sterile medical interventions and environments that can relieve pain and save lives. I've heard Christian women speak of this pain as if it is their spiritual duty, I sensed they felt guilty to escape the *natural* pain with modern medicine. For the record, I didn't want a needle in my spinal cord because I have rehabilitated too many side effects from this procedure, let's just call it an occupational hazard.

Each pregnancy is different, and the outcomes are not always in a woman's control or a reflection of a woman's morality. The Bible gives zero guidance on whether a pregnant woman should eat sushi or have an epidural. When it comes to maternal health, I personally have a bias toward evidence inspired data and skeptical of making it moralistic.

Having done the pregnancy and delivery thing twice before, and being a healthcare professional, I knew I didn't *do* anything "wrong"; however, I didn't necessarily feel exonerated. I was in and out of the hospital during the holidays, isolated from my kids. The doctor prepared me for a premature delivery, but my son arrived full-term on a cold February night. My new obstetrician, a woman, spent nearly forty-five minutes with me as I labored and delivered. I didn't need the Pitocin, so the contractions didn't come on so hard. I even came off a few of them with an orgasm! After delivering my baby boy I looked up to see a line of onlookers in scrubs, including a guilty looking janitor at the end holding her mop. They were all applauding and cheering for me as if my delivery was a performance. I remember a nurse noting I was "an old mom" because I was in my thirties, and later another nurse remarked about how my heart rate stayed under 78 during the entire labor and delivery. I felt strong, not old. The doctor immediately placed the baby on my belly, and my newborn smiled. Despite his smiles, his Apgar score was low, so he and I stayed in the hospital another week, beginning a difficult journey to meet his special needs.

There's an indescribable onus on an expecting mother's womanhood to deliver a "healthy" baby. *Healthy* is a veiled term for "normal." Pregnant women are expected to be happy – "glowing" – about having a "healthy" baby. Women aren't to complain about the leaky bladder, swollen ankles, punitory vomiting, unrelenting constipation, excessive fatigue, unforgiving heart burn, back pain, financial strain, or whatever else is impairing our health and well-being to bring forth a child. The physical and financial expenses of pregnancy are largely regarded as compensatory, though they can impair a woman's life for weeks, months, and even decades. While fetal health is essential, it cannot diminish the health needs of the woman who delivers the infant. My friend endured an excruciating headache for months after delivery and was told it was migraines, but it took her demanding care for doctors to discover it was from a small spinal fluid leak from the epidural. The back and pelvic pain I suffered was brushed off as "normal." I know now, as I have become a pelvic floor rehabilitation specialist, that many women's health issues are long-term side effects from childbirth that go untreated. Some of these issues include urine leakage, heightened urinary urge, heightened urinary frequency (eight or more times a day), back pain, pelvic pain, sexual dysfunction, and prolapse.[1] All these issues are preventable if a woman is properly rehabilitated after childbirth. Even if a woman didn't receive proper rehabilitation (and most American women don't) these issues can be relieved or even healed conservatively with individualized therapy.[2] While the medical system divides women up as if we are plumbing – urology, gynecology, gastroenterology – it too often overlooks the network of muscles and nerves that control and connect our pelvic floor orifices. A

---

1. Prolapse occurs when the muscular tissues can no longer hold the pelvic organs in place. Examples of prolapse include bladder drop, uterus drop, vaginal drop or internal organs bulging into the vagina.

2. Endometritis, pelvic pain, back pain, bladder issues, mood disorders, insomnia, appetite changes, cellulitis, neurological impairments, hernia, and surgical complications are only a few other short- and long-term ailments that can arise from birthing a child. Many people are generically told to do "Kegel" exercises (squeeze), which may or may not be helpful to their symptoms.

woman's pelvic floor muscles are strained and often injured when she carries a baby for nine months. Vaginal deliveries often cause stretch injury to the pelvic floor muscles and Cesarean section deliveries lacerate the abdominal wall. These type of muscle injuries would be rehabilitated in the left arm, right leg, or any other area of the body, but are largely ignored in postnatal women. Injuries from child delivery cause severe long-term health issues for many women. Urinary leakage is experienced by more than half of women over fifty and many are ashamed to get help or are unaware their "little problem" is treatable.[3] Chronic back pain, pelvic pain, and emotional instability are other adverse effects of pregnancy. The prevailing acceptance of women's ailments – "that's just part of it" – harms the lives of women and is even deadly. Maternal mortality, death from causes related to pregnancy up to forty-two days post-pregnancy, is also preventable; however, it continues to increase in the U.S. at astounding rates to where a woman's chance of experiencing a pregnancy-related death has more than doubled since I was a child in 1987.[4] *That's unacceptable!* Claiming power includes seeking and demanding the comprehensive care you need and deserve as a woman.

---

3. Carolyn Swenson et al., "Urinary Incontinence: An Inevitable Part of Aging?" University of Michigan, National Poll on Healthy Aging (November 2018), http://hdl.handle.net/2027.42/146144.

4. C.J. Berg et al., "Pregnancy-related mortality in the United States, 1987–1990," *Obstetrics and Gynecology* 88, no. 2 (September 1996): 161–167. Also, A.A. Creanga et al., "Pregnancy-Related Mortality in the United States, 2011–2013," *Obstetrics and Gynecology* 130, no. 2 (August 2017): 366–373. Fatality risks are significantly higher for black women and other minority groups than white women in the U.S., and death usually occurs in the weeks before or after delivery. Center for Disease Control and Prevention, Pregnancy Mortality Surveillance System, last reviewed August 7, 2018. It's my opinion that hospitals and insurance providers would save lives if they put their resources toward more involved perinatal care, rather than building Las Vegas style birthing suites or substituting phone calls for direct, in-home perinatal care.

Life didn't stop with my fourth pregnancy. I had three children under the age of five and was hoping to go forty *plus* weeks because I knew babies are easiest to care for in the womb. My water broke, and I didn't want Pitocin again so I asked to hold off on it; the medical staff was resistant but agreed. As time ticked by nothing happened, and I got the speech about the baby's safety and my safety. I waddled into bed and offered up my arm for the pic line. The contractions started, and I labored. Soon after, three nurses bolted in, stuffed an oxygen mask on my face, and started turning me side to side. Silent tears streamed down my face. I didn't know what was going on and didn't want to distract them from their work, which was hopefully keeping baby and I safe. I was willing to lie there and be cut open so my son would live. I thought about how grateful I was, knowing they could do a Cesarean section within minutes. That experience gave me a deeper respect for the brave Cesarean mothers, who should bear their scars with honor. The nurses told me they were turning up the Pitocin and called the doctor, who sliced in and announced the baby was coming out as soon as possible. My body was no longer a haven but had turned into a dangerous place for my son.

The contractions came on like hard punches that smacked-down my entire being. Full dilation eased my pain, and the doctor announced it was time to push. I was so exhausted that I faked some pushes; she called me on it. I gazed at the big red ball on the wall and wondered what it was like to give birth kneeling on all fours over that sturdy, flexible sphere; but instead, I was again on my back with people I had just met looking on, fettered to an IV stand. I looked in the mirror at the hairy head coming from me, and I wondered if I was ready for my fourth child.

The doctor interrupted my moment, telling me to push, *for real this time*. I wanted my baby and resolved to deliver his life. I took a deep breath and pushed with all my strength. Every orifice of my body let something out, but no baby. The medical staff was screaming at me to push – *push, push, Tara!* So I pushed again and out came my baby boy. They swooped him off, saying the baby was fine, but my husband followed them anyway. I was scared, so I occupied myself by inspecting my placenta in detail – I am a healthcare professional after all – and I knew it was the last time I would ever grow one of those special organs that was mostly made up of my husband.[5] Soon after, my husband brought baby to me. There he was; the child I had been holding in my womb for nine months.

Delivering life is a transcendency for women that unleashes our power. It is by far my greatest accomplishment. According to the Bible, delivering a child is the depiction of how God delivers power.

> **Eternal One:** As a woman fiercely strains to give birth, I will gasp, pant, and cry out.
> I have been quiet for a long time; I have held back in the face of it all.
> Well, *no more.*
> *When My power is loosed,* I will make level the heights and render them bare.
>
> (Isaiah 42:14–15, The Voice)

Through pregnancy, labor, and delivery, women embody the work and power of God in the business of creating and delivering life. How each woman conceives, carries, and delivers this power is as unique as each woman.

As I have delivered life, like many women I have also delivered

---

5. Xu Wang et al., "Paternally Expressed Genes Predominate in the Placenta," *Proceedings of the National Academy of Sciences of the United States of America* (PNAS) 110, no. 26 (June 2013): 10705–10710, https://doi.org/10.1073/pnas.1308998110.

death. In my backyard is a small gravestone etched with Isaiah 40:31, it belongs to my palm-sized stillborn. I loathe the word "miscarriage" because any other word with the same prefix implies an active mistake (i.e. misconstrue, misprint, misstep, miscalculated). Unexpected pregnancy loss is a common occurrence that ends at least 15 percent of pregnancies for a myriad of reasons including genetic, anatomic, autoimmune, endocrine, infectious and other unknown factors.[6] Despite the facts, surveys reveal most people believe accidental pregnancy loss is a rare occurrence caused by a stressful event, lifting a heavy object, or still being on birth control.[7] These myths place blame on women who are already grieving their losses. The pain of a losing a pregnancy is recognized in Scripture as a punishment for Israel (Hosea 9:14). To tell a grieving woman about God's plan or control cruelly robs her space to mourn, so please don't do it. And the "at least" comments about already having children are also insensitive.

Whether we are delivering life or death, we labor and experience the vulnerability of becoming weaker and then defenseless as the hour nears. As Jesus initiated his labor to deliver a new humanity, he comforted the disciples by likening what they would experience at his departure to a woman delivering a child. "In the same way that a woman labors in great pain during childbirth only to forget the intensity of the pain when she holds her child, when I return, your labored grief will also change into a joy that cannot be stolen" (John 16:21–22, The Voice).

The most crucial "hour" to deliver humanity is akin to a laboring woman. Christians are taught to remember the agony of

---

6. Holly B Ford, MD, and Danny J Schust, MD, "Recurrent Pregnancy Loss: Etiology, Diagnosis, and Therapy" *Reviews in Obstetrics and Gynecology* 2, no. 2 (Spring 2009): 76–83.

7. J. Bardos, D. Hercz, J. Friedentha, et al., "A national survey on public perceptions of miscarriage" *Obstetrics and Gynecology* 125, no. 6 (June 2015), 1313–20.

Christ's labor but conditioned to forget, dismiss, minimize, or even shame the shrills and gore of women giving birth. During my first delivery I remember the eye rolling and under-the-breath sighs that occurred when a woman in the labor room next to me let out her high-pitched screams, as if it was painful to listen to her and she somehow was not doing a good enough job. I wondered what they would think of my own cries, which were sure to come, and it made me ashamed to express my own pain. After that delivery I felt traumatized. I needed help to get out of bed and use the toilet, but the focus was on the baby, and I was just supposed to deal silently with one of the most painful and traumatizing events my body had ever experienced. It didn't matter that I couldn't feel my crotch, that I was so swollen I couldn't sit comfortably, or that I was bleeding everywhere. The nurse helped me get into disposable granny-panties, and I tried to force a smile. I had delivered a healthy baby. I delivered life. We women who give birth break our bodies and shed our blood to deliver life. Our sacrifice should *never* be reduced to "a part of life" or appropriated as "duty."

Of course we mothers value delivering our children and we shift our focus from the pain to the joy of having a child. But mothers rapidly go through tremendous physical trauma; our emotions bungee jump upside down off a cliff, and we naively enter an intensively profound life shift that consumes and challenges every part of our identity and well-being.[8] Mothers embody life's most important work. We are fleshed with God's power to deliver life, we are the deliverers. So I remember my labor as a mother; in fact, my labor is my greatest motivator, because when I need strength or courage, I remember how I gave life and know I can deliver!

---

8. Review to Action, "Report from Nine Maternal Mortality Review Committees," Review to Action, accessed February 11, 2019, http://reviewtoaction.org/Report _from_Nine_MMRCs.

Ask and see *for yourself*:
    can a man give birth *to a child*?
Then why do I see strong men *clutching themselves,*
    their hands on their abdomens as if they are in labor?
Why has every face paled, *looking sickly*?

                    (Jeremiah 30:6, The Voice)

20

THE POWER WITHIN

A champion is defined not by their wins, but by how many times they recover when they fall.

– Serena Jameka Williams (1981–),
American tennis champion

Nothing reveals faith more than transforming the flesh. It's an unearthing of oneself, a revelation. If you don't believe me, ask an athlete, someone who has lost fifty pounds, a person who has been paralyzed from disease or an accident, or someone who has learned to face the world again after having the muscles and skin of their hands scarred from fire. I have witnessed firsthand the mysterious power of physical transformation in my rehabilitation and fitness career. This proximity has helped me understand the value in pushing the comfortable boundaries of my body. Even though I'm dedicated to physical fitness, I need someone to see my blind spots and challenge me to "go there" (*but not go too far and hurt myself!*). A few years back a personal trainer challenged me to climb a nautical rope that was suspended from a thirty-foot gym ceiling. I didn't believe her when she said I was strong enough; but I resolved to do what the trainer said, because I have stood by many, many patients and clients and told them they, too, have what it takes, and I have been disappointed when they refused to follow my instructions. *I was terrified to make the climb!* Did I mention I don't like heights? With all the cheering, jeering, and prodding that goes on in a gym, the peer pressure veered up my courage (or insanity) and I inched up the rope. I followed the climbing technique she taught, one hand over the other; then I pulled my knees into my chest, keeping the rope weaved between my legs like the letter *J.* Having my arms hold my weight, without solid grounding under my feet, was *scary*. Splinters from the rope sliced into my hands as I held on for dear life, I dared *not* look down. The trainer calmly coached me over the back noise of hootin' and hollerin' for the rookie. At the top, I swatted the cowbell in victory while keeping my death grip on the rope as everyone cheered! I was thirty-feet above a cement floor; I looked down and froze as I realized that I hadn't prepared or trained for the descent, which required much less strength but more control to make sure gravity wasn't *too* helpful. *Why did I do this?!* About a third of the way down, I started to tremble and become paralyzed with fear. My tremors grew and became so fierce that the rope was gyrating. The shaking came from a place within me, deeper than what I could control. I felt like a little girl and wanted to cry, but I knew that wasn't going to help me get down. My coed cheering section realized something was wrong and toned it down to good old-fashioned encouragement, while they grabbed the gymnastics mat to soften the concrete floor. *Thanks!* What felt to be the longest less-than-thirty seconds of my life ended, and I was never so glad to feel the solid earth beneath my feet. I held back my ugly-cry because I felt like I may collapse *and there weren't enough tissues in that place to manage my snorts and sobs.* Though my feet were safe on the floor, I continued to tremble. In fact, the tremors lasted *three days* and came with more flood of emotion as my heart and voice trembled as well. I was a *hot mess*, to say the least, and it was difficult to breathe. I had seen this in patients before, especially around Christmas, and knew I was having a panic attack. It felt as if that rope was around my neck and body, and I wouldn't be able to take another breath *ever again*! I knew I wasn't going to die, but my body didn't believe that. My onslaught of perceived terror happened on a Friday, so I curled up on the sofa to gasp and tremble all weekend. "We are weak and do not know how to pray, so the Spirit steps in and articulates prayers for us with groaning too profound for words" (Romans 8:26, The Voice).

I'm not sure if climbing a rope at the gym is a prayer, but for me it was one that ignited something powerful beyond what any "Dear heavenly Father" laud could spark. During my weekend-long panic attack, I had flashbacks of the time Dad held Mom by her throat against a wall and threatened that I would no longer have a mother if I kept screaming. I learned quickly to keep my tears and panic to myself, until the day I climbed that rope. Episodes of tremors and flashbacks continue to randomly haunt me, without warning, often during my most vulnerable moments. My panic attacks flood me with memories of times when I felt powerless as a child. Sometimes I recall specific events; at other times it's a general feeling. I'm still learning to respect my panic attacks and listen to what my body is trying to tell me. My body doesn't know what time it is, if it's 2019 or 1981 – it only knows what it is experiencing, that I can't breathe and it's painful gasping for air. To end the agony, I've found that emotionally participating in what was too painful or dangerous to experience before somehow grounds me and allows me space to breathe.

Unbearable trauma can shut off memory, like turning out a light. But even if an episode is out of mind, our bodies don't forget, and they find ways to express our deepest feelings in a physio-logical way. A groundbreaking study, "Adverse Childhood Experiences (ACE) Study," correlates childhood traumatic experiences with physical ailments, including heart disease, diabetes, cancer, suicide, alcoholism, career success, and more.[1] An ACE score higher than four indicates the probability of post-traumatic disease. My ACE score is six.

In the U.S., women experience ACE scores over four at higher rates than men.[2] Medical research now shows how childhood traumatic experiences, as defined by high ACE scores, increases the risk of developing autoimmune disease.[3] In the U.S., autoimmune disease is the third most prevalent disease category for men and women, after cancer and heart disease, though nearly 80 percent of those with autoimmune disease are women.[4] The epidemiology of autoimmune disease is unknown; however, it's highly correlated with past emotional trauma.

This disproportionate occurrence of autoimmune disease in women begs researching as to how systemic sexism makes women ill. Childhood experience is not the only issue that affect

1. Vincent J. Felitti et al., "Relationship of Childhood Abuse and Household Dysfunction to Many of the Leading Causes of Death in Adults: The Adverse Childhood Experiences (ACE) Study," *American Journal of Preventive Medicine* 14, no. 4 (May 1998): 245–248.
2. Centers for Disease Control and Prevention, Kaiser Permanente, "The ACE Study Survey Data [Unpublished Data]," U.S. Department of Health and Human Services, Centers for Disease Control and Prevention, accessed December 19, 2018, https://www.cdc.gov/violenceprevention/acestudy/about.html.
3. Shanta R. Dube et al., "Cumulative Childhood Stress and Autoimmune Diseases in Adults," *Psychosomatic Medicine* 71, no. 2 (February 2009): 243–250. Autoimmune disease is where the body's immune system attacks the body to strongly it creates an impairing disease.
4. DeLisa Fairweather and Noel R. Rose, "Women and Autoimmune Diseases," *Emerging Infectious Diseases* 10, no. 11 (November 2004): 2005–2011, https://wwwnc.cdc.gov/eid/article/10/11/04-0367_article. Because the National Institutes of Health only measures certain classifications of autoimmune disease, there are various claims to the prevalence and cost of autoimmune disease that consider it more prevalent (American Autoimmune Related Diseases Association Inc. n.d.).

women's health, however. What we experience today can debil-
itate us next year. Most cancers, heart issues, and major illnesses
have an onset of approximately one year after a stressful life
changing event, such as moving, divorce, death of a family member or spouse, job termination, or even retirement.[5] With the
body's vital connection to our subconscious minds, it's no surprise
that medical research has found a correlation between trauma
and disease. Growing medical and health research shows that
every physical illness we experience in modern humanity – from
migraine headaches, arthritis, asthma and the common cold,
to heart issues and cancer – is influenced either positively or
negatively by our emotional health.[6] That women are twice as
likely as men to struggle with depression indicates their increased
vulnerability to health problems.[7]

My initial idea in writing a book was to explore this relationship
between body and spirit, emotional health and disease. Reading
the Bible through the lens of a twenty-first-century healthcare
professional, I see this as unexplored exegesis. As I stashed away
notes and articles, what became obvious to me is that I would not
be effective to influence the epidemic of women's health issues
if I did not first dismantle the harmful beliefs women harbor, the
theological beliefs that silently destroy our emotional health
and manifest themselves physiologically. Women are taught,

5. Thomas H. Holmes and Richard H. Rahe, "The Social Readjustment Rating
Scale," *Journal of Psychosomatic Research* 11, no 2., (August 1967), 213–218. This
scale is still used to measure health risks according to the "Life-Change Index."
6. Werner W.K Hoeger et al., *Lifetime Physical Fitness & Wellness* (Stamford,
CA: Cengage Learning, 2015), 403.
7. Debra J. Brody, Laura A. Pratt, and Jeffrey P. Hughes, "Prevalence of Depression Among Adults Aged 20 and Over: United States 2013–1016," National
Centers for Health Statistics, Centers for Disease Control and Prevention, NCHS
Data Brief 303 (February 2018), https://www.cdc.gov/nchs/data/databriefs
/db303.pdf. 1–7.

from Scripture, that we are the "weaker vessel," as if this is a God-ordained, scientific fact; however, many men I meet cannot climb a thirty-foot rope on their own strength.[8] That women are weaker than men is laughable to me, because I know physical strength is about genetics and training, not about gender. If you don't believe me, come work out with me (*and some of the very strong women I know*) sometime. During my fundamentalist years I was taught that God created women emotionally weaker than men, which "rightfully" places us in subservient roles to men. These partial teachers appeared to be intimidated by women's resolute display of emotion or any explicit display of emotion.

Why is the display of strong emotion a sign of weakness? Nobody stopped to consider how uncontrollably broken men can be while watching a football game. The "boys don't cry" culture is harmful to everyone, especially when it's a rite of passage for men to assume power over women. The fact that "Jesus wept" in front of his friends (John 11:35, NIV) is also dismissed. Jesus wept over Jerusalem as well (Luke 19:41). To shame emotion as weakness or as "feminine" is not biblical and linguistically assigns women to weaker places on the margins of power. How the church speaks about women matters, because language can be healing or harmful: "A joy-filled heart is curative balm, / but a broken spirit hurts all the way to the bone" (Proverbs 17:22, The Voice).

An undeniable connection exists between our body and spirit in Scripture, as medical research shows. Our minds, hearts, legs, hands, and feet (and every other part of us) are masterfully designed to work together in balance, in the way a symphony of individuals creates music. When women are taught to be under man's authority, or they need man's protection, they are denied the power to create their own song. The symbiosis of body

---

8. First Peter 3:7 calls the wife, not women, the weaker vessel. This may be because in the legal relationship of marriage, women were the weaker legally.

and spirit is a powerful mystery that holds the power to heal us. Explaining the synergy is like explaining the mystery of God. "If the Spirit of the one who raised Jesus from the dead lives in you, the one who raised Christ from the dead will give life to your human bodies also, through his Spirit that lives in you" (Romans 8:11).

God's power lives in each of our human bodies! Our bodies are incredible instruments that bear life's weight and support us. Even with their vulnerabilities they connect us to ourselves and each other. When our bodies function well, they allow us to see, speak, hug, share good news, earn money, give to our world, bring forth children, care for others, innovate, and create change. Our bodies connect us to God's power, even when they are injured and broken. What I love about my work in rehabilitation is that I help the injured create a new song for their lives, I help find this power in their broken bodies.

We are all unfinished symphonies and need to be healed or transformed in some way. It's fine to pray for healing. However, being in the business of healing people, I must point out that Jesus *never* taught us to pray to be healed but assigned action in healing, whether we are the healer or the one who needs healing. This is not to say we shouldn't bring our sickness to Jesus, but it's to highlight that Jesus sometimes gave an action item to folks who came to him to be healed.

"Go home. Your son lives." (John 4:50)
"I say to you, get up, take your cot, and go home."
    (Luke 5:24)
"Stretch out your hand out." (Luke 6:10)

Sometimes our responsibility is to act, which may mean we need to take that step, go to church using the walker, leave the abusive partner, join the gym, listen to the woman's explicit emotion, or climb the rope. If you're a chaplain or minister or just a friend, the next time you visit the sick, ask them about the home exercise program the therapist gave them, and do it with them after you pray with them. By doing so, you will be helping them embody God's healing power, and you'll help nudge them out of that paralyzing gap between hope and effort. Action can be the touch of power that is needed to activate the miracle, leveraging the power in your flesh with an action item: stretching your hand to make a difference, building an altar, taking your mat to the yoga class, being faithful in doing your home exercise program, or going home and trusting God.

I have observed that when people are aligned with God's power within them, they know if their action item is to fight illness or if it is to "go home" and submit by saying goodbye. Facing mortality, the transforming from our physical body to an eternal one, is perhaps the most challenging physical transformations we are called to do as humans. I truly respect my patients who have had the courage to tell their families and friends that their time has come, forgoing further treatment and entering hospice. They radiate God's Spirit as they prepare for the profound physical transformation that comes in leaving what they have come to know in this life. It's a physical transformation we all will face one day, and it is one that reveals our faith as no other: "My power is made perfect in weakness" (2 Corinthians 12:9, The Voice).

Since I'm not a sage I cannot tell you how to ignite God's power within you – whether you are to take a step or go home – that's between you and God. I can tell you that entering into the process of transformation ignites God's power in you. I see this in patients; I see it at the gym; I see it with musicians, scholars, business owners, and athletes; and I see it in myself, each time I allow myself to be challenged. Therefore, I'm still climbing that rope at the gym, even though it still scares me; and, as a middle-aged mom, I have zero plans to join the military. I know the rope challenge, and others, condition me to bear my weight and move my world, to be flexible and adapt. My next challenge is to create greater strength, to lift heavier and stronger; I can do aerobics and yoga all day but *loathe* weightlifting. These challenges – and more, many more – transform me. They are my groanings that are too powerful for words, my acts of faith, that articulate my weakness and give life to the power of God in me. So I encourage you too to find God's power in physical transformation; you have permission now so go!

> Little children, let's not love with words or speech but with action and truth.   (1 John 3:18)

PART 3

DO THE BRIGHT THING

I don't cause commotions, I am one.

– Elphaba
in *Wicked*

21

DRAMA QUEENS

There is a special place in hell for women
who don't help each other!

– Madeleine Albright (1937–),
first female American secretary of state

Penni was my best friend in high school. We met on the cheerleading squad and became fast friends. I picked her up for school each morning, and we listened to each other cry after school as both of our parents were divorcing. On weekends we cruised the town, blaring Garth Brooks on cassette and sipping fountain drinks with extra ice, while talking about hair styles, fashion, and everyone and everything else. We giggled, *a lot*. Like any rites of passage for teenage girlfriends, we found our fair share of getting in and out of trouble. We saved our money to eat Mexican chips and salsa with the white cheese. *Yum!* If we had enough money left over, Penni ordered a Coke and I ordered a Diet Coke. We both had part-time jobs in food service, and we rolled our eyes and smirked, and giggled some more, as we compared notes about our customers and managers. Leaving Penni was painful for me. I moved on to college and never found a friend quite like her. She stayed at her food service job back home and eventually became an aesthetician. There was never competition with Penni – for grades, boys, or social status – it was just friendship and fun.

I've had other friends, and still do. Some have championed me; some have betrayed me; others have given their time, ear, and fresh coffee (or cold beer). These are the friends who told me about what to expect when delivering a baby and the friends who've spilled the truth about how their body responds in down dog yoga. Often the conversations get deeper, and we talk about family and relationships. Some who have moved on still call or text on my birthday. My favorite friends are ones I can immediately pick up with after being apart, no matter the distance. Friends laugh and cry and give you a manicure, and the great friends will hold you when you ugly cry and tell you you're great even when you've demonstrated yourself to be an epic failure. Best friends believe in you and help *you believe in you!* I haven't always been the best friend, but I know I haven't been the worst either. With adult responsibilities I find I must be intentional about nurturing my female friendships, because it's easy to be consumed with being a mom, wife, and professional. Certainly it takes a lot of patience to be my friend because I have some big ideas, if you haven't yet figured that out from reading this book! I do my best to be patient with my friends and offer them my ear, a hug, and the gospel of Tara (*good advice, ahem!*) if they ask. I almost always invite them to yoga.

We want our daughters to have best friends but don't always give them the examples they need to grow up on. Princesses are all the rage for little girls, but when was the last time you heard a princess story that celebrates female friendship? They're rare. I don't recall Cinderella, Snow White, Belle, or any of the traditional Disney princesses having girlfriends or a "BFF." For the record, playing a motherly role to mice, fish, furniture, or desexualized dwarfs doesn't count – those are minions, not friends. The question begs to be asked whether the traditional princess stories subtly endorse *Mean Girl* (like the movie) behavior.[1] When a princess is rescued by a prince, she becomes queen; and there can only be one queen.[2] On the flip side, when women become the rescuers of women, they form a sisterhood by teaming up to fight together.

The Bechdel Test brings awareness to women actively working together in stories. It's a pass-fail test, and a pass requires that two named women talk to each other about something other than a man.[3] That's it. With so many of the male-centric plots in books and movies, the test reveals the mass gender inequality in our narratives. Nearly all the Bible stories epically fail the Bechdel Test. One exception is Mary and Elizabeth, who meet up to discuss their lives, their hopes, and their fears, with no talk of guys. They sing, hang out, talk about pregnancy, and pray. It's a great reflection of relationship between women who encourage each other. Ruth and Naomi come close to passing but eventually bring a man into the plot, so their story doesn't pass.[4] These ladies should get honorable mention, however, because they talk finances. I'm waiting for the Bechdel Financial Test to be created, because more women need to get together and talk money, right?

Unlike these biblical women, not all female friendships are family. At no place that I can think of does the Bible honor peer relationships between unrelated women. In fact, any of the biblical "girls' night out" examples seem to go really, *really* bad. Queen Vashti and her feast for the women was cruelly interrupted and

1. *Mean Girls*, directed by Mark S. Waters (Los Angeles: Paramount Pictures, 2004).
2. Peggy Orenstein. *Cinderella Ate My Daughter: Dispatches From the Front Lines of The New Girlie-Girl Culture* (New York: HarperCollins, 2011), 23.
3. Scott Selisker, "The Bechdel Test and the Social Form of Character Networks," *New Literary History* 46, no. 3 (Summer 2015): 505–523, https://muse.jhu.edu/article/601626/summary.
4. Ruth and Naomi talk about Boaz, which fails the Bechdel Test.

disassembled so they could be told to listen to their husbands. Jephthah's daughter and her friends displayed a seismic perversion to the idea of girls having fun crying together, knowing she would come home to die at the hands of her father. All of these women's social gatherings, from very different times in Bible history, resulted in appalling consequences for what began with amiable intentions. I suppose the men who did the Bible writing did not witness the power that women acquire from their female relationships so they *couldn't* record them.

We model what we see and experience in relationships. My experience has been that without examples of healthy female relationships from the Bible, Christian social circles tend to imitate the one princess and her minions dynamic, while overlooking female friendships among peers. A bride has her bridesmaids; a small group leader has her circle; a women's ministry leader has her flock; or the leader is male, and all the women are silent (outside of the kitchen anyway). Despite the many named women in the Bible, their relationships with each other appear to be undervalued. When I read the scriptures, I love to imagine the relationships the biblical women may have had, putting women at the center of the story. Even if we don't read about women directly working or interacting together in the Bible, we still have record of their alliances. One of my favorites is the story of the sisters: Mahlah, Noah, Hoglah, Milcah, and Tirzah (Numbers 27:1–11). These sisters appeared in front of the all-male court (aka priests, leaders, and assembly) and claimed, "Why should our father's name be taken away from his clan because he didn't have a son? Give us property among our father's brothers" (verse 4).

In a world that considered women themselves to be property, these women made a bold claim. *I love it!* Certainly these sisters met and scripted their statement for the court, though we don't read about their preparation. They were probably afraid, and we don't read that either. I am sure that people in the tent of meeting accused them of being "drama queens." *But they got their property!* I like to imagine that they held regular house parties on their property and used their wealth to support women in the development of business and politics in the new promised land. Their voices in court perhaps laid the foundation for women to serve as judges. Rather than envisioning women who were alone and rescued, this story gives me hope to envision women actively working together to rescue themselves. Because we don't read about their interactions with each other, we don't read about their conflicts either.

Conflict between women is too often a trump card to defeat. We are so sensitive to being called catty; I almost believe it's been programmed into our characteristic X-chromosome! I am bothered that even the slightest conflict between women – and especially teenagers becoming women – is considered "drama." It's easy to point the finger at men on this form of sexism, but I hear this "drama" complaint from many more women than men. I suspect it is rooted in the belief that we women are supposed to be sweet and caring princesses, quietly wiping tears and cleaning up messes, instead of asserting ourselves to achieve a goal. Yes, there are queen bees among us who will trample anyone and everyone to get ahead. My experience is that these women will take exclusive credit for anything good, blame anyone else for the bad, and then move along quickly – so let them go. If you are in an environment where a queen bee is dominating your life, it might be time to join forces and take her down, for the good of the community, or move on yourself. Asserting oneself as an individual or as part of a group isn't "drama." After all, we don't use that word when referring to men.

As women, we are up against the storylines that say we must be rescued princesses instead of women working together to make ourselves queens. *So work together* – even if there is competition, judgment, and potential "drama" conflict. The litmus test as to whether someone is a queen bee – and needs to be toppled – is whether the person acts as if she succeeded alone and refuses to attribute her success to the influence and help of others, not whether she hurt your feelings or did a better job than you.

Colleges can be competitive places to earn grades and post-graduation placement in limited jobs or graduate programs. Arwyn and I met in the dorm, and we both had the same goal to be accepted in the master's program for occupational therapy. In the mid-1990s the competition was extremely fierce, with only fifty positions available to top applicants from across the nation. Those would-be applicants whose GPA was below 3.4 need not apply. I am forever grateful for Arwyn's friendship and influence because she kept me on a strict study schedule and *expected* me to make the grades. She *believed* in me and helped transformed me from a B+ student to an A student. I graduated *cum laude* and made it into graduate school, largely thanks to her. She taught me how to dominate academics and get to the top by helping others. Arwyn was an A student, but studying with me, and the other women she helped, made her an A+ student. I thanked her a lot, and she was humble, saying that studying with me helped her too. But she was mostly proud of me. Arwyn didn't worry about turning me into competition for a position we both wanted to be awarded. We kept to our study schedule, came prepared for our study sessions, and made time to have fun – *and get in and out of a little bit of trouble, that's what are friends for!* When it came time to apply to graduate school, we filed our applications and loved each other enough to be glad if the other it was accepted and we weren't. Fortunately, we both got in. Arwyn is one of the many women who have fulfilled the scriptures to me: "So support one another. Keep building each other up as you have been doing" (1 Thessalonians 5:11, The Voice).

Many, many more stories of female friendship are coming out of the shadows, and need to, to help both women and our daughters learn to be better friends. Some of Disney's latest, Princess Tiana and Queen Elsa both had friends. As Disney redefines *princess* and *queen*, we, too, can redefine the role of women in Bible prose. We can give them voices in their collaborations and endeavors. We can also see how many of our own stories and relationships pass the Bechdel Test. If you are failing the test, you might rearrange some priorities with your friends! If they advise you to submit your power, just because you're a woman, "don't be deceived, bad company corrupts good character" (1 Corinthians 15:33).

Friends propel us into our power, and they celebrate it with us. They butter us up when we need it and have a way of setting us straight with their flattering hugs, words, (and manicures). Wherever you're headed, I assure you that you get there because of the friendships in your life, not despite them. Friendship is not a competition, so be a friend. And don't stop what you are doing just because someone accuses you of being a "drama queen." Real queens fix each other's crowns!

> The heart is delighted by *the fragrance of* oil and *sweet* perfumes,
> and *in just the same way*, the soul is sweetened by the wise counsel of a friend.
>
> (Proverbs 27:9, The Voice)

22

FORGIVE US OUR TRESPASSES

It's your obligation to speak the truth, and everyone can either take it or leave it. But truth must be in us.

– Mother Mary Angelica (1923–2016),
American Catholic nun and
founder of Eternal World Network

On a Sunday morning we presented a liturgy of Psalm 51, "Create in Me (a Pure Heart)." There was my friend, the clarinet player, aiming her horn into a microphone stage right. I stood near her behind a taller mic stand; and my friend's husband, the speaker, stood downstage, front and center, behind the pulpit. The clarinet began the melody and played the entire time, and I started the liturgy, singing the prayer for sixteen measures in my alto voice:

Create in me a pure heart, God,
*   and renew a steadfast spirit within me.*
Do not cast me from your presence
*   or take your Holy Spirit from me.*

And the male speaker followed me, speaking the previous three verses of the psalm:

Cleanse me with hyssop, and I will be clean;
    wash me, and I will be whiter than snow.
Let me hear joy and gladness;
    let the bones you have crushed rejoice.
Hide your face from my sins
    and blot out all my iniquity.

This liturgical sequence was repeated a couple of times until I kicked in the soprano with a rendition of verses 12–15:

Restore to me the joy of your salvation
    And uphold in me a willing spirit,
Then, I will teach transgressors your ways
    and they'll come back to you,
I will sing of your spirit.

We continued echoing the words with the clarinet in the background. I wrapped up the liturgy with a dynamic projection of the "Restore to me" chorus. I put my entire self into it, opening my arms wide with the crescendos as to hold the entire congregation, gathering them to all God offers and then bringing them inside with quiet reflective words. It was an incredibly moving experience with lots of tears, a few amens, and applause. If music cleans a heart, theirs were cleansed that morning. "Create in Me" is a ballad rendition of Psalm 51 set to music. Its words are a prayer from the depths of a remorseful soul, intimately sung to God. Music and poems are powerful. In fact, the holy words I sang that day were more powerful than the exact same spoken words at the pulpit.

I found it ironic that my church permitted me, a woman, to dramatically and *powerfully* sing the Scripture; however, I was not permitted to speak it. I mentioned this to the leaders and got a few chuckles as if my claim wasn't serious. They made me feel that my prescribed purpose as a woman was to be their entertainment. According to my leader's response, the words from Psalm 51:13, "Then I will teach transgressors your ways" were not for me because I was not permitted to "teach" the men.

Interestingly, our presentation that morning of these timeless words embodied the misdeed from which King David was "repenting": using a woman for entertainment. If you don't know the story, David used his high position of king to peep at Bathsheba, who was bathing at the time. Sexist theology turns her bathing into a sideshow, even though Jewish law required ritual bathing for women and there were no private bathing chambers. Anyway, David found out who the bathing woman was and summoned her. David impregnated Bathsheba and had her husband murdered. The scribes didn't bother to share Bathsheba's side of *that* story, so we can only speculate whether she was a victim of coercive rape or if she used seduction and adultery for her political gain. Since she was a woman, and David was the king, I see this as a classic case of coercion, but not everyone agrees on that. I took a poll on my Facebook page and 57 percent of the responders agreed Bathsheba was coerced, while 43 percent deemed her a seductress and opportunist. For the record, silence is not consent, and who says "no" to an all-powerful king?

While sexist theology assumes Bathsheba was putting on a show to seduce a king, her appearance gets judged as if she was a rape victim on the witness stand. *What was she wearing?* A bathing suit.[1] *Why was she bathing?* Well, duh. *Why was she bathing in front of David?* Wrong question. The question really should be:

---

1. In an ancient world where women did not have private bathrooms or indoor plumbing, the Bible doesn't reveal the amount of daylight or the location of her bathing. Historical evidence reveals that women did not bathe nude: "Now the women go into the baths with some of their garments on, as the men do with somewhat girded about them. And these are the customs of this order of Essenes." See Flavius Josephus, *The War of the Jews, Book 2* in *Josephus: The Complete Works*, trans. William Whiston (Nashville: Thomas Nelson), 729.

Why was he peeping from his all-access rooftop view, and why did he summon her? David *could* have used some self-control.

Rather than holding rapists accountable for trespassing onto a victim's body, a woman's appearance, reputation, and recollection gets put on trial instead of a man's actions when determining rape. *How disgraceful!* Questions include why she was there or whether she was drinking, as if a woman doesn't have the right to attend social events with alcohol and the man does.[2] Clearly, not all women's accusations are credible; however a woman's side of the story should be heard and taken seriously.

All Christians agree that David's adultery and subsequent murder of Bathsheba's husband was an atrocious abuse of his power. He used his power and high position to trespass onto Bathsheba's body, dismissing his many opportunities to say no and preventing the entire disaster that afflicted the kingdom. When Bathsheba is accused, the culpability shifts to her female form, assuming her unworthy by being female.

The female form has long been considered unworthy because it has the power to trespass on men's power. It has occurred to me that the only reason people can find to hold Bathsheba culpable is because her female image was "seen." My image was unworthy of the sacred space behind the pulpit because it trespassed on what the leaders saw as a man's place of power. When the image of "female" is unworthy and seen as inherently evil, boundaries of power are placed around her. Her testimony is automatically judged untrustworthy. She is positioned as a transgressor because

---

2. The Center for Disease Control (CDC) cites risky sexual behavior, pregnancy, and violence as potential health risks for women who drink. This denies responsibility of women who do drink responsibly and men who rape, impregnate or act in violence towards women. According the CDC's page "Alcohol Use and Your Health," last reviewed January 3, 2018, all women are a fertile womb and responsible for violent acts: https://www.cdc.gov/alcohol/fact-sheets/alcohol -use.htm.

she is female, and her power to teach male transgressors is considered trespassing upon "their" authority. Fortunately, Jesus didn't see women as guilty but empowered even a non-Jewish woman to teach transgressors, including the male transgressors. In fact, the Bible's very first Christian evangelist was a Samaritan woman.

Unlike the twelve male disciples, the Samaritan woman didn't need a death and resurrection to realize the deity of Jesus. This woman also broke multiple laws in her interaction with Jesus, including the many that forbade men and women to stand side by side in public or have a drink together while discussing literature, religion, and politics.[3] Jesus also broke the accepted social customs that segregated Jews and Samaritans. The unnamed Samaritan woman was not only considered by the Jews to be religiously unclean as a woman, but as a Samaritan she was toxic. I once heard a preacher call this woman "morally bankrupt" because of her sexual history of having five husbands and shacking up with another. Like the Bathsheba condemners, he, too, used sexist theology to hold the Samaritan woman guilty before hearing the details of her current situation. That she was remarried so many times likely meant she was widowed, since most men would not marry "rejects." If she had outlived five husbands, she was likely beyond childbearing years and could not produce a legitimate heir for a man as a wife.[4] Jesus didn't condemn this woman; in

3. Ally Kateusz, "The Samaritan Woman at the Well: Two Texts and Two Traditions in Art," December 4, 2013, https://www.slideshare.net/DivineBalance1/art-as-text-08-two-texts-two-traditions-the-woman-at-the-well.

4. Bronwen Speedie, "Samaritan Sinner, Celebrated Saint: The story of the first Christian missionary," *Mutuality: Men and Women Serving and Leading as Equals* 23 (Winter 2016): 6–9, https://www.cbeinternational.org/resources/article/mutuality/samaritan-sinner-celebrated-saint-story-first-christian-missionary. Widows were a contested political issue in that day. Most men did not want the financial responsibility of marrying a widow who was unable to give him

fact, he deemed her worthy to be the very first person to whom he revealed his identity. "Jesus said to her, 'I Am – the one who speaks with you" (John 4:26).

As the first of her community to believe in Jesus, the Samaritan woman was compelled to leave her task of fetching water and lead the first (and most successful) evangelism campaign recorded in the Gospels. She did this alone as a woman, leading the men and women of her village to also see Jesus. Jesus knew everything she had done; the men and women of the village were probably curious to find out if he knew everything about their lives too! Evidently leaving a vessel of water at the well to bring others to see Jesus isn't as "venerable" as leaving a fishing business to follow Jesus. Sexist theology is unwilling to recognize her power and didn't even bother remembering her name. It sees women as unworthy bystanders, just as the Samaritan woman has been accused of being "morally bankrupt" from the pulpit; Bathsheba was entertainment to David; and my liturgy was mere entertainment to the church leaders.

How easy it is to point the finger at men and cry "sexism"; however, many females also believe women should not rightfully hold power to influence men. Years ago, an exceptionally talented singer told me she didn't sing at church without being "covered" by a man because it was too powerful of a position for a woman. She likened it to a soldier playing the drums or horn and leading troops into war. She told me this after I sang the Psalm 51 liturgy, by the way. Her issue assumed the power of voice as a domineering force and not something that is shared.

---

children, but the law was trying to account for women without a guardian. Widows often became concubines or prostitutes. The Samaritan woman may have been a chosen concubine as a woman no longer able to bear children, and it was perhaps her only decision to avoid prostitution. We see the deliberation of how to deal with widows in 1 Timothy 5:3–14.

Many preachers say David should have been out fighting with his men. That is true, but that is to say fighting a battle that slaughters people is a righteous thing. It's been my experience that many men, and even women, see their faith as a fight, a struggle to win a zero-sum battle, and the battleground of faith too often becomes the power of women. Silencing, minimizing, and controlling the expressions of women are assaults on women's power and not a medal of faith. Women are also *expected* to use their ambition to teach transgressors, including men. "So then, brothers and sisters, use your ambition to try to get the gift of prophecy" (1 Corinthians 14:39).

While some women are given the distinguished gift of teaching (Romans 12:4–9), *all* women are expected to live according to Christ's teachings and teach others to find happiness through love, mercy, humility, hunger, peace, hope, and more (Matthew 5:1–20). As Christians we are called to elevate and develop the gifts of each other, not suppress spiritual maturity (Ephesians 4:7–14). Biological properties aren't justification to stunt spiritual gifts, or belittle the called. Jesus said, "Let the person who has ears, hear" (Matthew 11:15), not close your ears because of my messenger's biology. Whether a woman is singing, extending mercy to her teenager who screwed up, teaching behind a pulpit, evangelizing a village, hungering for the truth, teaching transgressors that spiritual gifts aren't priapic, or telling her side of a sex scandal (*harassed because she is righteousness* [verse 10]), the voices of women must be heard, and not be perceived as trespasses.

A motto I live by when making a grab for power is "Ask forgiveness, not permission." I didn't ask permission to write this book. I didn't ask permission to start practicing yoga. I didn't ask permission to wear my yoga pants when leading classes of men and women in Christian based yoga and meditation. I never asked my husband's permission to start my business with its banking account or to see a counselor when I felt confused. I never asked permission to change jobs, change churches, or stay at home on Christmas Day with my little children instead of visiting my mom. When the backlash came, I didn't always ask forgiveness unless I directly hurt someone...*Sorry, Mom, I missed Christmas Day at your home; we'll find another day to visit.* I'm not a total rebel; I *did* ask permission to sharpen my pencil in school and get an extension to submit a late paper in college, but I don't need permission to express who I am or do what I need to do.

I've created more than one rub as a woman who doesn't ask permission to take power. Of course, taking power is different than collaboration, which is what my husband and I exercise as a married couple who share a home, a family, and, yes, a bank account separate from my business. When people are offended by my "trespassing," I figure their offense is more reflective of their intimidation; a lot of people are sensitive to a woman who independently wields her power. When I'm feeling intimidating about pulling the trigger of power without permission, I try to remember that if the Samaritan woman had asked the religious leaders to run her preaching campaign, it wouldn't have happened. Jesus didn't ask permission to start his ministry either. At the heart of Psalm 51, David did not ask God for permission but forgiveness.

God is merciful. If God can forgive David – who never fully realized that his sin was against Bathsheba and her husband, in addition to God, with his statement, "I have sinned against you – you alone," (Psalm 51:4) – then God can forgive *anyone*. Yes, that means even a woman "trespassing" to claim the power that is rightfully hers or a person who has placed unjustified boundaries on women. Like the Samaritan woman who was the first female messenger of Christianity, we are called as Christians to teach transgressors God's way, and that is what Jesus did.

God knows everything about us – how to engage us; all our strengths, our shameful secrets – and yet God still invites us to stand eye to eye just as we are and converse over a drink. Jesus inspires us to share our lives and move the lives of others into a place of joy and great reward. When a woman's part in this invitation is dismissed, silenced, brushed off as entertainment, or even defamed as "morally bankrupt," we are considered trespassers. So sometimes the most righteous way to our power is to "trespass." Fortunately for us women, though we sometimes hurt a few egos to complete our work in Christ, Jesus forgives our trespasses as we forgive those who trespass against us!

> Forgive our sins as we ourselves release forgiveness to those who have wronged us. And rescue us every time we face tribulations. (Luke 11:4, TPT)

23

INFECTION CONTROL

We're going to have to let truth scream louder to our souls than the lies that have infected us.

– Beth Moore, (1957–),
American evangelist, Bible teacher, and author

Patient care is very sensitive work, especially in my area, with senior citizens in their "twilight years" who are dealing with mortality and loss of independence. As an occupational therapist in the U.S., I find there's lots of pressure to meet customer service standards, which often requires the delicate balance of being sensitive while pushing a patient beyond his or her comfort zone to achieve therapy objectives. My work has shifted from a traditional clinic setting into seeing patients, typically aged 85–100 plus, in their homes. Homebound persons of any age are a hidden and vulnerable part of our population. It is my job, as a skilled clinician, to advise and educate my patients on how to safely overcome the challenges of disability and disease to manage their daily activities – eating, dressing, bathing, going to the bathroom, getting groceries – the basic stuff they've done all of their lives, except now it's become a struggle to complete these basic tasks.

One patient, who had a large pressure wound on his coccyx

(i.e., tail bone) from prolonged sitting in his chair, became irate when I told him he needed to get himself his own glasses of water. He was expecting his wife do everything for him because he needed to use a walker and supplemental oxygen to make it to the kitchen. The twenty-five-foot walk made him short of breath and reduced the oxygen saturation levels in his body. He told me he never learned "women's work" – *such as getting a glass of water?* I educated him that he was capable, and I would teach him how to get his own glass of water safely, even with both hands on the walker and oxygen tubes in his pathway, because getting his own water was a functional opportunity to get out of his chair and decrease the pressure to his coccyx, and a safe way to exercise his heart. He began acting like a pouting child who was being made to do a chore. He followed my instructions; however he made a big mess splashing the water on the floor so that his aging wife had to clean it up – he was going to make her work one way or another as if he was punishing *her*. It pained me watching the eighty-seven-year-old woman kneel to the floor to clean up the spill, as if she was trying to wipe up his anger. I educated his wife not to bring him water unless he was "dying of thirst" because he needed to get out of that chair. I educated him about his physiological need for activity and the dangers of prolonged sitting and pressure areas that can become life-threatening.

On my next visit, the patient passively referred to me as his "aide" in front of his visiting brother. No shame to aides here; they do important work. However, aides are caregivers and not clinicians. If this were his *first* visit I wouldn't have corrected him, however he was being passive-aggressive towards me and minimizing my position. He knew very well I was his occupational therapist and he was still mad at me for making him get his own glass of water for the first time since 1950. We had been working together on the goal that he remains in his home and not have to move to a skilled facility for care. He was in his nineties, and he couldn't formally acknowledge that women have a role in his life outside of serving him. When I corrected his "aide" comment, he then referred to me as one of his "girls" His much younger brother and exchanged brief eye contact with an internal smile. I kept my warm and caring demeanor and kindly, *again*, clarified to him my role as his therapist. I reminded him of the goal in the plan of care that we agreed to and assured him I was trying to keep him healthy and safe in his home, which was becoming a dangerous environment to him because he was not engaging in activities such as getting out of his chair and completing his own self-care. I reviewed the importance of the exercises and activities I prescribed, and I took the opportunity to educate his brother on encouraging the patient to "get off his butt and get his own glass of water" because his life literally depended on it. I understand I am as young as many of my patients' grandchildren; however, as a woman, I could not accept his minimizing "girl" comeback.

What's crazy about this patient is that his life – in his home as he knew it – really *did* depend on his compliance with my intervention. This brought him to the "moral" dilemma of listening to a woman tell him what to do in his own home or lose his independence and live in a skilled nursing facility. Ultimately, I represent hope to my patients and work hard to deliver that because I want them to have hope in their lives. This patient was not willing to hear my instructions on how to reach what he hoped for because I was a woman.

In the Bible, prophets, too, represented hope to people. Yet, like my patient, people were often resistant to hear the prophet's instructions on reaching that hope. According to the Bible, we still have prophets among us today. I'm always baffled at how many Christian men and women have a difficult time listening to or recognizing the female prophets among us. These women share important messages that can save our lives! Many Christians who believe women cannot prophesy trust that God can speak through an "ass," because the Bible says so (Numbers 22:22–35, KJV) but cannot accept that God speaks through women, even though the Bible records such a wonder in multiple places. *Whoa!* Some women in the Old Testament who spoke the word of God as prophetesses include Miriam, Deborah, and Hulda (Exodus 15:20; Judges 4; 2 Kings 22:14–20). The New Testament also records the prophetess Anna as the first to speak of Jesus in the temple (Luke 2:36–38), and the daughters of Phillip who were in the work of prophecy (Acts 21:9). Jesus himself provoked a woman to speak in the temple, as the men around them listened (Luke 13:10–17, more on her in reflection 24, *Raise Our Voices*) and inspired the foreign Samaritan woman to share the good news. Moreover, on the day of Pentecost, the day in which the church was established, Peter reiterated the prophecy from Joel 2:28–29 that women will speak as prophets:

> I will pour out my Spirit on all people.
>   Your sons and daughters will prophesy.
>   Your young will see visions.
>   Your elders will dream dreams.
>   Even upon my servants, men and women,
>   I will pour out my Spirit in those days,
>   and they will prophesy. (Acts 2:17–18)

Clearly, the daughters are called to prophesy and aren't awarded some alternative type of Holy Spirit. God spoke through women in the Bible and still speaks through women today. Prophets bring a message of hope, but the message often comes with homework in order to change the course of one's life for reaching that hope. As with my patient, God may send a woman to warn us how to not lose everything we have. Despite the fact that women have credibly delivered God's messages in the Bible, many men, and even some women, atrociously use two sentences from the Bible to suppress the Spirit's power in women's voices. They claim the Bible is clear on this matter, forbidding women to be heard as an authority in a public Christian platform of men and women. It's as if two verses are a trump card to deny women their call to prophesy or an excuse for anyone to not have to listen to them.

The verses they use come from Paul's personal letter to Timothy.[1] Timothy was the pastor of the church in Ephesus nearly two thousand years ago, and the verses are found in 1 Timothy 2:11–12. Despite the obvious pull against the grain of Scripture, and the inconvenience of silencing half of the church (or at least the married women), some Christians find it too painful to listen to women and uphold these words to be an instruction to all Christians for all time, rather than personal, pastoral instructions for Timothy during a time of controversy. The church in Ephesus was the armpit of churches that Paul oversaw. Political relationships among the leaders were heated. On top of that, cultic influences were taking hold in the area, and the church was desperate for some crisis management, which came in the form of social instructions described in Paul's personal letters to Timothy.[2]

Later in his first letter, Paul recommended putting a heavy filter on who could supervise and serve, which would include preaching and teaching, excluding almost all the men and all women in the church (1 Timothy 3:1–13).[3] In addition to the

---

1. Cynthia Long Westfall, *Paul and Gender: Reclaiming the Apostle's Vision for Men and Women in Christ*, (Grand Rapids, MI: Baker Academic, 2016), par. 9.1.3.

2. Westfall, par. 9.2–9.3.3

3. Using the logic to silence women in chapter 2, the restrictions in chapter 3 would also include silencing: single men, married men without children, married men with only one child or children who were too young to profess faith, married men with disobedient children (that's everyone at some point!), married men whose children were obedient but not respectful in all things (did Paul ever meet kids?), men who were new converts, men who were prone to alcohol or violence, men who were unfaithful to their wives, men prone to greed, men who did not have good reputations in the community, and women. See Gilbert Bilezikian, *Beyond Sex Roles*, 137–138.

exclusion of women speaking in that church at that time, Paul gave recommendations to women on attire that excluded gold, pearls, braids, and expensive clothing (1 Timothy 2:9). Most modern Christians agree it is fine for a woman to braid her hair or wear gold and pearls to church, seeing the command of attire as cultural, while also believing God somehow used karyotyping to determine who could prophesy publicly, ignoring the fact that female prophets spoke to the people (including the men) throughout Scripture. "The Lord announces the word, / and the women who proclaim it are a mighty throng" (Psalm 68:11 NIV). Christians will often hear single men, who were a restricted group to teaching in Ephesus (1 Timothy 3–5), speak but will still disqualify women. Because of the sexist double standard some Christians use to uphold 1 Timothy, there are continents full of churches infected with the belief that men should not listen to women, even though women are clearly called to prophesy. This infection has been festering in our churches for two thousand years and has created a wound that has certainly killed the spirit in many women, girls, boys, and men.

Instructions should always be taken within context. I don't use microwave instructions to ride a bicycle. I also don't use the instructions my husband received in the mail from the State of Indiana to renew his Indiana license plates to renew my Indiana occupational therapy license. (I also don't read my husband's mail, nor does he read mine). When I advised my one patient to get his own glass of water, those instructions were for him personally and did not necessarily pertain to all my patients. Generally, it is good and healthy for patients to get their own glass of water; however, for some patients, it would be very dangerous for them to get their own water due to a variety of medical and environmental complications. Some patients may not be able to drink thin liquids, or they may not be able to walk or use a wheelchair safely to get the water. The reasons can go on and on and get very specific. The specific provisions listed in 1 Timothy were personal instructions to Timothy for pastoring his church in Ephesus at that specific time; they were written within their specific culture context for specific reasons that we will never know.

While we have a right to read Timothy's personal letter, we must read it in context. The instructions Timothy received from Paul were never meant to usurp how God pours out the Holy Spirit or what kind of dreams women can dream. They weren't intended to contradict the overarching themes of equality in Christianity (Galatians 3:28). They certainly weren't a hall pass for all men to skip out on listening to all women for all time. God said through the prophet Joel, "I will pour out my spirit on *everyone*" (Joel 2:28, italics mine), not just males. We have a responsibility to hear our brothers *and* sisters in Christ.

For many years I was unable to reconcile the grace of Jesus with 1 Timothy 2:11–12, because these verses had been used in the church I attended to limit my call to prophesy. At times I spoke at church but only to the women. Women seemed just as opposed as the men were to allowing women to speak God's Word to an audience comprised of both men and women. We have an obligation as Christians to determine who is and is not a false prophet (1 John 4:1). Assuring that our prophets meet the specific biological qualification of being male is speaking in the image of men as God, *guydolatry!* (Deuteronomy 18:20). As a woman I can attest firsthand that when the Spirit puts a message on your heart it will get communicated to the world; but it's up to men and women to choose to listen, and listening just might save our lives. As the prophetesses and prophets of the Bible often delivered their messages of hope, sometimes packaged in a warning to take responsibility, we, too, must hear the words of our prophets, whether they are coming through the mouth of a man or woman, and yes, even if they come through the mouth of an "ass"! (1 John 4:1).

Prophecy has never been a product of human initiative, but it comes when men *and women* are moved to speak on behalf of God by the Holy Spirit. (2 Peter 1:21, The Voice)

24

RAISE OUR VOICES

The womens' stories are not yet fully told.

– Nancy Beach (1957–),
American minister and author[1]

O n March 23, 2018 the Chicago Tribune broke a story about sexual misconduct allegations against the founding pastor of a prominent Midwest megachurch, Willow Creek Community Church.[2] Willow Creek had previously rede- fined the church experience for Christians worldwide through "radical" actions, such as putting women in leadership positions, making it permissible to wear jeans on Sunday morning, and cre- ating a concert-like experience for worship. The accused leader was a global heavy hitter and "father" of the modern evangelical church. According to the Tribune, the board of elders knew about the accusations for years but had not taken serious action to investigate them. My family attends a church that has been

---

1. Nancy Beach served as programming director and teaching pastor at Willow Creek Church, one of the world's most influential megachurches. She spoke out for herself and for other women who said they were assaulted by the leader.
2. Manya Brachear Pashman and Jeff Coen, "After Years of Inquiries, Willow Creek Pastor Denies Misconduct Allegations," *Chicago Tribune*, March 23, 2018, https://www.chicagotribune.com/news/local/breaking/ct-met-willow-creek -pastor-20171220-story.html.

associated with Willow Creek, and we are friends with people who were directly affected by this leader's influence. So when I read through the shocking Tribune article, I was appalled. The allegations themselves were disturbing, but the church's response in their "family meeting" was a standing ovation in support of their beloved leader, the accused!

Now, just because a person is accused of sexual misconduct certainly does not mean he or she is guilty; however, in this case, Willow Creek was acting as if the accused were himself a victim! Who was listening to the voice of the women who were accusing this man of assault? I could barely keep my skin on and could not sleep that night as if the prayers of these women who spoke out would not let me rest! The next morning I went to my keyboard and clacked out a commentary. I'm no reporter, but I was becoming more and more aghast by the silence of the Christian reporters and publications. It was deafening! In my opinion, these silent Christian publications were becoming just as guilty as the Willow Creek members who gave this accused man a standing ovation. As I was in my kitchen office, typing away and reading my rhetorical phrases out loud for my husband and children to comment on, my teenagers said, "Mom, are you sure you want to do this?" I gave my mom sermon about doing what is right, even if it makes people uncomfortable...*and that includes myself.* I have a sign in my kids' bathroom that reads, "Never confuse the will of the Majority with the will of God."

I submitted my article to the web manager of a Christian women's group to which I belong. My blog article, "Hey, Bill Hybels – Where There's Smoke..." was published April 3, 2018, eleven long days after the story broke, which is ancient history in a news cycle.[3] I was a lone voice in an atmosphere of pious

---

3. Tara J. Hannah, "Hey, Bill Hybels – Where There's Smoke...," Viewpoint Blog, *Christian Feminism Today*, April 3, 2018, https://eewc.com/hey-bill-hybels/.

disbelief, all while Willow Creek was talking about how to take care of their leader and his family and continuing to ignore the accusing women. My article went viral. I received private messages from across the world with varying thoughts; some were critical, many were grateful. I found it ironic that the blog article had no public comments as it sat on the front page of a "Bill Hybels" Google search, yet I was receiving a significant number of private messages. Why couldn't people discuss this issue publicly? The Christian conversation on the web felt as if it was a twilight zone full of people who wanted to appear like mindless sheep, waiting to hear what their official response should be.

It got weird for me at church. People wanted to pretend nothing was wrong and would give me a look and then wave from a distance as to keep me away. Nobody wanted to discuss the scandal, especially with me, as if I might *say* something. A friend told me that someone came to her office and shut the door to discuss the scandal. Ironically, we were talking privately as she complained about the topic being so *hush-hush*. I brought up the scandal in my women's small group and shared my article. I was shocked to hear how divided even the women were. Those who had been directly shaped by this leader and Willow Creek were defensive of him and angry towards the women who came forward, as if the women were the guilty ones. Others had not heard; one woman said she wanted to hear more, which is always a good idea. In my article I didn't accuse the leader but highlighted sexist comments and behaviors in which I had seen him publicly engage – sexist behaviors that are normally accepted in church environments, such as assuming women want to talk about their families instead of the topic at hand. I determined that with all the missing emails and accusations, lots of smoke was lingering over him at Willow Creek and anticipated Jesus would sort it all out with his fire, as Paul discusses in 1 Corinthians 3:10–15.

That's exactly what happened. Since the article, Bill Hybels was forced to resign though maintains his innocence.[4] More serious sexually criminal accusations toward him have surfaced,[5] and he was exposed overseeing settlements of child sexual abuse that occurred on his watch.[6] Much has been written on the significance of Willow Creek's response, which was resistant initially to listening to the women despite the revelation of prior investigations. I'm grateful for the victims who risked, and even sacrificed, their careers to raise their voices and break the silence. I'm grateful to the courageous board members who believed the accusations and elevated the issue beyond the church, as they realized the church was unwilling to take the accusations seriously. They, too, raised their voices.

Sexual misconduct is a silent subculture in Christianity that has been around for centuries. I know personally what it's like to get the Sunday morning side-eye or have the worship leader stand a little too close when giving instructions. If you haven't read the news lately, sexual misconduct allegations are rampant in our churches as victims, both women and children, are coming forward and going public. The scandals are not restricted to one denomination or group; however, the more patriarchal the denomination, the more widespread the allegations.[7] Not all

4. Emily McFarlan Miller, "Willow Creek Names NAE Head, 3 Others to Oversee Hybels Investigation," *Religion News Service*, September 18, 2018, https://religionnews.com/2018/09/18/national-association-of-evangelicals-president-others-to-oversee-new-investigation-of-hybels-willow-creek/.

5. Laurie Goodstein, "He's a Superstar Pastor. She Worked for Him and Says He Groped Her Repeatedly," *The New York Times*, August 5, 2018, https://www.nytimes.com/2018/08/05/us/bill-hybels-willow-creek-pat-baranowski.html.

6. Robert McCoppin, "Willow Creek Paid $3.25M to Settle Lawsuits over Child Sex Abuse by Church Volunteer," *Chicago Tribune*, August 13, 2018, https://www.chicagotribune.com/news/local/breaking/ct-met-willow-creek-paid-3-million-to-settle-lawsuits-over-sexual-abuse-20180810-story.html.

7. The Catholic Church has demonstrated a global pattern of long-term sexual abuse of children. It's difficult to stay up to date on the allegations and cover

victims are women, but the perpetrators are a crushing majority, if not all, men. [8] Traditionally, churches have silenced the accusers and swept the messy story under a theological blanket that silences and even blames victims in order to protect the church. A woman told me once that she was sexually involved with her pastor when she was seventeen years old. She was forced to apologize to him for "leading him into sin" and quietly left the church so the pastor's wife and congregation would not know. This woman is now an adult; and when I talked with her last, she realizes how she was coerced and blamed but was unwilling to speak about it publicly because of the social backlash she would receive from her community. I hope she finds the courage and support to raise her voice.

Just here in my Midwest, midsize Indiana hometown, I know similar stories, and so do others because these stories are everywhere. As a collective group, churches are only starting to take these abuses seriously; largely because of the accountability from the non-Christian press. Thanks, *Chicago Tribune*, *New York Times*, *The Houston Chronicle*, and every other news agency who has stuck its nose in the church's business to sniff out the truth! (And please report the complete truth for us and not partial ones to bump your ratings).

Silencing women is crippling to our spirits. Luke's Gospel tells about a woman at the temple "who had been disabled by a spirit for eighteen years. She was bent over and couldn't

---

ups because they come out so frequently. Wikipedia keeps an ongoing list by geographic region at: https://en.wikipedia.org/wiki/Catholic_Church_sexual _abuse_cases.

8. In February 2019 *The Houston Chronicle* ran a three-part series titled "A Chronicle Investigation: Abuse of Faith," citing 380 male leaders and volunteers who have faced allegations of sexual misconduct. You can read about their investigation here: https://www.houstonchronicle.com/local/investigations /abuse-of-faith/.

stand up straight" (Luke 13:11). With the weight of the world on her shoulders, the disabling spirit left this woman without a voice. I work with disabled persons in my profession, and I am proud this woman made the sacrifice to leave her home and go the synagogue, which likely did not have handicap-accessible accommodations. We don't know whether she was looking for Jesus, but Jesus saw her. "When he saw her, Jesus called her to him and said, 'Woman, you are set free from your sickness.' He placed his hands on her and she straightened up at once and praised God" (verses 12–13).

Most of my life I've heard this story as being about Jesus healing on the Sabbath. In fact, the Common English Bible titles the scripture section "Healing on a Sabbath." This is a similar title to other English translations, completely ignoring God's commission for this woman to raise her voice. There is absolutely no instruction in the Old Testament (which was the Bible of Jesus' day) forbidding a woman to speak on the Sabbath in the synagogue. However, at the time of Jesus, only men could teach and participate in song or liturgy, and women were segregated.[9] The tradition of "laying hands" is attributed to apostolic succession; however it started with Jesus laying his hands on *this* crippled woman, releasing her to raise her voice in the temple. Receiving her call, her disabled spirit was set free, and she stood up and praised God in the synagogue, on the Sabbath, for all the men and women to hear.

---

9. History teaches us there was a *mechitza* (barrier) that segregated women in the synagogue. That Jesus taught near the *mechitza* where the women could hear shows how Jesus wanted women to be a part of the conversation. See Bushnell, *God's Word to Women*, (Minneapolis: Christians For Biblical Equality, 2003), par. 191. Jesus taught where he could see the women, and saw within this crippled woman the power and ability to stand tall and speak, so he "placed his hands on her." A minimum of ten men were required to start a temple service (the women did not count), so we know men were there listening. See Scanzoniand Hardesty, *All We're Meant To Be*, 3rd ed. (Grand Rapids, MI: William B. Eerdman's, 1992), 83.

The synagogue leader, who was highly upset that Jesus had healed on the Sabbath, and was probably more offended a woman was holding a spontaneous worship session in *his* synagogue, responded by blaming the woman instead of taking it up with Jesus. He reprimanded her for coming to the synagogue to be healed on the Sabbath and not another day! If you read the passage carefully, this woman did not ask to be healed; she didn't call to Jesus, and Luke doesn't say she was even looking at Jesus. All this kyphotic woman did was push through her physical pain and show up at the synagogue for the Sabbath. Jesus wanted her healed that she might raise her voice, and she did; but she was blamed by the very church where she was moved to praise.

Raising my own voice when led by God has cost me too. I ask a lot of questions that are sometimes interpreted as offensive. My experience is that most churches don't want to engage in the messy soul-searching that is needed to cross the line they have helped drawn between biblical teachings that silence women and perpetuating the subculture of hidden sexual misconduct. I don't believe most churches are trying to silence women intentionally; however, communicating theology in a way that dismisses women's experiences silences women, which makes them vulnerable to sexual assault. It can be challenging to recover the truth of biblical women because translators did not often relay woman's words (or names); however, biblical women have survived the marring and erasing. They also survived in religious systems that normalized sexual assault. Until we, as a church, are willing to take the time and energy to confront the bias in our theologies and explore how it enables sexual misconduct within our numbers, we will continue to feel the repercussions of #MeToo (#ChurchToo) among us. Remember it's okay for a woman to help clear up a preacher's understanding: "So, when Priscilla and Aquila heard him speak boldly in the synagogue, *they discerned both his gift and his lack of full understanding.* They took him aside and in private explained the way of God to him more accurately and fully" (Acts 18:26, The Voice).

When Jesus said, "You are set free from your sickness" (Luke 13:12), the woman raised her voice in praise. The same was true for me; I felt sick about the sexual bias in my faith, but once I decided to raise my voice through writing this book, I didn't feel sick anymore. I'm empowered by how Jesus defended the woman he empowered to raise her voice, even though the religious authorities of the synagogue didn't recognize her to rightfully have a voice in the temple. They were blind to see how her voice supported their mission, but maybe that's because their *real* mission was to support their own power (Matthew 15:14). Jesus deviated from his church tradition and called her a "daughter of Abraham" (Luke 13:16).[10] Before this statement, the Jewish tradition only recognized "sons of Abraham" in the Old Testament. To be a "son of Abraham" was an intimate link to God in this life and the life after, and this relationship was consummated with circumcision. The Pharisees were blind to how a woman could have a relationship with God (who was believed to dwell in the temple) without a man, because only a man could be circumcised. Only "sons of Abraham had the right to raise their voices in the temple.[11]

Jesus understood how women were denied a direct heritage with God. As the Pharisees recognized spiritual authority to be only within the sign of the covenant inscribed onto the flesh of

---

10. Scanzoni and Hardesty, 78.

11. Being in the lineage of Abraham was a requirement for participation in the covenant God made with Abraham. The covenant extended to his descendants, – or "seed". This became thought of as taking the land or inseminating the land to produce more "sons of Abraham." Women were not considered part of this lineage – they couldn't be circumcised or seed the land – but were eligible to "join [the] ancestors in peace" (Genesis 15:15) through consummation with the "sons of Abraham." Basically, women were thought to be saved through

men, many churches continue this practice. When church groups and denominations only recognize the flesh of men worthy to communicate God's authority, it teaches Christians to distrust the voices of women. When the voices of women are distrusted, male power goes unchecked creating probability for sexual abuse. The Pharisees also dismissed the part of Abraham's covenant that was for his offspring (*which included daughters and foreigners through Hagar*) and for his wife (Genesis 17:9–15).[12] Jesus enabled the woman in Luke 13 to assume a radical posture as a spiritual daughter, "daughter of Abraham," and she was given direct relationship with God; she raised her voice in the temple as heiress.[13] We, too, must elevate the voices of women in our churches to be heard with the authority of heiress. As my kids would say, Jesus "roasted" the synagogue leaders in verse 15, because he revealed how these leaders considered women to be no more important than animals, pointing out how they gave water to their animals on the Sabbath.

As a follower of Jesus, I encourage you, too, to raise your voice and speak out against the absence of women's voices, confront those who silence women or see them no greater than animals. As a woman, stand tall and raise your voice, knowing God sees you and wants to hear you and trusts women to speak with the authority of an heiress. Remember this woman from Luke's Gospel. All she did was show up! The abuse and silence women suffer can be risky and crippling to witness. The only evidence can be subtle, like listening exclusively to women talk about how

men. See Malul, *Knowledge, Control And Sex* 172–174. Tamar, Rahab, and Ruth received honorable status in the lineage because they were "taking the land" and produced more "sons of Abraham."

12. Gaffney, *Womanist Midrash*, 35; Scanzoni and Hardesty, *All We're Meant To Be*, 142.

13. Robert F. O'Toole, "Some Exegetical Reflections on Luke 13,10–17," *Biblica* 73, no. 1 (1992): 84–107, http://www.jstor.org/stable/42611233.

they serve men, multitudes of hunched church women without a voice, or patriarchal hierarchy. But like the woman in Luke, we, too, must show up and believe God will set us free to raise our voices in praise as we stand tall and speak out, no matter what *they* say!

"But when we do what pleases God, we can expect unfading glory, true honor, and a continual peace – to the Jew first and also to the non-Jew, for God sees us all without partiality.
(Romans 2:10–11, TPT)

25

INTERRUPTING WOMEN

If women want rights more than they got, why don't they just take them, and not be talking about it.

– Sojourner Truth (unknown–November 26, 1883),
African-American escapee of slavery,
abolitionist, and women's rights activist

"You have a hair in your face." What does that have to do with what we are talking about? Reaching for the lone hair dangling in front of my face was a distraction to shift the topic of conversation to my appearance, as if my credibility is dependent on my appearance. This subtle interruption was a symptom of the larger issue that as an American Christian woman I have been "churched" to make my appearance a moral priority over making myself heard. That pastor didn't really want to talk about my discussion with the elder's wife. He was more concerned about my misplaced hair, my appearance as a woman in his flock. After interrupting the topic by noting my misplaced hair, he inquired, "What does your husband think of this?" He believed if I disagreed with my husband over this issue, it would disqualify my opinion. Was I not allowed to have my own opinion? I shared with him that my husband and I share a daughter who is coming of age, and we both feel it's important she not only have a voice of her own but that she sees that women have a voice at the table in church.

The elder's wife agreed that the rhetorical idea of not allowing her daughter to speak at the dinner table, *ever*, would be serious emotional neglect and abuse. Out of the other side of her mouth, though, she, the pastors, and everyone else refused to see how our church was doing the same to God's daughters, not allowing us to publicly speak at the table where we met as a church family. I had already discussed this issue with the elders, who told me that I needed to discuss this with my husband. I was hoping my analogy might move the elder's wife to consider the harm in not hearing women; however she was clearly unwilling to think for herself on this issue, or at least outside of her husband's "company line" opinion that upheld women's submission as a litmus test to faith. She was quick to quote 1 Corinthians 14:34–35 and instruct me to further consult with my husband, and her husband would follow up with him as well. *Sorry Dear!* As a good Christian I was slow to be angered and knew better to than to answer a fool in her folly.

On the subject of Christian women and wives being heard in church, the Bible appears to communicate opposing messages. In Romans 16 the apostle Paul lists women by name, describing them as colleagues, anointed, deacons and apostles – positions in which these women would have been heard by the church. Prisca is a married woman who is mentioned multiple times in Acts 18 as a fellow worker of Paul, and even listed before her husband Aquila, indicating she may have carried more responsibility in the ministry.[1]

---

1. Margaret Mowczko, "At Home With Priscilla And Aquila" Arise, CBE International, November 9, 2015, https://www.cbeinternational.org/blogs/home-priscilla-and-aquila. Also, Carolyn Osiek, "The Women in Paul's Life," *Biblical Theology Bulletin: Journal of Bible and Culture* 42, no. 2 (2012), 90–95.

Though I respect my husband's opinion, I don't believe it's necessary for mine to be congruent with his on every spiritual matter. When reading scriptures that appear to oppose a woman's right to be heard apart from her husband, it's important to look at context. We don't always realize the political issues the early church faced. The Judaizers in Corinth were challenging Paul's right to be an apostle and attempting to discredit him for his employment of women in his ministry. They were offended by women's high positions in Christianity and bent on silencing and segregating the women as part of their agenda to return the new church back to its Jewish roots. Interestingly, in Paul's first letter to the Corinthians, he reverses his nontraditional practice of listing Priscilla before Aquila, the thought exists that by listing Priscilla after Aquila that Paul may have been showing sensitivity to their prejudices.[2]

Paul appointed women to positions of authority in the church, but because the church in Corinth was grappling over whether to embrace women's authority, it was at great risk of splitting (1 Corinthians 1:10). In this letter to the Corinthians, Paul precariously tells women they are not allowed to talk in church meetings and should ask their husbands any questions, the very Scripture the elder's wife used to silence me (14:34–35). This is a sharp contrast to his earlier sentiment towards women as fellow workers in leadership positions and his practice of employing women in ministry (Philippians 4:2–3; Romans 16:1–2).

I find it hard to believe that the apostle Paul, who is credited with writing most of the Epistles in the New Testament, was so flippant that he would validate women and wives in ministry and then decide they must be quiet and consult their husbands on matters for all posterity. Note that Paul refers to Euodia and

---

2. Bushnell, *God's Word to Women*, par. 193–196.

Syntyche, both women (Philippians 4:2–3), as fellow workers in the gospel as he did Timothy (Philippians 2:22).

Despite the obvious fact that Paul encouraged brothers *and* sisters to use their gifts of prophecy publicly in chapter 14 of 1 Corinthians, many churches hold that Paul was quoting a blanket policy towards all women for all time in verses 34 and 35, telling them to be quiet and ask their husband questions, while ignoring verses 39–40: "So then, brothers *and sisters*, use your ambition to try to get the gift of prophecy, but don't prevent speaking in tongues. Everything should be done with dignity and in proper order" (emphasis mine).

Paul encouraged both men and women to speak! Sometime when all four of my children are talking at the same time in the minivan, I tell them to be quiet. That doesn't mean I want them to pipe down forever – just in the minivan so the drive is not so chaotic. If you read *all* of chapter 14, the people were all speaking at the same time, which was making their services chaotic. So, either the apostle Paul is a hypocrite and contradicts himself in the same letter on his intent for women to speak publicly, or he was giving specific instructions to this setting to create order, as I do in my minivan. When today's church leaders pull out verses 34–35 in an attempt to silence women, it is essentially an interruption to the direct calling Paul gives to men and women to be heard in versus 38–40. That interpretation also brings serious implications for women to even be allowed to learn at church without a husband. Thus, using the Bible as a weapon to silence women has wounded my soul because it doubly communicates I am unworthy to be heard because I am a woman. When this attitude is coupled with my being demonized because of my questions, or giving greater pastoral attention to my hair, I am honestly wary of participating in church environments in which I do not hear women.

First Corinthians holds yet an additional scripture that is often used to usurp women's right to be formally heard. At first glance the passage appears to represent a God-ordained human hierarchy between the sexes, which some claim women inhabit the lowest rank. "Now I want you to know that the head of every man is Christ, and the head of the woman is the man, and the head of Christ is God." (11:3). Those who are interested in silencing women will use "head" as meaning authoritative position; when in fact Paul was discussing a "point of origin" in connection with creation. When we consider "head" as "point of origin," like the head of a river that feeds the momentum of the water, for example, we are naturally able to read this passage in consensus with Christology from Genesis, which promotes equality and diversity.[3] "Head" in the Bible is not a prescription for hierarchal relationships between men and women in church and marriage. It does not mean "authority" in the Greek, which is the original language of the New Testament. Christology validates that Christ existed first, man second, and since and man needed help, God brought in a woman, and through her the world was changed.

> And the LORD God said to the serpent...
>   I will put enmity
>   between you and the woman,
>   and between your offspring and hers;
>   he will crush your head,
>   and you will strike his heel.
>
> (Genesis 3:14–15, NIV)

First Corinthians 11 moves to make an egalitarian argument of the headship hierarchy points and then discusses women

---

3. Pierce, Ron, "How Should We Interpret 1 Corinthians 11: 2–16?" *Mutuality: Men and Women Serving and Leading as Equals* 18, no. 2 (Summer 2011), https://www .cbeinternational.org/resources/article/mutuality/how-should-we-interpret -1-corinthians-11–2%E2%80%9316.

covering their heads: "As woman came from man so also man comes from woman. But everything comes from God. Judge for yourselves: Is it appropriate for a woman to pray to God with her head uncovered?" (verses 12–13).

Think about this: the fact that a woman covering her head during prayer or prophecy was even being discussed in this context indicates women were leading service in Corinth. In the Jewish Orthodox tradition, only men preached, and they covered their heads to lead service. Paul responded that a woman should be heard as an independent person who came from God. She can pray and prophesy publicly at the church service with or without a head covering, with short or long hair, it doesn't matter. It's is up to the woman. A woman's appearance doesn't matter.

This is pretty incredible because a woman with her head uncovered could have indicated sexual availability. So not only could she publicly lead prayer and share prophesy, but she could do it with her head uncovered, *scandalous!*[4]

Pitifully, in my former church, when I expressed my exacerbation over the absence of women's voices in church messages, church leaders have interrupted my concern – if not steered the topic to my physical or moral appearance. *We were discussing the lack of women's voices being heard, not my sinful rebellious nature.* If my voice was offensive to anyone, it was considered sinful. To be accepted as a woman in that church required a tightrope act to not fall into accusations of a sinful rebellious nature if I offended anyone.

Also in my former church, the evangelists' wives were the women's ministry leaders. The authority of the women's ministry

---

4. Philip Barton Payne, "Wild Hair and Gender Equality in 1 Corinthians 11:2–16," *Priscilla Papers*, The Academic Journal of CBE 20, no. 3 (Summer 2006), https://www.cbeinternational.org/resources/article/priscilla-papers/wild-hair-and-gender-equality-1-corinthians-112%E2%80%9316.

leaders was not their own but was displaced to their husbands who "covered" them; hence their sexual relationship gave the wives permission to be heard. I never quite felt the women's ministry leaders were being fully authentic because they created messages to empower women, but they ultimately taught women's submission to men as a woman's highest virtue. These women certainly hold power with authority and pay, but they will never truly empower women until they honor the spiritual power of women as they do the power of men. It's as if their role was to serve the male leaders in witnessing to the women – *so the men didn't have to?*

In other churches, pastor's wives often function as a mom to a congregation – decorating the church facilities, planning the food, making sure the messes are cleaned up, and wiping the tears. Being the wife of a pastor can be some of the most taxing ministry work, without the formal title and pay. Pastors' wives serve in different capacities, some officially co-pastor and others have separate work and a career. A patient once told me that when she married in 1953, the role of "preacher's wife" was an aspirational role for her and other women who wanted to minister. She married the preacher and served their church in that role for nearly fifty years, until her husband died. The closest she got to preaching was writing plays for holidays or special events.

Women's voices and trajectory are constantly interrupted by erroneous interpretations of Scripture and traditions that have tried to dismiss, silence, veil, and even obstruct women's place to share spoken word. Above the baptismal in the Saint Venantius Chapel in Rome, a framed Madonna hides a mosaic of Mary, who is standing in the middle of the apostles, her hands uplifted as she leads them in prayer. She wears a white pallium with a red cross – the symbolic garment bestowed to the pope. It's a starkly different image from the Madonna and a clear demonstration of how the Catholic Church is resistant to upholding Mary seen with power.[5] Scholars have record of female bishops, however Bishop Theodora's mosaic at the Church of Saint Praxedes in Rome shows that a renovation tried to make her a man.[6] Historical evidence doesn't support the notion that women were managing the homefront while men were leading the business of the church (unless they were fighting the Crusades; I'll give them that one). Saint Teresa of Avila actively rebuked church fathers for not teaching women.[7]

In Cambridge, December 1653 public records record two women were stripped naked to their waist, restrained to the whipping post, and publicly whipped until their backs bled because they were preaching; evidently they angered the mayor when they reported "they had no husband but Jesus Christ." The mayor, of course, called them whores before he had them whipped![8] One of my favorite stories is from Dr. Anna Shaw, a missionary preacher from the late1800s whose outreach to an isolated timber camp drew a full house because the men heard she held her driver at gunpoint on the all-night journey after he tried to rape her.[9]

And how can we forget Sojourner Truth? In her 1851 "Ain't I a Woman" speech; she starkly pointed out that because she was an African-American woman, nobody helped her into carriages, she watched her thirteen children be sold into slavery, and boldly attested that "no man could head me." She was prophetic in her warnings to abolitionists about leaving women behind.[10]

The U.S. government granted women the right to vote fifty-two

5. Ally Kateusz, PhD, "Two Marys, Two Traditions," Powerpoint presentation, http://allykateusz.com/art-as-text-powerpoints/two-marys-two-traditions/.
6. Ally Kateusz, PhD, "Making Bishop Theodora Male," Powerpoint presentation, http://allykateusz.com/art-as-text-powerpoints/making-bishop-theodora-male/.
7. Miles, Who Cooked the Last Supper, Kindle loc. 2127.
8. Miles, Kindle loc. 2479.
9. Miles, Kindle loc. 3464.
10. Miles Kindle loc. 3394–3947.

years after black men upheld the underlying "Christian" belief that man is "head" of women.[11] These stories, and many more help to explain why we don't see women in pulpits. My spiritual lenses have become fogged from years – okay, decades – of listening to preachers who believed women are unqualified to preach publicly because of biological disqualifiers or that a woman's "place" is in the home. This history of male authority in the church is really male supremacy that demands female inferiority; it idolizes the masculine – it's *guydolatry*!

With the low numbers of women being heard in church, I, personally, have had a difficult time finding authentic female role models. As I interviewed women preachers, I was told of the many challenges these women face. After service, these women receive firm greeting line handshakes, frequently given by an incensed man to express how God does not allow women to preach! I asked local female pastors about their process in creating their messages, and many shared a notion of being restricted from full-throated preaching. Though they were heard, the narrative was not yet theirs.

I have personally seen female speakers being treated as if they were a cover act to the person who wrote their script. One woman told me she was fully supported by her church, as they voted to leave their denomination so she could be ordained by her husband. She and her husband co-lead the church, and she runs an influential ministry to women in the county jail. I could not find a local woman who was a founding pastor of a fellowship; however, I follow a couple on social media because I want a piece of their soaring spirit. I also follow female pastors who found their way to serving in senior pastor positions, and I support women-founded ministries.

---

11. Nina Morais, "Sex Discrimination and the Fourteenth Amendment: Lost History," *The Yale Law Journal* 97, no. 6 (May 1988), 1153–1172.

According to a Pew Research Center article, many women serve in church positions; however, few have made it into the positions that ensure they occupy the platform, or pulpit, in order to share their authentic words.[12] It's time we stop interrupting women and silencing them with Scripture. Both Jesus and Paul led ministries that interrupted the systematic silencing of women. In fact, they interrupted the system and interjected women into it. Perhaps, as women, *we* need to do more interrupting, listing women first on church bulletins as Paul listed Prisca in Romans 16:3. At minimum, we need to interrupt the systems that prevent women from being heard, remembering that we, too, came from God and are gifted with prophecy and the ability to create order, even when we interrupt to preach!

Always be eager to present yourself before God as a perfect and mature minister, without shame, as one who correctly explains the Word of Truth.   (2 Timothy 2:15, TPT)

---

12. Sandstrom, Aleksandra, "Women relatively rare in top positions of religious leadership," Blog, Fact Tank, Pew Research Center, http://www.pewresearch .org/fact-tank/2016/03/02/women-relatively-rare-in-top-positions-of-religious -leadership/.

26

BEARING WITNESS

I'm sure that there are people who are skeptical that a woman can do this job as well as a man, I am blissfully unaware of such people – and have been gifted with the ability to ignore them completely.

– Frances Arnold (1956–),
2018 Nobel Peace Prize winner in chemistry. Her work
led to new pharmaceuticals and cancer treatments.

Mock clinicals were examinations that evoked anxiety during my second year of graduate school. They were weighted like an exam, but were scored as pass/fail, with less than 100 percent being a fail. We were told there was not room for mistakes in clinical judgment. I agree (*and so does every patient!*). These scheduled role-play sessions, which the professors simulated, were designed to get student novices ready for a real-life rehab clinic. A professor handed us a mock chart and pretended to be the patient. We were given a ten-minute time frame, and multiple professors judged our clinical performance. What has become second nature to me now felt like a pressure cooker then, determining on the spot what treatment protocols would be best for that patient and then implementing them in the mock treatment session. The director of the occupational therapy program at that time, Dr. Pearl Myers, would typically sit in and deduct points if we young clinicians didn't "say it with authority." She was relentless. If our voice became high-pitched from nerves or sounded immature, she interrupted "with authority" and would deduct points, which meant fail. There is a significant underrepresentation of men in occupational therapy, so most of our class was young women in our early twenties. Pearl understood that the world has a difficult time taking young women seriously; she knew our credibility would be questioned. She told us to sound assured, even if we weren't (and then assured us we knew more than we thought we did and instructed us to trust the process).

Moreover, when an occupational therapist is ordered, the patient has typically had their life turned upside-down with significant impairment, and they are nervous and vulnerable. Giving instruction to patients "with authority" puts the patient at ease by establishing a tone that says, "You can trust me." It also promotes patient compliance, an essential component to effective intervention. By slowing down and using a deeper, more confident voice, I was perceived as being more credible to assist the patients with what was frequently one of their most challenging life issues. Dr. Myers taught me an incredible lesson to own my authority, for which I will always be grateful.

In the days of Jesus, it was more difficult for a woman to own her authority. The domestic sphere was thought to be a woman's place, while the social and religious spheres were considered to be for the men, according to the Roman household codes. If a woman did go out in public, she was expected to remain quiet. The Jews had a long history of adhering to these codes and even believed a woman's voice was dangerous.[1] It is well documented that rabbis considered burning the Torah more honorable than

---

1. Meredith Blackman, "American Orthodox Jewish Women and Domestic Violence: An Intervention Design" The University of Chicago School of Social Service Administration,. accessed September 29, 2018, https://www.ssa.uchicago

to commit its teaching to a woman, "Let the words of the Law be burnt rather than be committed to women"[2] When Jesus came on the scene, he was, in fact, a radical because he invited women to "sit at his feet" to learn Scripture.[3] Martha of Bethany was even criticized by Jesus for fussing about her domestic duties as if they were more important than joining her sister to learn from him (Luke 10:38–42). Some Christians are unwilling to see how Jesus taught that a woman's most faithful position is *not* in the kitchen serving men. They hold that a woman's sphere is the home, permitting women to learn Scripture, while silencing them to bear witness with authority.

One of the most exemplary and authoritative confessions of faith recorded in the Gospels is from Martha of Bethany. Martha and her sister were caring for her sick brother, Lazarus, who died while Jesus delayed the requested visit to heal him. As Jesus came into town, four days after Lazarus had died, Martha went out to meet him and charged that her brother would not have died if Jesus had been on time. Though accusing, she still exhibited faith: "Even now I know that whatever you ask God, God will give you"

.edu/american-orthodox-jewish-women-and-domestic-violence-intervention-design.

2. Arthur M. Silver, "May Women Be Taught Bible, Mishnah and Talmud?" *Tradition: A Journal of Orthodox Thought* 17, no. 3 (Summer 1978), 75–76. The 1983 Barbara Streisand Film *Yentl* depicts this tradition in the setting of early twentieth-century Poland.

3. New Testament Scholar N.T. Wright as quoted, "As is clear from the use of the phrase elsewhere in the New Testament (for instance, Paul with Gamaliel in Acts 22:3), to sit at the teacher's feet is a way of saying you are being a student, picking up the teacher's wisdom and learning; and in that very practical world you wouldn't do this just for the sake of informing your own mind and heart, but in order to be a teacher, a rabbi, yourself" in, "The Biblical Basis for Women's Service in the Church," *Priscilla Papers* 20, no. 4:5–10, Accessed September 29, 2018, http://www2.cbeinternational.org/CBE_InfoPack/pdf_files/wright_biblical_basis.pdf.

(John 11:22). Her statement of faith is one that most of us could not utter after losing a loved one, but it wasn't authoritative enough for Jesus. He challenged her to bear witness *with authority*. "Jesus said to her, 'I am the resurrection and the life. Whoever believes in me will live, even though they die. Everyone who lives and believes in me will never die. Do you believe this?' She replied, 'Yes, Lord, I believe that you are the Christ, God's Son, the one who is coming into the world'" (verses 25–27).

Martha professed her faith with authority. She had faith that Jesus was powerful enough to raise her brother from the dead. We read almost the same words verbatim from Peter as he bore witness to Jesus as Christ prior to the resurrection; but his faith confession did not evoke authority to heal the dead in the same way Martha's did.

A Christian woman encounters many obstacles to being accepted as an authority in her church and community. Man-made requirements often have little to do with speaking with authority in bearing witness of Jesus. My religious experience has certainly communicated to me, both directly and indirectly, that my most important job and purpose as a woman is to be in my home to serve my family. This teaching upholds the household legal codes during the *Pax Romana*, highly influenced by Aristotle, above Jesus![4] Jesus never said to a woman, "Go home and serve your husband," or "Your focus should be on your children." We have no idea if Martha had her own family, or how many other women Jesus taught, but it doesn't matter. Martha is a model for women to move out of domestic constraints and become a godly force who bears a powerful witness that moves the world.

But it wasn't only Martha who spoke with authority about Jesus. Perhaps the most important witness of Jesus was Mary of

---

4. Shi-Min Lu, "Woman's Role in New Testament Household Codes: Transforming First-Century Roman Culture," *Priscilla Papers* 30, no. 1 (Winter 2016): 9–15.

Magdala or "Mary Magdalene." Each time we share the gospel, we are led by the testimony of this ancient woman and her female associates. Lots of alternative facts have been spread about Mary of Magdala. I had always thought of her as a prostitute, though the Bible claims nothing of the sort. Looking into this, I discovered her smear campaign can be traced back to a Roman Catholic Pope who lived 540–604 CE and was trying to diminish female authority in the church.[5] His campaign fooled the Anglo-Saxon branch of Christianity, but the Coptic Orthodox church didn't buy in. Copts still honor Magdalene as the "apostle to the apostles," being the first messenger of the resurrection. And, yes, she witnessed to the men. Mary is listed with the Twelve and is noted for traveling and financing the ministry of Jesus." The Twelve were with him, along with some women who had been healed of evil spirits and sicknesses. Among them were Mary Magdalene (from whom seven demons had been thrown out), Joanna (the wife of Herod's servant Chuza), Susanna, and many others who provided for them out of their resources" (Luke 8:1–3).

Considering the cultural context in that day and the fact that women did not have a place in social or religious authority, I would love to have overheard the conversation when Jesus told his disciples that the women are not only traveling with them but paying for them! The Twelve were a charity case for the women. In our modern world, a woman financing a project isn't such a shock; but in the days of Jesus, it was inconceivable, because with the ability to finance something comes the power to influence it. If it doesn't, you are being swindled.

---

5. The propaganda was believed to have been created by the church as weapon against women to effectively control and manage the legend of "Magdalene" so that a woman would not be associated with authority and intelligence. See Jane Schaberg. *The Resurrection of Mary Magdalene: Legends, Apocrypha, and the Christian Testament.* (New York: Continuum International, 2004), 80–81.

Jesus's choice to travel with women was radical. The traditional image of Jesus and his disciples is a gang of guys, but the accurate historical picture is that women were on the forefront and even ahead of the men, and not just because they *paid for them*. Mary of Magdala did not deny Jesus; she was one of the women who demonstrated the highest of courage and leadership, staying loyal to and beside Jesus during his execution while all of the men except John ran away in fear, she was chosen by Jesus to be one of the first witnesses to his resurrection and then preach it widely.[6]

For much of history, the authority of women has been diminished. History records less than 1 percent of women's stories, while women have been half the population.[7] Many believe this is because women did not participate in notable acts, rather than their stories were erased. The truth is men wrote history, and the Bible, so they dominate it. I have a difficult time believing women were inconsequential to trade, peace treaties, health practices, development of communities, education, fighting of wars, growing of food, religious practices, or anything else for that matter. Fortunately, the Bible is an ancient book that has preserved much of women's authority. It's fragmented with women largely being unnamed or excluded, but we're there because of God's plan to use women as a power to move the world. When Christians diminish women's authority it is because they are too sensitive to hear a woman speak with authority. Nothing makes people as insecure as women who speak with authority. It would be easy to make a joke about powerful men being insecure to hear a

---

6. Ann Graham Brock, *Mary Magdalene, the First Apostle: the Struggle for Authority*, (n.p., Harvard Divinity School, 2003). I must add that I consistently witness my Coptic relatives reverence for Mary Magdalene.

7. English Heritage Digital Team, "Why Were Women Written Out of History? An Interview with Bettany Hughes," English Heritage, February 29, 2016, http://blog .english-heritage.org.uk/women-written-history-interview-bettany-hughes/

woman speak with authority; however, many women become just as insecure when women hold power.

For many years I couldn't see how to shrink myself to fit under the authority of male leaders who were offended by me, when I spoke with authority. I was called "disrespectful," when I knew something they didn't. The silencing tactic worked for a while. I learned to pleasantly smile and keep my mouth shut so I didn't appear as having authority. I had no idea that women were leaders and spoke powerful words of faith in the ministry of Jesus. I was told women could not bear witness to men with authority...*and on and on*, thus says the Lord. The pulpit is undoubtedly a position of authority but obviously not the only position of preaching. At the end of the day, the chauvinistic church environment of which I was a part pulled all kinds of mental gymnastics to ensure women are *not* heard as authorities, anywhere in the church.

Bearing witness to Jesus may be our greatest calling as Christians, with faith being the measure of our authority. Women's righteousness is often equated wrongly with passivity, even though Jesus taught women to bear witness with authority. We all bear witness in many ways: singing, healing, teaching, financing, praying, and, yes, *even cooking!* As I bear witness, while healing through my work as an occupational therapist, empowering men and women as yoga instructor, and pulling from all my spiritual gifts and even borrowing a few as a mother, it is now my privilege to bear witness through authorship. As Dr. Myers taught me, I'm "saying it" with authority, no matter how stressful the circumstances. Many other women bear witness as teachers, nurses, military personnel, sales women, legislators, advocates, CEOs and CFOs. One of my patients spent her career working with men on telephone poles; another was the first engineer in her factory. I'm encouraged to see women entrepreneurs, global investors, world leaders, movie directors, and others changing the narrative of Hollywood entertainment and combatant command leaders. These women help me realize my power. I cried when I learned my high-school classmate led the first "un-manned" (all-female) B-52 mission. She reminisces how it never occurred to the Air Force that women could be pilots!

We all have our little corner, or big corner, of the world and need to shine our womanly light there – share our power – it's how we bear witness to God's power. Jesus had amazing words for Martha when she finally learned to take some time out of her kitchen: "Didn't I tell you that if you believe, you will see God's glory?" (John 11:40). Sometimes we need to look in the mirror and own our power to change the world by bearing witness with authority.

As I see real patients these days, instead of professors as mock patients, many of them hope to bear witness to their one hundredth birthday. If they do, the dynamic is interesting months, even years, afterward. Outside of a birthday message on the Today Show, the world really doesn't have a place for someone over one hundred years old. I often hear their lament, "I don't know why I'm still alive." No, there isn't much they can do anymore. I also hear this from my "younger" eighty-plus-year-old patients who, too, have lost much of their ability and struggle to find meaning in their lives. I let these patients know there is still a job for them. Their job is to tell stories because only they can tell their stories, and their stories are dying. It's how they wield their power. I then ask them to tell me a story; sometimes I prompt story-telling with "What did you do during the war?" or "What was your first job?" These lonely, frail people with worn down senses then bear witness to a story that only they can tell. And I hear some amazing stories. These folks no longer have the strength to get out to the grocery store, but they still have power to move the world. They become the authors, even as frail, vulnerable, and dependent persons. They reach into their soul, which isn't bound by their weakening, dying body, and they "say it" with author-ity.

Women are curing cancer and fostering world peace. We have no excuse; each of us is expected to bear witness to God's power in this world, and preaching is not the only way to do that (1 Peter 2:9). When Martha learned her place was not in the kitchen, she found her faith, and her power helped conquer death. Mary Magdalene was bold enough to stare death in the face and she, too, witnessed the conquering of death. Our highest calling as Christians is to bear witness to God's power. As women we must do this with authority. So "say it" with authority, grow your power, be blissfully unaware of the naysayers, and do it all with excellence and love.

> For the Spirit God gave us does not make us timid, but gives us power, love and self-discipline. (2 Timothy 1:7, NIV)

27

SHINE YOUR TALLEST LIGHT

*You must never be fearful about what
you are doing when it is right.*

– Rosa Parks (1913–2005),
African-American Civil Rights activist

The adults circled around the children, and we sang "This little light of mine…" Children always add an element of inspirational authenticity. My boisterous three-year-old daughter, whose voice naturally commands attention, proclaimed she was going to shine her *tallest* light and proudly raised a right-handed bird for all! The chuckles were reflexive in the adults and older kids, but my daughter was too innocent to be shamed into silence with laughter. Her childlike faith had not been varnished with the hard "polishing" of social and religious norms. She was brilliant and simply shined taller and prouder among the saints who were trying not to let the amusement interrupt their song. Satan couldn't blow *her* light out, and her valiant tallest light shined on as a one finger salute, radiant and pure. The more other people wouldn't shine *their* tallest light, the higher she stuck it in the air with emphasis, not understanding why people wouldn't want to shine their tallest light for Jesus.

Shining our "tallest" light can be offensive, but we are called to do it anyway.[1] A little light from women is acceptable in most Christian circles so long as someone has control on the dimmer to keep her from shining her tallest light over a male. If a woman's little light grows into a flame, some just can't take the heat. If you haven't read the Gospels lately, Jesus wasn't exactly an ally of the religious establishment, though most churches never emphasize the radical side of Jesus that set the system afire. If they do give him a nod, it's to fire up the followers to a specific task, such as an evangelical campaign or political protest. Growing up Christian, I never knew following Jesus could mean cultivating the heart of a rebel. But in Jesus' last days he came into Jerusalem riding an ass and attempted to whip the religious system into shape.[2] He never tried to destroy it; he only struck at its heart and cleaned house, so to speak (Matthew 21:1–13; Mark 11:1–11, 15–17). So, when we follow Jesus, shining our tallest light may mean riding an ass or turning over a few tables in church!

In Matthew 10:34, Jesus said, "Don't think that I've come to bring peace to the earth. I haven't come to bring peace but a sword." So, who preaches the gospel of the rebellious, anti-peace Jesus? Embodying this side of Jesus can be damning for girls and women who feel called to speak out on controversial issues at church. Following the protesting side of Jesus requires some holy chutzpah! For me, a person who prefers to work within the system, I find it noteworthy that Jesus became a radical example and teacher of the law, within the system, actively speaking out against its injustices before he went and vandalized it. I've turned over a few tables and upset a few leaders, but I have also done it while understanding the call – it was never a knee-jerk reaction but a meditated assault the same as Jesus' preplanned temple raid. We each have our own call, and it is imperative we recognize

---

1. Matthew 5:14–16.
2. Matthew 21:1–17.

that some women are called to wage war in broadcasting the gospel. "God Almighty declares the word of the gospel with power, / and the warring women of Zion deliver its message" (Psalm 68:11, TPT).

If you haven't felt the heat of a woman delivering the gospel with power, you haven't seen the full light of God. As women, shining our light may mean we need to blaze through some dogma, which might stir up the anti-peace of Jesus and be (*gasp!*) loud. Women are taught to be quiet and submissive; but the gospel is good news, even for loud women, because sometimes the loudest, most combative woman gets the miracle:

> A Canaanite woman from those territories came out and shouted, "Show me mercy, Son of David. My daughter is suffering terribly from demon possession." But he didn't respond to her at all.
>
> His disciples came and urged him, "Send her away; she keeps shouting out after us."
>
> Jesus replied, "I've been sent only to the lost sheep, the people of Israel."
>
> But she knelt before him and said, "Lord, help me."
>
> He replied, "It is not good to take the children's bread and toss it to dogs."
>
> She said, "Yes, Lord. But even the dogs eat the crumbs that fall off their masters' table."
>
> Jesus answered, "Woman, you have great faith. It will be just as you wish." And right then her daughter was healed.
>
> (Matthew 15:22–28)

Let's be real: the men shunned the Canaanite woman, and Jesus was flat rude to her. Why? I think to teach us ladies to pipe up. Despite these holy men's rejection and prejudices towards her (on her side of town), the Canaanite woman argued directly with religious authority *and* the very face of God...even in a kneeling position! She persisted in claiming her power from God, despite receiving the typical treatment women who asserted themselves received – ignoring, shunning, and then being referred to as a female dog. She didn't ask – she insisted.

Scripture does not record an instance when a man won an argument with Jesus, but this woman did. This foreign woman, who practiced a foreign religion and faced God alone, is the only person to win an argument with Jesus in all of the Gospels.[3] *Way to get it sister!* Jesus didn't "correct" her, telling her to be respectful or tell her to not be so rude or demand that she fit into a behavior that made him more comfortable. He didn't call her a "feminist"! In fact, he granted her request because she was faithful, despite her unprivileged position as an outsider.

As women, if we want the blessings of God, we must have faith in our right to God's power and be resolved to claim it, which may mean confronting religious authority and going face to face with God. Women are worthy and deserving of God's power but must come to peace that God's power is available to us. If you haven't noticed, a woman with power makes some people very, very uncomfortable – to the point of them losing faith in God! When women come to peace in claiming the power of God in their lives, they can wield real power to help the poor, hungry, meek, and disabled; they honor the children; they see the woman; they change the heart of the corrupt government worker, preach in the temple, speak for those who cannot speak, and turn over a few tables at church.

I didn't become at peace with my power right away – it took a while – and I still need a bit of meditation to become unconcerned about making a scene, hurting feelings, or turning over tables in protest to claim God's power, which rightfully belongs

---

3. Susan McLeod-Harrison, *Saving Women from the Church: How Jesus Mends a Divide* (Newberg, OR: Barclay Press, 2008), 107–119.

to me. Even as I've studied the scriptures, I still have a knee-jerk reaction to smile and please like a little girl. In my own life I have surrendered my power as a woman when I did the work to fit into the small scope created for me. I only saw that view, and I believed the lie that I didn't have any power or didn't have the right to assert whatever power bubbled up from me. But nothing or no one has moved me more to protest and challenge the injustices in Christianity than my children – I want a better church for them. I don't want their vision limited by a Christianity that prefers men or "happy-clappy," noncontroversial women to a faith that moves the world. Like the Canaanite woman, I, too, have pleaded and demanded that God move heaven and earth for my children. The mama bear side of my faith is fierce; so fierce that the Bible equates it to God: "Like a bear robbed of her cubs, I will attack them and rip them open" (Hosea 13:8, NIV).

The church upholds a single heavenly Father as God, and Jesus called him Father; however, as in the previous verse and others, God also exhibits motherly attributes. The motherly side of God isn't only that of a fierce momma bear, but it comforts as well:

As a mother comforts her child,
    so I will comfort you;
    in Jerusalem you shall be comforted.   (Isaiah 66:13)

There are other motherly references to God in the Bible, including Jesus comparing himself to a mother hen. But, even then, God is also more than a parent. God takes on a variety of forms in the Bible: cloud, fire, judge, lion, shepherd, friend, branch, bread, shield, spirit, father, and more. I don't know that I've sang to "God the cloud" or "God the bread" in church. We give thanks to a heavenly Father for the bread but avoid recognizing the parable of the woman shaping the bread or God as anything but male. This blinds us from seeing female images of God and the power of God in the female form:

"Or what woman, if she owns ten silver coins and loses one of them, won't light a lamp and sweep the house, searching her home carefully until she finds it? When she finds it, she calls together her friends and neighbors, saying, 'Celebrate with me because I've found my lost coin.' In the same way, I tell you, joy breaks out in the presence of God's angels over one sinner who changes both heart and life." (Luke 15:8–10)

Our greatest value as women is not in our silver coins, or even our children, but understanding our worth as having been created in the image of God. If we are to shine our "tallest" light over the doctrines that reduce us, we must search ourselves carefully until we find our value, our power, our last coin. Personally, I want *every* coin. Some women prefer not to clean house to find their lost coin because they fear unearthing embarrassing situations or prefer to not have the responsibility of handling power. However, our call isn't to have nine coins but to hold all ten. I don't want just nine-tenths of my value, I want to be a "ten" as the image of God, so I keep cleaning house and changing my heart and life to embody a greater image of God. And as the woman in the parable, I celebrate this with my girlfriends![4]

It's felt uncomfortable and even unnatural to view God in the image of a woman; however, it is biblical. It's also necessary for women to claim their power and for all Christians to recognize God's power in women. Until the Christian status quo recognizes and teaches God's female qualities in addition to God's male attributes, women will continue to blindly surrender our power and do the difficult work of squeezing ourselves into the narrow lens that has been created through which to see us. Each of us, and the church as a whole, must give sober reflection that God

---

4. The Greek term for friends and neighbors is feminine plural. See Hultgren, *The Parables of Jesus*, 63.

accused, revolted, and denied the prayers of those with such limited discernment: "You ignored the Rock who bore you/ and forgot the God who gave birth to you (Deuteronomy 32:18, The Voice).

If *all* scripture is "God-breathed" (2 Timothy 3:26, NIV), then we need to uphold *all* the women of the Bible who wielded power, and the scriptures that share imagery of God as female.[5] Biblical women often found their power of God and ended up challenging the system, breaking all kinds of religious protocols and offending lots of people. Some of these greatest offenders were the women who witnessed the resurrection. The angel told these women to not be afraid, which is exactly what Jesus reverberated (in addition to instructing them to tell the men what to do): "Don't be afraid. Go and tell My brothers to go to Galilee. Tell them I will meet them there" (Matthew 28:10, The Voice).

The first witnesses of the resurrection were women who were then instructed to bear witness of God. Where would our Christian faith be if these women had told Jesus it was not proper or natural for them to witness to the brothers or tell men what to do? Mary Magdalene and the other Mary had the courage to tell the story about their encounter with a man who had risen from the dead (Matthew 28:1–9; Luke 24:1–9). Their witness to God's story changed the world forever. The resurrection is arguably the most important story in the entire world, because it gives our lives meaning beyond our circumstances, beyond our body, beyond death, beyond what any of us can accomplish with our human power. I don't have all the answers to Christ's mysteries; however, I do have my experiences of how God's story has moved me two thousand years after Christ walked the earth. I, too, can

---

5. For further discussion on biblical imagery of God as female, please read Virginia Ramey Mollenkott, *The Divine Feminine: The Biblical Imagery of God as Female* (Eugene, OR: Wipf and Stock, 2014).

bear a personal witness to how the life of Jesus has moved and empowered me. When we can observe who God is and how God works in our everyday lives, even in the smallest of things, we are claiming our power of God.

Shining your "tallest" light means claiming your God-given power. The table of silencing and ignoring women needs to be turned because it has robbed us of the faith to claim our power to witness. Each woman uniquely embodies God's image and power, no matter how ugly, boring, or ideal their story. Jesus brought these stories out from the shadows, and so should we. Recognizing God's power in the witness of *each* woman helps us roll away the stone of oppression and resurrect hope and love for all. It has the power to break the chains that restrain women in the church and in the world. So, "don't be afraid." Let the power of God burn through you as you shine your tallest light and bear witness loudly. Those preventing you from seeing your power will eventually run away in fear when you are faithful to claim the power of God.

Eternal One: Now do you see that I am the One,
　　　and there is no other God besides Me?
　I have power over life and death;
　　　I wound, and I heal;
　　　no one can resist My power!
　　　　　　(Deuteronomy 32:39, The Voice).

28

THE PRICE OF LOVE

*Having family responsibilities and concerns just
has to make you a more understanding person.*

– Sandra Day O'Connor (1930–),
First female Supreme Court Justice,
serving from 1981–2006

B efore I had children, a crying child was a rude interruption. Babies wailed over injustices such being tired, hungry, or having soiled britches, and I looked to the mom (not the dad) to remove the child from church or the restaurant for my convenience. It never occurred to me the mom had other children or that she, too, wanted to relax. When I waited tables in college, I marveled at how messy children were and wondered why moms (not dads) didn't teach young children to be tidier eaters. Hah! After I had children, the cries and messes came from my own offspring, signaling me to do something. It all added up to years of cry rooms, nursing rooms, hall pacing, diaper changing, and extra tipping at the cost of my social isolation. Fortunately my husband was eager to share this responsibility the best he knew how.

Children, especially young children, require total care, and the impatience to meet their needs has led to a binary world where most women with young children occupy a realm isolated from socioeconomic resources. Children are absent in large chunks

241

of society. Now, my husband sometimes works in a high-voltage lab, and I see patients; those places aren't appropriate or safe for children. However, our workplaces can certainly do more to recognize children instead of pretending they aren't supposed to exist. Not including young children is an American moral pathology that infects every part of society, including some churches. I cannot begin to count how many church events I have skipped because there wasn't an appropriate place provided for my children. If churches, restaurants, stores, employers, political groups, or schools want to attract young families, they are wise to acknowledge and accommodate young children.

Including children in the lives we live is an obligation of our faith. The first book of the Bible, Genesis, declares children as blessings for all people (15:5; 22:17; 28:14). As society evolved, this blessing to the Hebrew people become contingent on teaching God's ways of being "right and just" to children (18:19, NIV). Later, when society became even more complex, Hebrew law included instructions to live life with children, as God knew they could easily be forgotten on the margins:[1] "Make the things I'm commanding you today part of who you are. Repeat them to your children. Talk about them when you're sitting together in your home and when you're walking together down the road. Make them the last thing you talk about before you go to bed and the first thing you talk about the next morning. (Deuteronomy 6:6–7, The Voice). These instructions to include children apply to more than wedding ceremonies and church events. Including children has spiritual significance in everyday life. Even in the ancient days life's ebb and flow could get busy and leave children behind, out

---

1. Terence E. Bretheim, *The Child in the Bible*, ed. Marcia J. Bunge, Terence E. Fretheim and Beverly Roberts Baventa (Grand Rapids, MI: Wm. B. Eerdmans, 2008), Kindle loc. 234–304/7015.

in the margins, or see them as too weighty of a load. So God gave us instructions to include children.

Children are a lot of work, *a lot of work*, and women have shouldered most of that work as caregivers. Women have paid inequitable costs with children, not only because of our physical expenses, but because we are often expected to sacrifice above and beyond what men are expected to sacrifice to care for children. When was the last time you asked a dad if he was going to quit his job and stay home with the new baby? The expectations surrounding children are much higher for us women, and women are often the ones upholding the status-quo. According to my mom, and initially my husband before we fixed that, it was *my* job as the mother to care for children, and my husband was "babysitting" or "giving me a night off." My mother-in-law elevated my "stay-at-home" status to say I "worked in the home," but didn't get sick days.

Sacrifice is an idolatrized virtue of motherhood. Women are expected to smoothly dissolve into motherhood, with any loss of self as "worth the sacrifice." For me, I have felt pressure to elevate the well-being of my child over my own. After the baby arrived, I felt as if nobody cared what was happening with my body, mental health, bladder control, career, or identity, because my identity was supposed to be wrapped up in the pounds of growing flesh that cried, pooped, peed, and sucked on me. It was risky for me to share about my desperation, because my vulnerability was punished with a reminder that the decision to have four children was mine, and therefore it was my own fault if I was upset. I didn't want to devalue my children. As a woman, being angry about anything, especially the inequitable sacrifice of motherhood, is taboo. "Blessed" and "grateful" are feelings I have about my kids, but they don't trump my other feelings in motherhood.

Shaming mothers for sharing these dark realities, as if we're really supposed to "cherish each moment," is cruel. I have sacrificed economic resources, opportunity, sleep, peace of mind, showers, and exercise; and that's just a drop in the ocean of motherhood liabilities. These imbalanced caregiving expectations often pushed me beyond my physical limits, and I have collapsed in fatigue. Emotionally I have felt lost and, at times, out of control. It has ultimately fallen my duty as Mom to clean messes (who gets the grime out the back of the fridge in your house or makes sure the front and back of the toilets are cleaned?), arrange activities, and oversee the kids' education and medical care, which I did often at the "sacrifice" of my own. There were also the years of giving up what was on my dinner plate because, according to children everywhere, Mom's food always taste better than Dad's, or their own, even when it's the *same thing.* Bathroom privacy or peace and quiet are luxurious during motherhood.

Moms pay a high price to nurture children, and sometimes it feels as if we're paid in terms of zealous judgment. There are a million wrong ways to be a mom. Surf through the blogosphere and you'll find an endless supply of advice to moms coming from other moms, grandmas, scientists, religious zealots, fathers, politicians, and even kids. I've received mothering "advice" from literally everyone from my financial advisor to my boss, my kids (hah!), church, other moms, teachers, politicians, and even another shopper at the grocery store. The judgment, packaged as "help," can individually be appropriate; however, it accumulates and feels like an avalanche pouring in from *every* walk of life, while real help to nurture children is slim. As a young mother I caught on to this quickly and made it a personal policy to filter the "help." If the advice required another thing for me to do, I listened with a grain of salt and reserved the right to ignore it, even if the advice came from family or church.

Mothering is perhaps the most difficult job in the world, so difficult that Moses was exacerbated by it:

Did I conceive all these people? Did I give birth to them, that you would say to me, "Carry them at the breast, as a nurse carries an unweaned child," to the fertile land that you promised their ancestors? Where am I to get meat for all these people? They are crying before me and saying, "Give us meat, so we can eat." I can't bear this people on my own. They're too heavy for me. If you're going to treat me like this, please kill me. If I've found favor in your eyes, then don't let me endure this wretched situation." (Numbers 11:12–15)

I find it ironic that the Common English Bible titles this passage as "Moses' Complaint About Leadership," but church tradition ignores *this* is the kind of leadership mothers do. Every. Single. Day. Rather than uphold mothering or caregiving as leadership; or learn how to care for the hunger and cries of children; or learn from a mother how to meet these primitive needs that come with an overwhelming amount of emotion, mothers are often paid with judgment, as if they are selfish for not doing or being *everything*.

I have often been made to feel ashamed about my imperfections as a mother, as if the moral fabric of society hinged on how much television my kid watched, their selection in music, or their clothing choices. It felt as if the character of the children was under a microscope and that I might lose my salvation if they consistently were wry or they scowled.

When my kids were young, I felt the women in church weren't interested in listening or helping me to find choices that were best for my children and me, but they were implicit to give me a preconceived prescription for a motherhood that expected my full sacrifice and submission as a woman. If I veered from the sacrificial motherhood prescription, there would surely have been eternal consequences and the ruin of my family and society as God designed it. I quickly became insecure to console these "friends."

Outside of the religious "sacrifice" dogma, there are double-binding social contracts on mothers. Moms wait at the bus stop with their kids to keep them safe but then are condemned as "helicopter moms." If a kid breaks an arm while on Dad's watch, people chuckle about him being busy watching football, but if the same injury happens while Mom is watching a talk show, she is subject to arrest. I'm all about keeping children safe; however, I have four kids and can't possibly watch all of them every minute of the day, so I must rely on neighbors, coaches, God, and even strangers. I do my best and am pragmatic and concern myself with more likely threats such as childhood anxiety and diabetes, rather than public bathrooms or the bus stop. All this ranting isn't to say I don't value advice, the development of my children's character, or that I can't manage, but it's to relate the pressure a mother can face.

Ironically, Christian tradition upholds the biblical woman Hannah as a sacrificial mother, even though she didn't raise her own child. Hannah didn't exactly live up to the expectations put upon her, because she didn't have babies, and when she did have a child, she didn't raise him but handed her prized son over to God by dropping him off at the temple. Personally, I'm not sure I would have been so "sacrificial" or "faithful" as to hand my kid over to service the temple without camping outside to have dinner with him each night or getting a job there too. I want to be near my kids. But maybe Hannah's faith understood God's sentiment that women are at no higher calling to raise up children than men and that society has an obligation to include children. Her son was involved directly in the everyday work of the temple, which was the highest form of educational, political, and religious law of that day.

Hannah's story flies in the face of the "cross to bear" mentality held over today's Christian mothers. Motherly sacrifice is a huge badge of honor in many Christian circles; however when Hannah, or even Jochebed, are upheld for their motherly "sacrifice," it reveals how sacrifice is really a guise for "suffer." Glorification of suffering has a long history in Christianity, especially with women; and when women openly share their suffering of motherhood, society is held accountable. Motherhood brings indescribable joy and pain, we mothers need to be authentic in sharing both.

My greatest challenge in motherhood continues to be this deliberation: At what cost of myself I should sacrifice for my children? The price of loving my children should not be my silent suffering so everyone else can get along with their business. Yes, everyone loves moms; but despite our popularity and sacrifice, a special parking space at Walmart isn't enough. We get propped up on Mother's Day, lavished with perfumes and flowers, but nobody gives us a discount! We're saints when we have a baby, but they send us a bill and tell us we have to "sacrifice" and be liable for the burdens of mothering.

As mothers we can cry sexism all day long, but the truth is that much of the discrimination towards women is really towards the work of mothering. In much of American society, women *have* reached equality with men, and even surpassed them, but we've reached it at the cost of not having children or keeping our children invisible. Second-wave feminism gave mothers opportunity to provide financially for their children; however, it left the work of mothering behind. It forgot the children. Mothers want to be with their children, so if women are to achieve the highest levels of power in society, we need to do it on our own terms, with our kids by our side.[2] God's way is to include the children.

---

2. It's a shame, because more than 80 percent of the world's women become mothers, and motherhood is a central part of women's lives. "Matricentric Feminism" is a relatively new study, doing the research we need to determine how best to include children in our lives or work as women. This is starting to

Research shows mothers are stereotyped as less committed and less competent than women without children, even when they are equality qualified.[3] Moreover, when it comes to the gender pay gap, women without children earn 96 percent of what men earn, while women with children earn 71 percent.[4]

The virtue of sacrifice isn't only held out for mothers but to daughters of aging parents as well. I work in this area and see how often daughters are expected to sacrifice to care for their aging parents. U.S. law is recognizing the open discrimination of moms and caregivers in the workplace and has created a class of family-responsibilities discrimination; however, these laws provide greater social protection for men because it's difficult to prove caregiver discrimination of a woman since most women are caregivers.[5] American policy has a long way to go. Liberty can't be at the expense of women's free domestic labor, insulated at home with children.

---

change, however. Andrea O'Reilly is working overtime to produce a feminist theory for mothers through her "Motherhood Initiative for Research and Community Involvement (MIRCI)." https://motherhoodfoundation.files.wordpress.com/2015/05/procreate_andrea_oreilly_july_1_2015.pdf.
I believe her "matricentric feminism" is an ideal that honors mothers and children which is consistent with the teachings of Jesus.
3. Shelley J. Correll, Stephen Benard, and In Paik, "Getting a Job: Is There a Motherhood Penalty?" *American Journal of Sociology* 112, no. 5, (March 2007): 1297–1339, doi:10.1086/511799.
4. Michelle Budig "The Fatherhood Bonus and The Motherhood Penalty: Parenthood and the Gender Gap in Pay," *Third Way*, September 2, 2014, https://www.thirdway.org/report/the-fatherhood-bonus-and-the-motherhood-penalty-parenthood-and-the-gender-gap-in-pay. This report also revealed that 71% of mothers who are caregivers work, and women are breadwinners for 40% of American households.
5. Equal Employment Occupation Commision, "Enforcement Guidance: Unlawful Disparate Treatment of Workers with Caregiving Responsibilities," *Equal Employment Occupation Commision*, accessed November 25, 2018, https://www.eeoc.gov/policy/docs/caregiving.html.

In the church, we can start progression by toppling the motherly sacrifice idol and find ways to include children in society instead of isolating them at home with Mom. Jesus honored children and even elevated them as a standard of faith (Matthew 18:2–4). I've often thought that the women who traveled with Jesus also brought their children since one was readily available to plop on his lap.

The price of motherhood is high, and the pay is low. The job of mothering children is undervalued socially, in the workplace and in public policy; it has been well established that society financially and socially punishes women who have babies.[6] There is no social protection for a woman who chooses to bring a child into this world and care for the railing cries of hunger, wreaking diapers, and the primitive need to be held.

I don't believe God intended motherhood to be a liability. Mothers deserve better choices to include the lives of their children within their own. I have yet to read in the Bible where a mom is called to sacrifice for a child more than a dad or anyone else. Both men and women are equally capable of caring for children; however, estimates say that women spend ten times more time doing the unpaid work of caregiving than do men.[7]

I'm encouraged by the growing numbers of dads who are putting their careers on hold to care for young children, a practice

---

6. Damian Grimshaw and Jill Rubery, "The motherhood pay gap: A review of the issues, theory and international evidence," International Labour Organization, *Conditions of Work and Employment Series, no. 57* (Geneva, 2015), http://www.ilo.org/wcmsp5/groups/public/@dgreports/@dcomm/@publ/documents/publication/wcms_348041.pdf.

7. Gaëlle Ferrant, Luca Maria Pesando and Keiko Nowacka, *Unpaid Care Work: The missing link in the analysis of gender gaps in labour outcomes*, OECD Development Centre, December 2014), https://www.oecd.org/dev/development-gender/Unpaid_care_work.pdf .

that 82 percent of Americans support.[8] These dads who work in the home likely don't get a day off, are too financially liable, and are potentially isolated from the playgroups that moms arrange, yet they largely escape the criticism for mothering. Research shows much of this comes from women's families, which can be a nesting place for gender discrimination.[9] The next time you hear someone judging a mom, question them; challenge them to offer some grace and real help instead of unsolicited judgment. It doesn't matter whether the mom was right or wrong; you haven't walked in her shoes, and it's none of your business. And, mothers, let's stop playing by the rules that other people make for us and teach the world how to *love* children. The world needs our wisdom and to follow our guidance. The world may forget children, but we mothers don't.

> **Eternal One:** Is it possible for a mother, *however disappointed*,
> *however hurt*, to forget her nursing child?
> Can she feel nothing for the baby she carried and birthed?
> Even if she could, I, *God*, will never forget you.
> (Isaiah 49:15, The Voice)

Like a mother, God promises to never forget us as children. As God doesn't forget us as children, we should never forget our children and those who mother them. Mothering is the very work of God, and while men can't carry or nurse a child, they can

---

8. Barna Group, *Barna Trends 2018: What's New and What's Next at the Intersection of Faith and Culture,* (Grand Rapids, MI: Baker Books, 2017), 73.
9. Mott Poll Report, "Mom Shaming or Constructive Criticism? Perspectives of Mothers," C.S. Mott Children's Hospital, Michigan Medicine, Volume 29, Issue 3, June 19, 2017, https://mottpoll.org/sites/default/files/documents/061917_criticizingmoms.pdf.

nurture children. Nurturing children is the work of God that we must embody together as Christian men and women.

Eternal One: Listen, you who count yourselves among
       Jacob's descendants,
     all the remnant of Israel.
It is you, *not I*, who have been carried from before you
       were born.
     Indeed, when you were still in the womb, I was taking
       care of you.
And when you are old, I will still be there, *carrying you.*
     When your *limbs grow tired, your eyes are weak,*
And your hair a silvery gray, I will carry you *as I always*
      have.
     I will carry you and save you.

                     (Isaiah 46:3–4, The Voice)

29

FARING THE VILLAGE

Certainly, travel is more than the seeing of sights; it is a change that goes on, deep and permanent, in the ideas of living.

– Miriam Beard (1876–1958),
American writer and suffragette

Maui was a much-needed vacation destination after eight straight years of either being pregnant or nursing. My children no longer needed my body, so I was free to travel 4,500 miles away from them, wear a bikini, and go snorkeling in the Pacific Ocean. Before my week-long luau, the longest I had been away from our children was a short weekend here and there. Getting babies ready for a weekend with their grandmas seemed more like moving than a visit: the playpen and stroller; the toys or blankets they must have to sleep; bottles, prescription lotion, bibs, diaper cream – I spent the first day of the weekend getaway catching up on sleep; and by the second day I was rested enough to go out and have some fun. When we returned home, the children were coming down from a sugar high and suffering amnesia regarding any prior schedule or expectations.

Young children are exhausting, with the never-ending messes of soiled diapers, drools, handprints, runny noses, bathroom sink magic potions, and crumbs on the kitchen floor. Generally, kids cry for Mom, so it was to my delight that my youngest preferred Dad when he was upset or needed comforting. I relished him crying for Dad because I knew I couldn't do it all alone, especially when the other three cried for Mom.

While I was in Hawaii it became real to me that there was absolutely nothing I could do if my curious preschooler decided to break the safety locks on the bathroom vanity or pull out the cleaners and drink them like Kool-Aid. The kids' grandmas had experience in successfully keeping children alive, so I believed they would be fine (both the grandmas and the kids!). But being so far away made me realize how little power I have in my children's lives. Those miles and week of separation instilled a deeper sense of faith in me and helped me to find solace in how God keeps special watch over children: "For I tell you: they are watched over by those *most beloved* messengers who are always in the company of My Father in heaven" (Matthew 18:10, The Voice).

It takes a lot of faith to be a mom. Moms are God's greatest resource for protecting and nurturing children; however, as a woman I am limited. Knowing my children have distinguished angels has helped me accept my limits of power as a mom. I've also weaved together a village of family and friends around my children, and sometimes I believe special people may just be angels in disguise!

I'm often asked, "How do you do it all with four kids?" and here's the answer: I don't...and I'm not supposed to. As my children grow, it occurs to me that perhaps our most important business as mothers is deciding who we weave into the village surrounding our children. We have a tremendous responsibility, as gatekeepers, to our children, and that responsibility starts with choosing who their dad will be. Mothers are central in deciding which schools our kids attend, what instruments and sports we introduce them to, which babysitter or nanny will care for them, which doctor they will see, and what faith community they will grow up in. The choices aren't always easy or within our control. I can't control what schools or healthcare is available in my community; and if mothers aren't partners with their child's father, at least legally through parenting, then much can be out of a lone parent's control as well. The developmental health and safety of my children is my top priority, so I consider very seriously what will and will not influence my children. And, sometimes, we mothers must overcome obstacles, endure resentment, and even navigate competition to make sure our children are in the best environments and have the right people on their team.

Weaving the village around our children becomes tricky when some family members have proved themselves harmful. I have endured some harsh judgment by my family when I have thrown a monkey wrench into our "Norman Rockwell" Christmas in order to protect my children from repeatedly witnessing bad behavior. In the Bible we read the dark history of Jesus's extended family; his kin were some of any family's worst offenders. This may be why Jesus violated traditional "family values" – hate your mother and father (Luke 14:26) – and created a new kind of community. The new community bears a family resemblance as we are adopted by God and united by God's Spirit in a *kin-dom* of family.[1] "God destined us to be his adopted children through Jesus Christ because of his love (Ephesians 1:5).

The familial nature of God's community is not through blood relationships but through love and grace. We are kin with Christ, called to serve each other. I consider much of my family to be a part of this *kin-dom*, in addition to teachers, coaches, neighbors,

---

1. Deb Saxon, "That Family Resemblance – The 'Kin-dom' of God," *Unfinished Symphony: Faith. Life. Family. Cats. And Chocolate. Always Chocolate!* July 15, 2018, https://unfinishedsymphony.org/2018/07/15/that-family-resemblance-the-kin-dom-of-god/.

my appointed angels, Sunday school teachers, youth group leaders, and (gasp) sometimes even strangers. We mothers need the community of faith because passing along faith is the most important thing we do as parents. I'm not talking about faith that keeps score on church tithing and attendance, or how many Bible verses we make kids memorize. Authentic faith is much greater than that; it's grace that hems us into a community where we can be supported, loved, and inspired. [2]

My faith community has been important with all of my children, but it became vital with my middle son. He has a long story of hospitals, developmental delays, therapy, seizures, special education, and special needs. Early in his life I was consumed with keeping him healthy – so consumed that my older kids began to complain that I didn't care about them when he got sick or needed to see a doctor, which was *all the time*. I spent many nights with him in the hospital, helplessly watching him struggle to breathe. The images of his small frame being restrained, tortured with needles, ice packs, and breathing masks is seared in my memory for eternity.

Eventually my son was identified as having an incurable, possibly fatal, genetic disease. The doctors prescribed a medicine – which was basically a bodybuilding supplement – for him to take three times per day and said there was nothing else they could do. I was devastated. I thought of the people in the Bible who sought out Jesus to heal their children. I remembered the parents of the pediatric polio patients I saw in Cambodia who pushed their crippled child in a wheelbarrow for miles and miles and then waited to see me, a therapist, who could make splints for him. If only Jesus were still on earth, I would push my child for miles

2. Reta Halteman Finger, "From Kingdom to Kin-dom – and Beyond," *Christian Feminism Today*, accessed October 5, 2018, https://eewc.com/kingdom-kindom-beyond/.

in a wheelbarrow, too, to see him. In all my pleading, begging, screaming, cursing, demanding, and ugly crying to God, and anyone else who would listen, it occurred to me that Jesus is with us through our kin-dom, and I could bring my son to Jesus to be healed. In fact, the Bible gives specific instructions on this: "Are any sick? They should call the elders of your church and ask them to pray. They will *gather around and* anoint them with oil in the name of the Lord. Prayers offered in faith will restore them from sickness *and bring them to health*" (James 5:14–15, The Voice).

The answer was within the kin-dom. Weeks later we participated in a small healing ceremony in the home of an elder who lived in the Chicago area. It consisted of a Hebrew prayer, anointing oil, and an informal sermonette about faith and healing. I had finally found some peace. We had done everything we could, and now we were faithful in giving the uncertainty of our son's fate to God.

Later that week I told my mom about having our son anointed, after she asked how he was doing. Mom is typically private about her faith and doesn't involve herself in religious conversations; however, this time she piped up with profound words that hit me like a bombshell: "You did the right thing; now it's your faith that will heal him." He wasn't healed, he was just anointed; it was my faith that would heal him, but I was numb and all out of faith. Honestly, I think I was in shock. Mom sensed my hopelessness and explained that having faith meant faithfully giving my son his medicine – the bodybuilding supplement – and following through with the services he needed. Hearing Mom's advice reminded me of how I, too, was a child in God's kin-dom. I needed healing as well. I had endured the trauma of being powerless as a mom, and I was refusing to be gathered and nurtured by God. Jesus said, "How often I wanted to gather in your children as a hen gathers in her chicks under her wings, but you were not willing to come to Me (Luke 13:34, The Voice). I needed God's protective wing. I had flown the coop because I was afraid. I had no more power, so I let God be mother hen to me and slowly grew more faithful.

My son is eleven now. He has no idea he's walking on water because he's too busy being a curious and ornery child. We are still faithful to give him his medicine – a teaspoon of citrus supplement with a shot of orange Gatorade to make it taste better – and he will need it for the rest of his life. The doctors and teachers have become vital members of my son's village; they're some of those suspected angels! We all marvel at him because he is defying the odds. The children's hospital has asked permission multiple times to do research on him, and I politely refuse, because I'm not letting another needle go into my child that is not a necessary vaccine or medicine. As he grows in faith, I hope he will choose to serve others with his condition by making himself available for research. I sometimes tell the doctors we had him anointed, and they give me a knowing smile. I work in healthcare too, and I have seen the miracles. They give me faith in the midst of the tragedy I witness.

Not every story ends up "happy." Some mothers lose their children. As a kin-dom of faith, we cannot forget those moms, but we can serve as God's protective wing for them. I realized this in Hawaii as I went for a break from kids and then fretted about them all week.

Early one morning I sat on the private oceanfront deck to have a quiet time, but it wasn't so quiet. I cried tears as I realized my children are mine on loan from God, and they will one day fly the coop. Children had already been my greatest glory and pain, and they were still so little. As I reflected on my motherhood, I felt vulnerable, powerful, and naked; but that could be because I *was* naked at the time, but I was not ashamed. My body had done the vital work of giving life. My belly had wrinkles and remembered the shape of children within me. I had a few more gray hairs here and there, and even though my breasts had been sucked on for years, they somehow could still gaze over the ocean's horizon and feel the warm breeze. I was a mother, but I was still a woman; so I bared it all, body and spirit, looking at paradise and reading my Bible through my pink sunglasses. It was the grace I needed as a woman; I had a beach, privacy, I was exposed, and I was loved by God, all at the same time. Motherhood had scarred me, leveled me, empowered me, and somehow even saved me.

Going back inside to put on some clothes, I realized I not only needed to take time away from my children to relax, but I deserved to. All us moms deserve to sit on a beach every now and then and just be ourselves. My kids were at home, loved and protected by their angels and the village I helped create for them. And I could just be me, alone in paradise.

> Then it dawned on me that this is good and proper: to eat and drink and find the good in all the toil that we undertake under the sun during the few days God has given, for this is our lot *in life*. (Ecclesiastes 5:18, The Voice)

30

GIRL POWER

*I want every little girl who's told she's bossy, to
be told instead she has leadership skills.*

– Sheryl Sanburg (1969–),
author, feminist,
and Facebook chief financial officer

My mom was an educator, my sister was an educator,
and, most of the women in my life were educators. So,
naturally, I wanted to grow up to be a teacher. I watched
my teachers direct class, studied their posture, and listened to
how they spoke. When I got home I played school and imitated
them as I played the teacher. Girls watch closely the women in
their lives to gain a vision of their future selves. How we women
interact with men, women, carry ourselves, and use our power
matters, because girls are watching and take our cues. I *believed*
I could be a teacher because I identified with them.

Later, when I was in high school, my mom was in a severe car
accident and spent time raising us teenagers from a hospital bed
in the middle of our living room. The occupational therapist was
often working with her when I got home from school. Seeing her
work with Mom started my journey into the field of rehabilitation.
Decades later, I'm the occupational therapist working in the
homes of patients. Before I pursued healthcare I was interested

in being a mortician, but a guidance counselor discouraged me by suggesting the hours weren't suitable for a mom with kids, and it would be a struggle for me to break into the male-dominated, racially divided, family run funeral industry. Looking back, the power characteristics of the funeral business are like churches. When girls sit in church, they most often see men at the pulpit, men making decisions, and women wielding soft power from a familial relationship with one of the men. Girls are yet at a disadvantage to break into the church business for several reasons, but we cannot dismiss that when church breaks open the Bible, the stories of biblical women are not given much attention. The Bible is peppered with stories of women but scarce on girls. There are stories about boys who are chosen or wield some power to save the day; however, girls are most often getting sold, sacrificed, or taken as booty. Despite the imbalance of girls and boys in the Bible, there are a few girls who wielded their power to change the course of the Hebrew people.

The most powerful girl in the Bible is Miriam. Miriam saved the life of her little brother Moses, reunited her family, and contracted financial resources for her enslaved mother, quickly and peaceably, all with one sentence. I'm not sure there is another Bible personality who intervened so efficiently. "Then the baby's sister approached the princess. 'Should I go and find one of the Hebrew women to nurse the baby for you?' she asked" (Exodus 2:7 NLT). Miriam negotiated with the government forces that were working to her kill her family and people. She was brave, wise, and humble – so humble that we forget to uphold her as a hero – but that could be because we don't uphold girls as the image of heroes. Since heroes are in the business of saving people, families, cities, and nations – and Miriam did all this – we *should* uphold her as a biblical hero.[1]

---

1. Mary Strommer Hanson, "Miriam Who Negotiated," in *Bold Girls Speak: Girls of the Bible Come Alive Today*, (Eugene, OR: Wipf and Stock , 2013), 1–17.

Another girl, an unnamed slave girl, made Bible history because she changed the life of Naaman. Naaman was a powerful Aramean general and is upheld as a model of humility. Naaman's most genuine demonstration of humility, however, was not in following the message of the prophet Elisha but in following the suggestion of his wife's Hebrew slave girl, an orphan and spoil of war. The slave girl suggested he see the Hebrew prophet regarding his skin disease, and Naaman's wife made sure the girl's voice was heard. Naaman's healing is a powerful testimony to the faith of a girl. God can work through even the least of children, including a migrant girl who worked as a slave. So, how many more of us would be healed if we listened to the voices of girls?

Girls have a lot to say but don't always have the confidence or ability to make themselves heard. They risk being called "bossy" or even a "know-it-all" when they speak confidently (banter that stalks girls "from the playground to the workplace").[2] The fact that Christian girls do not hear Sunday school stories about girls who wielded power robs them of confidence. It's no secret that girls experience lower rates of confidence than boys, especially during puberty. A recent study revealed that the confidence level of American girls ages eight to fourteen drops 30 percent, and the self-assurance rate of girls is the lowest at age fourteen. In the details, it appeared teenage girls not only worry about having perfect selfies but about academic and career performance to beat the wage gap.[3]

Girls understand that women's leadership is unfairly scrutinized. Looking to their faith communities for support may only

2. Cathleen Clerkin et al., *Bossy: What's Gender Got to Do with It?* Center for Creative Leadership, 2015, https://www.ccl.org/wp-content/uploads/2015/04/Bossy2.pdf.

3. YPulse, "Teen Girls are Less Confident Than Boys and It's Affecting Their Futures," YPulse, April 12, 2018, https://www.ypulse.com/post/view/teen-girls-are-less-confident-than-boys-its-affecting-their-futures.

be contributing to the trend. Girls watch women and are acutely aware that we work harder and are paid less. Much of this harder work is in the invisible, emotional labor of homemaking, such as making sure the kids have enough socks, scheduling the pediatrician visit, researching which formula is best to feed the new infant who constantly vomits (and then washing the vomit off the onesie), knowing the time and bus number the kids are to catch for school. The list that that makes homemaking quite time consuming, labor intensive, and emotionally draining is never ending. Domestic and caregiving work has been largely considered "women's work"; and even as men are stepping in to do their part, when a kid misses an activity, coaches hold Mom accountable for an explanation.

One of my greatest insecurities as a mother is not demon-strating an egalitarian marriage for our children when it comes to managing our home, and I worry about them gleaning these imbalanced gender dynamics. Girls watch us moms scurrying around, carrying the load of others' schedules, health, hygiene, and participation in household chores. Who makes sure toilet paper, toothpaste, or something to pack for lunch is available? Who knows which brand of soap is best for the kid's skin allergy or which ointment to use if the kid's allergy does flare? Who knows where to look for the missing shoes that were supposed to be in the box by the door? Who makes sure a science project doesn't grow behind sofas or underneath kids' beds?

Women manage homes, often while managing jobs outside the home, and the work in the home goes largely unrecognized. From an outsider's view it may appear the domestic work is divided evenly, and it may be; however, girls see the invisible emo-tional labor moms spend to make sure our homes don't resemble a men's dormitory (and our children don't grow rashes).

When moms believe *they* are supposed to predominately manage the domestic sphere and neglect to hold capable house members (including the kids) accountable for their share of the work, girls will glean the idea that they are *supposed* to silently be responsible for the messes and needs of those they love. Girls hear how we keep domestic work invisible with our language choices, using phrases such as "stay-at-home mom," instead of "working in the home." Girls hear Mom's tears during the late-night kitchen fight over the dishes, then learn to dismiss Mom's pain when they watch her chuckle along at church as the pastor makes a self-deprecating joke about how he "got in trouble" for leaving the large pans in the sink for his wife to wash (which is really a comment to publicly belittle his wife for getting on his case). These things teach girls to dismiss their own pain. Girls and women have occupied a place of forced, coerced, or learned servitude; however, God does not forget them and even upholds their perspective as a way to look to God:

> Just as a maid carefully observes
> > the slightest gesture of her mistress,
> In the same way we look to *You*, Eternal One,
> > waiting for our God to pour out His mercy upon us.
> > > (Psalm 123:2, The Voice)

The maid, or "slave girl" (NLT), is an eye of hope as she meticulously perceives her mistress. My daughter has watched me this way, and I watched my own mom with years of intimate proximity. Daughters can predict their mother's priorities and reactions, often better than the mother herself! The mistress is like a mother to the girl and is likened to God as the girl's in-depth insight is upheld as a way to see God.

Girls deserve to understand that their capabilities to be like Mom, a teacher, the professional who comes to their home, or other role models in their lives (yes, even male role models, *go dads!*) is a desire honored as turning their face towards God. I imagine the mistress as the Proverbs 31 mistress who delighted in operating a business outside of the home, while managing her homemaking responsibilities (verses 13–15); a woman who invested her money (verse 16) – a wise woman who strived for excellence, her accomplishments worthy of public recognition. I so wish someone would have shared with me the power of women from Scripture. I remember being a girl and not so much identifying with the men, kings, sons, or disciples served up to me at church because I didn't see myself in those stories. When girls don't see themselves with power in Scripture, they will be less confident to use their power as God's hand in their own lives. Girls may be young; but they, too, are capable of faith that can level the playing field for women.

When girls look out to see the fate of girls and women around the world, they can understandably feel defeated. I look at the numbers and also feel like a helpless girl. There are 131.7 million girls without access to education because of financial challenges and engendered social restraints.[4] Globally there are now 650 million women who were child brides, and one in five girls is projected to become a child bride.[5] Approximately two million girls become pregnant each year, not by their choice, and approximately sixteen million adolescents give birth each year.[6] There are 250 million girls who are at risk of losing out on the means to create a future because they lack access to menstruation

4. UNESCO Institute, "One in Five Children, Adolescents and Youth is Out of School," United Nations Educational , Scientific, and Cultural Organization, Fact Sheet 48, February 2018, http://uis.unesco.org/sites/default/files/documents /fs48-one-five-children-adolescents-youth-out-school-2018-en.pdf.

5. UNICEF, *Child Marriage: Latest Trends and Future Prospects*, accessed November 18, 2018, https://data.unicef.org/wp-content/uploads/2018/07/Child -Marriage-Data-Brief.pdf.

6. United Nations Population Fund. *Girlhood, Not Motherhood: Preventing Adolescent Pregnancy* United Nations Population Fund, 2015, accessed November 18, 2018, https://www.unfpa.org/sites/default/files/pub-pdf/Girlhood_not _motherhood_final_web.pdf.

products.[7] It's estimated over 200 million women suffered female genital mutilation as a child, and three million girls are at risk to have their genitals "cut" each year, a barbaric practice based on the idea that the female flesh is inherently evil.[8] Because of engendered social beliefs, girls and women are disproportionately more undernourished than males.[9] Estimates say that 126 million females are "missing" from the world because of gender-biased sex selection – femicide – where female fetuses are aborted or female infants are killed because parents prefer sons.[10] And issues, such as sexual assault, violence and abduction into sexual slavery are not even trackable.

More than 2.7 billion women are denied equal employment opportunities as men, and many women must legally receive permission from their husbands to work.[11] Globally, rural women without access to land, bank accounts, or Internet access face more risks of violence because they are female.[12] Girls across the globe have specific issues that face them because they are female.

---

7. Rosalinda Kowalczewski, "Lack of Access to Feminine Hygiene Products: A Global Issue for Women," Gender, Politics, and Global Cultures, April 15, 2018, https://blog.ecu.edu/sites/genderpoliticsculture/blog/2018/04/15/lack-of-acc ess-to-feminine-hygiene-products-a-global-issue-for-women/.
8. World Health Organization, "Female Genital Mutilation." World Health Organization, January 31, 2018, http://www.who.int/news-room/fact-sheets /detail/female-genital-mutilation.
9. Asian Development Bank, Gender Equality and Food Security: Women's Empowerment as a Tool against Hunger, (Manilla, Phillipines, Asian Development Bank, 2013 http://www.fao.org/wairdocs/ar259e/ar259e.pdf.
10. United Nations Population Fund "Gender-biased sex selection," accessed November 18, 2018, https://www.unfpa.org/gender-biased-sex-selection.
11. World Bank, Women, Business and the Law 2018, The World Bank, http:// wbl.worldbank.org/.
12. United Nations Economic and Social Council, Commission on the Status of Women, "Challenges and opportunities in achieving gender equality and the empowerment of rural women and girls," December 20, 2017, http://undocs .org/E/CN.6/2018/3.

Understanding the violations of girls and women is daunting and can suck the spirit from a girl.

So what would our world look like if we empowered our daughters to solve a few of these problems? How would our Sunday morning lessons need to change? In that spirit, perhaps the most important story we can tell girls is how Jesus resurrected the life of a girl: "But he took her by the hand and said, 'My child, get up!' Her spirit returned, and at once she stood up. Then Jesus told them to give her something to eat" (Luke 8:54–55, NIV).

When others saw the girl's situation as hopeless, Jesus reached out and touched the girl, took her by hand, and pulled her up. He didn't expect the girl to serve him but told others to give her something to chew on. We, too, must reach out and touch our girls – give them a hand and pull them up out of seemingly lifeless situations. We, too, must give our girls something to chew on. What kind of faith are we feeding our daughters?

Girls deserve to see a future where they are not expected to carry the domestic ignorance and irresponsibility of those they love. Girls and women need to be free to chew on bigger problems than how to keep the kitchen and bathrooms clean. They deserve to be heard regarding the plight of girls and women from around the world. God calls girls to solve global issues (Micah 6:4). We adults must elevate their voices and teach them a faith beyond the approval of men (John 5:44). Perhaps if we teach them about a couple of ancient slave girls who spoke up and changed the world, and the biblical women who wielded their power, they, too, will find the courage to become ambassadors of hope and level the playing field for girls and women, using their girl power.

Little children, let's not love with words or speech but with action and truth. (1 John 3:18)

PART 4

OUR FUTURE IS SO BRIGHT

It's time to trust my instincts, close my eyes,
and leap, it's time to try defying gravity

– Elphaba
from the musical, *Wicked*

31

A GREATER VISION

*Don't assume that the answers are out
there in the form of somebody else already
doing something. Sometimes they are.
But you have to think beyond that.*

– Abigail Johnson (1961–),
American businesswoman and
CEO of Fidelity Investments

One day in 2018 I awoke and fell to my knees. I wasn't praying; no, athletic yoga instructor me literally fell to the floor and stayed there. I had to go pick Mom up and take her to her first appointment at the women's oncology office that morning. My mother, my foundation, had been diagnosed with breast cancer. It felt as though the earth was ripped from underneath me, and I didn't have a leg to stand on. So I stayed curled on my bathroom floor and sobbed wails – loud wails – from a place within me that was too deep for words. Only months prior my sister had been declared cancer-free after her battle with stage IIA breast cancer that had metastasized to her lymph glands. It took her hair and pounds of her female flesh, and it nearly took her life. On the day she went to her first oncology appointment I texted her that she wasn't going to die, but she would lose her hair. It's a perilous humor we share; she told me later how that text comforted her at just the right time. In her year of hell, I played with the blonde wig she wasn't too crazy about, and she lamented how the world hates bald white women. We stayed in each other's hair, even without any; it's where sisters belong. My sister and I were both dying that she could not be with Mom on her first day at the women's center. My sister had been through this; she knew the ropes and the staff. She made sure her doctor was now Mom's doctor and her surgeon was Mom's surgeon as well. This was *their* mother-daughter journey that I wanted no part of but couldn't escape. My sister coached me on what to ask the doctor. It felt like taking your first child to his or her first day of kindergarten, with all the emotional weight of knowing your child's life will change forever; except with Mom, her first day was about learning her chances of staying alive. All my healthcare training and emotional deflection skills could not have prepared me enough for that day. I felt utterly powerless.

I dwelled on the idea of losing Mom, and memories of her doing my hair came back to me. I remembered her so precisely sculpting my curls each morning in her bathroom. I had never felt gratitude to her for that until I was threatened with losing her. She cared about my hair. I remembered how for weeks she faithfully picked each parasitical nit of head lice from my thick hair so I wouldn't have to cut it. Mom groomed me to always look good; she knew how a groomed appearance would help me.

My daughter *loathes* my being anywhere near her hair. I've seen *Tangled*, and I still have emotional scars from Mom's snagging and pulling through my frizz and curls. This is why I have been known to let bed head ravage my daughter's tresses. *Why make her cry over hair?* Letting my young daughter run around with messy hair was an unintentional silent revenge to my mother's entanglement with hair (who never thought to ask my husband to "fix it"). But really, *why should a little girl hurt to look good?*

My daughter isn't a crier, so her preschool strategies to escape my brush usually involved eliciting her power over body functions: silent farts, then the noisy ones, snorting out a hawker (and then licking the thick yellow mucus with her curled tongue, *eww, I know!*). Sometimes she preoccupied herself playing fishbowl tag with "Dorothy" the goldfish – anything to avoid enjoying her forced submission to the grooming process. I had doted over my daughter's hair until after my dad died in an accident. After that, I didn't have the emotional energy to doll up her hair, so I didn't.

My mom survived breast cancer, as did my sister. It's still their mother-daughter bonding thing that I want no part of. Unlike my sister, Mom didn't have to lose her hair. While she can no longer haul her brush through my hair, she keeps her business in it by commenting on its presentation. Every. Single. Time. I. See. Her. Something is drastically wrong if my mom doesn't comment on my hair (or clothes or weight). She's not always critical; sometimes it's a simple "that blouse looks good on you," and other times it's the foxlike "I like your hair better curly." What's crazy is that my mom is at the stage in life where she attends friends' funerals several time a year, *so why does she still care about my hair?* Women may be denied power in many areas; however, when it comes to grooming hair, especially our daughters' hair, mothers reign supreme.

So, what if we groomed our girls to feel worthy of power? How different would our world be if girls believed power was their God-given right? As a child, the presentation of biblical women groomed me to submit my power; these women were framed as weak, victims, villains, and "morally bankrupt" vixens; instead of survivors, thrivers, victoresses, righteous, and godly. I mirrored the perceived weakness in my spirit because the spirits of women in the Bible were presented as evil and weak: I thought that's how God wanted women to be. Nobody taught me about the businesswoman Lydia from Acts 16:11–15 who financed Europe's first church in *her* house.[1] Nobody taught me it was righteous to multiply my talents and take power. My religious teaching spent lots of time shaming the appearance of biblical women and over-sexualizing them,[2] while spending zero time teaching that women are to persist in pursuing power (Luke 15:8; 18:1–8). I had no idea about the patron Phoebe (Romans 16:1–2) or that the Proverbs 31 woman invested (verses 16–18). I never knew Deborah led an army (Judges 4–5). As the feminism in each story was made to be invisible, I was groomed to be invisible in faith.

As women, hair is perhaps our most distinguishing feature; it gives us power to be seen. I'll be the first to admit that hair is empowering. It feels great to have fabulous hair! Women have infinite preferences and opinions about what is and what is not "good" hair. While "good" hair can be a confidence builder and loads of fun (and its pursuit a provoker of many tears), I've noticed women have many opinions about botched-up hair but few opinions regarding botchy Christian teachings. Shouldn't we hold Christian teachers who do a poor job of grooming our faith more accountable than hairdressers? *Why yes!* Acts 17:11 says, "The Beroean Jews were more honorable than those in

---

1. Margaret Mowczko, "Lydia of Thyatira: The foreign woman who became the foundation member of the Philippian Church," Women in the Bible, Fixing Her Eyes®, November 29, 2017, http://www.fixinghereyes.org/single-post/2017/11/29/Lydia-of-Thyatira-The-foreign-woman-who-became-the-foundation-member-of-the-Philippian-Church.

2. The ancient women of Scripture were presented to me as nemeses: poor (2 Kings 4:1); crippled (Luke 13:10–17); nags (Luke 18:1–8); overly sexualized (John 4:17–18); overly sexualized some more (Genesis 38; 2 Samuel 11:2); sexualized into something to be pitied (Genesis 29:23) or sexualized into something shameful (Genesis 39:7); suspicious (Proverbs 7:5); or sexualized into something to justifiably fear and punish *all* women for *all* posterity (Genesis 3:3). The sexualization of biblical women silently groomed my faith to believe I was unworthy of power and my sexuality was a liability to whatever invisible worth I had.

Thessalonica. This was evident in the great eagerness with which they accepted the word and examined the scriptures each day to see whether Paul and Silas' teaching was true." The Bereoans were honorable because they challenged the apostle Paul! Would we feel honorable challenging our own teachers this way, or would it make us feel as if we are having a bad hair day, or worse yet, as if we are one of the villainous vixens they teach about? As Christians we are called to examine our Bibles and challenge our teachers and preachers about what they teach, including what they teach about the power of women.

So, ladies, when a Christian teacher oversexualizes or minimizes the power of a biblical woman, what about shifting our focus from our physical appearance (our hair) to the importance of being able to discern whether we are being taught correct theology? And how about we become more concerned about what churches teach our daughters than we are our daughters' hair? Christianity's first female evangelist, the Samaritan woman, didn't have a problem challenging Jesus about his interpretation of Scripture (John 4:11–12). As a result, she determined his message was legitimate and invited her neighbors to come and hear (verses 13–30). Jesus' teaching activated the power of God within the Samaritan woman. The teachings of Scripture should always activate the power of God within us, not hide it.

If you've made it this far through these reflections, you already know the issues of the day that rob women of power, so I challenge you to challenge your teachers! Study the Bible for yourself so you can judge whether what you are being taught is scriptural.[3] Studying for ourselves is how we grow in faith. And lead by

---

3. I recommend using the *Women's Bible Commentary* with your Bible study to further your understanding of a feminist lens in Scripture. See, Carol A. Newsom, Sharon H. Ringe, and Jacqueline E. Lapsley, eds., *Women's Bible Commentary: Expanded Edition* (Louisville: Westminster John Knox Press , 2012).

example by letting your daughters watch you as you study and as you question. Like the servant woman who stuck her nose into Peter's business and forced him to reveal his heart (Mark 14:66–72), we, too, can bring leaders to repentance by asking them some fairly simple questions.[4]

- Have you ever given a message championing Deborah? Miriam? Martha of Bethany? Priscilla?
- Was Bathsheba a seductress or victim of King David?
- What do you believe about the Samaritan woman before her interaction with Jesus?
- How do you teach Ephesians 5? 1 Timothy 2:8–15? 1 Corinthians 11:2–15?

Simple questions such as those will give you a good idea about how your church leaders view women. Your leaders may not understand biblical feminism, so just as Priscilla and Aquila pulled Apollos aside "and explained to him God's way more accurately" (Acts 18:26), you can too!

My mom is normally a thought-out and vocal person; however, the day I took her into the women's oncology center, she was overwhelmed and could not produce questions for the doctor. She lost her voice because she felt powerless. The weight of her issue was too heavy, so I carried some of it for her. I asked the questions my sister had suggested and found other great questions from the handbook Mom had been issued about navigating breast cancer. It's normal to feel powerless or without a voice when confronted with profound issues, so I encourage you to research some questions and bring a trusted friend who will carry some of the weight when discussing the power of women with your church leader or leaders.

---

4. Mary Stromer Hanson, *Bold Girls Speak: Girls of the Bible Come Alive Today* (Eugene, OR: Wipf & Stock, 2013), 102–119.

If Ephesians 5, 1 Timothy 2:8–15, or 1 Corinthians 11:2–15 are used by your leaders as trump cards to rob women of authority, you may want to consider leaving and finding a church that loves and values the power of women. They do exist! While loyalty is a biblical virtue, it should always be built on the foundation of honor (Romans 12:10).

We're not called to blindly follow man's interpretation of the Bible. Jeremiah 8:8 asks,

How can you say, "We are wise;
we possess the LORD's Instruction,"
when the lying pen of the scribes has surely distorted it?

Teachings that deny women power are a venomous fruit we must no longer swallow. Some Christian colleges and seminaries actually teach that a woman's place is "sex, supper, and submission" to her husband.[5] Does God want me, a woman, to hold power? God does! So challenge any underlying messages that withhold power from girls and women.

I have come to the realization that sexism is an ideology, an idolatry of a gender, but not a gender itself. Sexism is *not* something that lives exclusively in the hearts of males. My feminism has been defended by multiple men who are fierce defenders of women's power – *Thank you, gentlemen!* My husband and I are raising our sons to honor the power of women. Conversely, I have heard from multiple Christian women about how God does not want them, as woman, to hold power, especially in relationship to their husbands. These women see their Christian faith through the lens of 1 Timothy 2:11–15 and not Galatians 3:25–28:

5. Zach Lambert, "Sex, Supper, Submission," January 11, 2018, The Junia Project, https://juniaproject.com/sex-supper-submission/.

But now that faith has come, we are no longer under a custodian.

You are all God's children through faith in Christ Jesus. All of you who were baptized into Christ have clothed yourselves with Christ. There is neither Jew nor Greek; there is neither slave nor free; nor is there male and female, for you are all one in Christ Jesus.

Our modern theology has been a cancer to the power of women; it eats at our souls and assumes our female flesh. It denies us of seeing our power and individuality. Stop defending, or passively accepting, a faith that denies power to women. To deny God's power to any person on the basis of their gender is to deny an image, a power, of God. One of my favorite things about teaching YOGATHEA® is awakening the presence of God in every body. We often think of God as being "out there," while Scripture tells us God dwells within: "Don't you understand that Jesus Christ is in you?" (2 Corinthians 13:5).

As I continue to grow in this understanding, that verse has become my most empowering truth of Scripture. My female flesh is a home to God, even with the gray, kinky hairs that stick out from my head; or if my cleavage is revealed when I bend forward; if I lose my patience with my kids; if I'm sharing smiles or snarls; feeling sexy or dried up; making an error; assuming authority; climbing a rope; mastering a toe stand; flailing that Olympic lift; or running errands in my yoga pants. In fact, the Holy Spirit can live in any size woman wearing yoga pants, or any woman!

I am encouraged to learn that the Greek word used for the Holy Spirit, the substance of God that works through us, is feminine![6] As a woman, I want to impersonate feminine beings in

---

6. Gary W. Deddo, "The Trinity and Gender: Theological Reflections on the Differences of Divine and Human Persons," *Priscilla Papers* 22, no. 4 (Autumn 2008): 4–13.

my faith, including the being of God. I was created in the image of God, and I am more than a womb and some breasts. I'm not a sexual liability or less than man or unworthy of power. I am forgiven. I am more than the hairs on my head, (although Jesus evidently cares about those too, even if they've all fallen out [Luke 12:7]). I do some pretty incredible things. And so do you!

As moms, it's imperative we take the power to groom our daughters so they may believe in their own power. Let's groom them for power, not just an appearance to gain the attention of men. Our daughters deserve a greater vision of faith. We give this to them by modeling our power, and they will mirror what they see in us. Show them how to honor the power of women that is rightfully ours. There are many problems in this world that unfairly harm and destroy women. We can no longer support Christian teaching that says women are unworthy of power. Let's choose to be like the widow who got involved and persistently confronted the judge "who neither feared God nor respected people" (Luke 18:2-5).

Let's use our power to lift the voices and experiences of women, in Scripture, in our communities, in our nation, and in our world. Each woman has a right to health, safety, food for our children, respect, agency, pleasure, and the opportunity for prosperous careers that honor both our talents and our motherhood. We each have a right to raise our voices and raise our power. The politics of denying women power are pervasive; but as women and men of God, so are we.

As we move into a postmillennial Christian faith, we have the power to honor the power of girls and women. So take a leap of faith, get involved wherever you feel called. And the next time you are ready to comment on your daughter's hair (or weight or clothes), bite your tongue (it's okay if it bleeds a little) and empower her to be fierce in the war on women of which none of us asked to be a part. Commission her with the girls and women in Scripture who seized power over their circumstances. Authorize her to raise her voice in the courts of her home, church, work, community and state. Equip her with confidence to argue for a better position and negotiate her reality. Let's entitle our daughters and women everywhere to celebrate our bodies and not be ashamed. Teach them about the goodness of their bodies, and grant them agency and ownership of themselves. Show them how to be seen and how to interrupt the conversation. Take your daughters with you wherever you are creating change and defend their position; children have a right to be with their mothers, and mothers should be everywhere decisions are made. Be the mother eagle and encourage your daughters to fly; hover over them; help them; catch them when they fall; carry them on your wings, and lift them high (Deuteronomy 32:11). Get out of your daughters' hair and ignite their power!

"God didn't give us a spirit that is timid but one that is powerful, loving, and self-controlled" (2 Timothy 1:7). These virtues of "authentic faith, which first lived in [Timothy's] grandmother Lois and [his] mother Eunice," empowered some of Christianity's most influential founders (verses 5–6). Their authentic faith should empower us yet today. So let's groom each girl and woman to know her power, be fierce in love, and deliberate to recognize her authority in creating a better world. Let's inspire each other with models of feminism that "build each other up on the foundation of your most holy faith" (Jude 1:20). And may we honor each girl and woman as a dwelling of God's power and grant them greater vision and faith through pink sunglasses.

Clothed in strength and dignity, *with nothing to fear,*
she smiles *when she thinks* about the future.

(Proverbs 13:25, The Voice)

I invite you to continue this conversation
in the Facebook Group:
Pink Sunglasses and Yoga Pants: 31
Reflections on Biblical Feminism.
You may find this group on the YOGATHEA® Facebook Page.

And please join our movement to
Breathe the Peace
Which Transcends All Understanding
~ Mind + Body + Spirit
By visiting www.yogathea.com
YOGATHEA® Christian Yoga + Meditation.
There you can learn about upcoming
retreats and workshops
to awaken the power of God in you!

TARA J. HANNAH is the founder of YOGATHEA® Christian Yoga + Meditation, which provides videos, instructor training, and retreats. She is an occupational therapist in private practice and spends her days rehabilitating women's health impairments. Tara wants everyone (both men and women) to recognize God's power and goodness in the bodies of women and girls, or at least do a better job of honoring women.

Tara has been a waitress, published researcher, beauty queen, grieving daughter, and full-time domestic goddess; she has been harried from graduate school, in counseling, and pulled over as a teenager for riding a snow sled hitched to a skidding pickup truck.

Pink Sunglasses + Yoga Pants: 31 Reflections on Biblical Feminism is Tara's debut book as an author. She has never been a historian, scholar, or theologian, but she wrote *Pink Sunglasses* because God wouldn't let her sleep if she didn't. She prays to grow into a very old woman who doesn't wear a bra and is still teaching yoga. She is very proud of her kitchen herb garden that she nurtures through Indiana winters, and she really wants a greenhouse. Find Tara at www.yogathea.com or on the YOGATHEA Facebook page (Tara prefers to work out and sleep instead of keeping up with any additional social media).

www.ingramcontent.com/pod-product-compliance
Lightning Source LLC
Chambersburg PA
CBHW020526270326
41927CB00006B/461